Regimes of Mobility

Mobility studies emerged from a postmodern moment in which global 'flows' of capital, people and objects were increasingly noted and celebrated. Within this new scholarship, categories of migrancy are all seen through the same analytical lens. This book builds on, as well as critiques, past and present studies of mobility. In so doing, it challenges conceptual orientations built on binaries of difference that have impeded analyses of the interrelationship between mobility and stasis. These include methodological nationalism, which counterpoises concepts of internal and international movement and native and foreigner, and consequently normalises stasis. Instead, the book proposes a 'regimes of mobility' framework that addresses the relationships between mobility and immobility, localisation and transnational connection, experiences and imaginaries of migration, and rootedness and cosmopolitan openness. Within this framework and its emphasis on social fields of differential power, the various contributors to this collection ethnographically explore the disparities, inequalities, racialised representations and national mythscapes that facilitate and legitimate differential mobility and fixity. Although they examine nation-state building processes, the anthropological analysis is not confined by national boundaries.

This book was originally published as a special issue of the *Journal of Ethnic and Migration Studies*.

Noel B. Salazar is Research Professor of Anthropology and Founding Director of Cultural Mobilities Research (CuMoRe) at the University of Leuven, Belgium.

Nina Glick Schiller is Emeritus Professor of Social Anthropology and Director of the Research Institute for Cosmopolitan Culture at the University of Manchester, UK.

Regimes of Mobility

Imaginaries and Relationalities of Power

Edited by
Noel B. Salazar and Nina Glick Schiller

Routledge
Taylor & Francis Group

LONDON AND NEW YORK

First published 2014
by Routledge
2 Park Square, Milton Park, Abingdon, Oxon, OX14 4RN, UK

and by Routledge
711 Third Avenue, New York, NY 10017, USA

Routledge is an imprint of the Taylor & Francis Group, an informa business

British Library Cataloguing in Publication Data
A catalogue record for this book is available from the British Library

ISBN 13: 978-1-138-01303-2

Typeset in Garamond
by Taylor & Francis Books

Publisher's Note
The publisher accepts responsibility for any inconsistencies that may have arisen during the conversion of this book from journal articles to book chapters, namely the possible inclusion of journal terminology.

Disclaimer
Every effort has been made to contact copyright holders for their permission to reprint material in this book. The publishers would be grateful to hear from any copyright holder who is not here acknowledged and will undertake to rectify any errors or omissions in future editions of this book.

Contents

Citation Information

The chapters in this book were originally published in the *Journal of Ethnic and Migration Studies*, volume 39, issue 2 (February 2013). When citing this material, please use the original page numbering for each article, as follows:

Chapter 1

Regimes of Mobility Across the Globe
Nina Glick Schiller and Noel B. Salazar
Journal of Ethnic and Migration Studies, volume 39, issue 2
(February 2013) pp. 183–200

Chapter 2

The Great Departure: Rethinking National(ist) Common Sense
Dace Dzenovska
Journal of Ethnic and Migration Studies, volume 39, issue 2
(February 2013) pp. 201–218

Chapter 3

Tibetan Peregri-nations: Mobility, Incommensurable Nationalisms and (Un)belonging Athwart the Himalayas
Chris Vasantkumar
Journal of Ethnic and Migration Studies, volume 39, issue 2
(February 2013) pp. 219–236

Chapter 4

International Migration: Virtue or Vice? Perspectives from Cameroon
Michaela Pelican
Journal of Ethnic and Migration Studies, volume 39, issue 2
(February 2013) pp. 237–258

Chapter 5

Cultivating Hustlers: The Agrarian Ethos of Soninke Migration
Paolo Gaibazzi
Journal of Ethnic and Migration Studies, volume 39, issue 2
(February 2013) pp. 259–276

Chapter 6

Development Mobilities: Identity and Authority in an Angolan Development Programme
Rebecca Warne Peters
Journal of Ethnic and Migration Studies, volume 39, issue 2 (February 2013) pp. 277–294

Chapter 7

Jembe *Hero: West African Drummers, Global Mobility and Cosmopolitanism as Status*
Pascal Gaudette
Journal of Ethnic and Migration Studies, volume 39, issue 2 (February 2013) pp. 295–310

Chapter 8

Moving Subjects, Stagnant Paradigms: Can the 'Mobilities Paradigm' Transcend Methodological Nationalism?
Barak Kalir
Journal of Ethnic and Migration Studies, volume 39, issue 2 (February 2013) pp. 311–327

Please direct any queries you may have about the citations to clsuk.permissions@cengage.com

Notes on Contributors

Dace Dzenovska is Senior Researcher and Marie Curie Fellow at the Centre on Migration, Policy and Society, University of Oxford, UK.

Paolo Gaibazzi is Research Fellow at the Centre for the Modern Orient (ZMO) in Berlin, Germany.

Pascal Gaudette is a PhD Candidate at McGill University, Canada.

Barak Kalir is Associate Professor of Sociology and Anthropology at the University of Amsterdam, The Netherlands.

Michaela Pelican is Assistant Professor of Cultural and Social Anthropology at the University of Cologne, Germany.

Rebecca Warne Peters is Assistant Professor of Public Administration and International Affairs at Syracuse University, USA.

Noel B. Salazar is Research Professor of Anthropology and Founding Director of Cultural Mobilities Research (CuMoRe) at the University of Leuven, Belgium.

Nina Glick Schiller is Emeritus Professor of Social Anthropology and Director of the Research Institute for Cosmopolitan Culture at the University of Manchester, UK.

Chris Vasantkumar is Associate Professor of Anthropology at Hamilton College, USA.

Introduction

Regimes of Mobility Across the Globe

Nina Glick Schiller and Noel B. Salazar

Mobility studies emerged from a postmodern moment in which global 'flows' of capital, people and objects were increasingly noted and celebrated. Within this new scholarship, categories of migrancy are all seen through the same analytical lens. This article and Regimes of Mobility: Imaginaries and Relationalities of Power, *the special issue of* JEMS *it introduces, build on, as well as critique, past and present studies of mobility. In so doing, this issue challenges conceptual orientations built on binaries of difference that have impeded analyses of the interrelationship between mobility and stasis. These include methodological nationalism, which counterpoises concepts of internal and international movement and native and foreigner, and consequently normalises stasis. Instead, the issue offers a regimes of mobility framework that addresses the relationships between mobility and immobility, localisation and transnational connection, experiences and imaginaries of migration, and rootedness and cosmopolitan openness. The introduction highlights how, within this framework and its emphasis on social fields of differential power, the contributors to this collection ethnographically explore the disparities, inequalities, racialised representations and national mythscapes that facilitate and legitimate differential mobility and fixity. Although the authors examine nation-state building processes, their analysis is not confined by national boundaries.*

Introduction

Anthropology, the social sciences and the policy and business world recently experienced a period of interest in and even celebration of mobility. In discussions of mobility over the past two decades, all those who travelled within a country or circled the globe—whether they were seeking refuge or were students, consultants, volunteers, tourists, labour or return migrants—came to be studied through the same analytical lens (Frändberg 2008; Lindquist 2009; Salazar 2011a; Urry 2000). As research on tourism, exchange students, retirement, labour contracting and forms of professional work-related travel developed, scholars questioned the division between categories such as international migrants and temporary travellers (Bell and Ward 2000; Hall and Williams 2002; Kesselring 2006; King and Ruiz-Gelices 2003; King *et al.* 1998; Nowicka 2007; Nyíri 2010). Some writers began to insist that all forms of movement, from walking across the room to the flowing of water downstream, be addressed within the same 'new mobilities' research paradigm (Hannam *et al.* 2006; Sheller and Urry 2006; Urry 2007). The new emphasis on mobility as an inclusive category echoed and renewed concerns expressed in 1980s migration research, such as that on population mobility in developing countries (Chapman and Prothero 1985; Prothero and Chapman 1985; Skeldon 1990). Recent work in the study of mobility recognises that 'mobilities create an integrated system, which can be observed at a range of scales: family/household, community, national, and the constellation of countries linked by migration flows' (King and Skeldon 2010: 1640).

However, the current global economic crisis seems to be accompanied by a normalisation—once again—of national borders and ethnic boundaries, even as the crisis itself reveals the degree to which the world is intricately networked and interdependent. National sovereignty once more becomes a topic of concern in the domains of economics, control of labour, debt, culture and identity. Demagogues and national security experts now look askance at many of those who move, defining mobility as dangerous and threatening, while immobility is seen as normal and necessary for political and personal security (Isotalo 2009; Turner 2007). How are scholars of migration, travel, tourism and refuge to understand the rapid glamorisation and then demonisation of categories of mobile people?[1]

Given the rise, at the beginning of the twenty-first century, of new 'mobilities studies', followed by a growing repudiation of the celebration of mobility, the time is ripe for an assessment of the analytical category of mobility and its relationship to social theory and global transformation. This assessment gives rise to several questions that previous cohorts of mobility scholars did not fully address. First, how do we theorise mobility as basic to human social life in ways that normalise neither mobility nor stasis? Secondly, how do particular developments in the global political economy of a specific era shape and/or become reflected in the dominant social theory? That is to say, what is the global context that produces first the development and then the repudiation of mobilities studies? Third, why, despite the recent inclusive moment of migration studies that was able to encompass forms of movement from international tourism to labour migration, were some kinds of human mobility sidelined? For example, as Russell King and Ronald Skeldon (2010) have pointed out, migration studies retained a division between internal and international migration though, since the 1990s, internal migration has been generally ignored.

This special issue addresses all three questions by bringing together a seemingly disparate set of case studies that allows us to assess what is gained and what is lost through a perspective that normalises various forms of movement within a single category. The articles ask whether speaking of 'mobilities' adds anything to past scholarship on forms of human migration and mobility. Is speaking of 'mobilities' just part of the passing fads and fashions of the academic world, as it is of the policy and business world, or are there crucial questions of social theory and political action at stake? In various ways that are in dialogue with each other, all seven authors respond to these questions not only by providing ethnographic descriptions of the everyday activities and communications that link people transnationally, to each other and to specific places, but also by contributing to an emerging theory of society as globally but unequally relational. In this modelling of society, various circuits of interconnection are part of the ordinary structuring of human sociability.

Moving Beyond Recent Mobilities Studies

If we think historically about the human condition, it might seem that we should really have a *stasis* studies rather than migration or mobilities studies. After all, in the long view, mobility is the norm of our species and it is stasis that should be regarded as something to be queried (Maryanski and Turner 1992). Across the millennia, migration or seasonal movements of people have been a significant aspect of the human experience of space and time. The academic disciplines of geography and demography began by focusing on human movement from one place to another rather than movement across borders. However, as various fields of research became differentiated and consolidated within the twentieth century, they not only ceased to look at the world as a whole but also fostered the growth of national scholarships and a legitimisation of methodological nationalism. Methodological nationalism is an ideological orientation that approaches the study of social and historical processes as if they were contained within the borders of individual nation-states. In a parallel development in the anthropological imagination, where diffusion studies initially had been important, the territorial fixity of cultures became a common-place (Salazar 2012a). Some contemporary anthropology and much of ethnic studies have continued to approach cultures as discrete webs of signification (Geertz 1973). From such a perspective, transnational processes are novel and transgressive, occurring in response to dramatic changes in communication technology and global capitalism (Gupta and Ferguson 1992). As they frame outcomes of transnational processes as hybridity, scholars of such 'mixity' have often implied that previous stages of cultural production were unblemished by diffusion.

As is the case with the broader metaphor of 'flow' and the globalisation studies that engendered its popularity (Rockefeller 2011), the recent field of mobilities studies emerged as a critique of the academic tendency to ignore either past or present histories of human movement and interconnection. Mobilities studies called attention to the myriad ways in which people and their cultural practices are not confined to a fixed territory but are parts of multiple spatial networks and temporal linkages (Greenblatt 2009; Salazar 2010b). They encouraged scholars to work against the narrative of stasis and sedentarism as normative (Malkki 1992). Identities and loyalties could be understood as products of social relations rather than of fixed relationships to territory.

Yet narratives of movement can actually endorse the normality or historicity of stasis. As the scholarship critical of globalisation studies has noted (Freitag and von Oppen 2010; Glick Schiller 1999, 2003; Held *et al.* 1999), those who have spoken of 'flows' of people, capital and ideas—such as Arjun Appadurai (1996), Manuel Castells (1996) and Zygmunt Bauman (2000, 2002, 2007)—imagined these flows as novel and exceptional, disrupting previous fixed relationships between culture, territory and identity. Moreover, the language of flows has been strangely agentless and frictionless (Rockefeller 2011; Tsing 2005). When binaries of difference—or, in Rockefeller's (2011) words, 'covert dualisms'—are constructed between fixity and motion, social life cannot be seen as processes in which both fixity and motion are relative and interrelated. Unless grounded in a broad historical perspective that moves beyond binary logics, including that of then and now, the study of mobility can obliterate the understanding that movement and interconnection are fundamental to the human condition—past, present and future.

Moreover, those caught up in the initial exuberance of the new 'mobilities studies' not only understated the degree to which the poor and disempowered find themselves contained but they also projected movement itself as liberating, valuable and the basis of a new contemporary cosmopolitanism (Canzler *et al.* 2008). In some iterations of this perspective, only the mobility of 'elite travellers' was recognised, and their ability to consume difference in various settings around the world was defined as cosmopolitan (Hannerz 1990). By serving as the connecting points for immobile 'locals', these 'cosmopolitans' were said to be building a 'world culture', marked by diversity rather than homogeneity.

Diversity, mobility and the differential ability to travel were thus linked and positively valued. Craig Calhoun's (2002) subsequent critique of the 'class conscious-ness of frequent travellers' questioned the bias of this positive valuation and its taking for granted of differential power but did not sufficiently query whether non-elite travellers could also be cosmopolitan and what that word would imply when linked to those who were impoverished and undocumented. Soon a number of scholars were changing the terms of the debate by linking cosmopolitanism to mobility, regardless of the class positioning and relative power and status of travellers (Vertovec and Cohen 2002; Werbner 2006). For example, Ulrich Beck has argued that 'in the struggles over belonging, the actions of migrants and minorities provide examples of dialogic imaginative ways of life and everyday cosmopolitanism' (2002: 30). Steven Vertovec (2009) has outlined a 'habitual concept' of cosmopolitanism by considering culture as a kind of 'toolkit' that migrants take on their journeys. Much of this literature, despite attributing the cosmopolitan stance to poor as well as to rich and empowered travellers, maintained a binary of difference by defining cosmopolitanism as a rejection of ethnic separateness and an openness to difference. Some scholars, however, have taken a further step by not only discarding the binary between sameness and difference but also refusing to see rootedness in territory and culture, and cosmopolitan openness as oppositional (Appiah 2006; Glick Schiller forthcoming; Salazar 2010a; Werbner 2008).

Reconciling Rootedness and Cosmopolitanism

As the new mobilities studies emerged, the challenges became clear. How could researchers reject the theorisation of mobility as problematic and asocial, cast mobility in all its dimensions as an aspect of the human experience, overcome binary thinking and yet not minimise the differential barriers to movement? As they address the dynamics between mobility and stasis within unequal fields of globe-spanning power, the authors in this special issue respond directly to these challenges. Several contributors address the question of unequal fields of power by illustrating the simultaneity of rootedness and cosmopolitanism.

In his article, 'Jembe Hero: West African Drummers, Global Mobility and Cosmopolitanism as Status', **Pascal Gaudette** illustrates the way in which broader identities, aspirations and mobility strategies are linked to, rather than separated from, local cultural roots. Local knowledge becomes part of mobility strategies (Canzler *et al.* 2008). Gaudette examines how, against significantly increasing barriers, young musicians in Guinea are leveraging the commoditisation of their roots to follow their elders into global mobility. Through the establishment of crucial strategic alliances, many *jembefolas* attempt to escape a considerable apparatus of exclusion. The successes and failures of these Mande drummers 'are not only illustrative of the commodifying effects of globalisation on culture, but also of the great desirability and empowered nature of the cosmopolitan status' (Gaudette, this issue).

Cosmopolitanism in this instance is neither about being mobile *per se* nor a consumption of the other. Rather it is by becoming the 'other' and marketing an African musical persona that these men seek to enter the uneven global musical playing-field and achieve a 'cosmopolitan status' (Salazar 2010a). Similarly, **Rebecca Peters**, in this issue, offers the concept of 'development cosmopolitans' to critique concepts and representations of mobilities. She notes that, in recent discussions, being cosmopolitan means having experience and engagement with the foreign or cultural other (e.g. Nowicka and Rovisco 2009). Yet, as her work illustrates, there are not only different ways in which the cosmopolitan mobile other is constructed within transnational flows of knowledge, professionals and resources, but also different 'foreigns' with which to engage.

To move away from binary thinking and create a study of mobilities in which migration and stasis are seen as interconnected aspects of the human condition, the temptation is to build on those social theorists who use terms such as 'deterritorialisation' (Deleuze and Guattari 1987) or 'actor-network' (Latour 2005) to speak of relationality and connectivity. These theorists *do* challenge binaries that deny simultaneity of connection and differentiation. However, they do so in ways that provide no theoretical framework within which to address differential and multiple forms of power. And yet a study of mobilities must be able to simultaneously normalise an array of forms of mobility but not minimalise the ways in which legal status, as well as global racialising categories, can make a world of difference in terms of the ease of travel, the repercussions of trying to move, and whether or not the traveller gains or loses status from being from elsewhere. In this article we deploy the term 'regimes of mobility' rather than mobility studies to explore the relationships between the privileged movements of some and the co-dependent but stigmatised and forbidden movement, migration and interconnection of the poor, powerless and exploited (Franquesa 2011). It is the labour of those whose movements are declared illicit and subversive that makes possible the easy mobility of those who seem to live in a borderless world of wealth and power (Cunningham and Heyman 2004; Rees and Smart 2001; Shamir 2005). It is for this reason that Gaudette (this issue) traces a 'diagnostics of power', noting that these 'global power dynamics have a direct influence on the relations between the various actors . . . and on the microdynamics of power in social relations'.

By recognising the on-going dynamic between situations of settlement and those of mobility within situations of unequal power, the authors in this special issue move beyond categorical opposites such as fixity and motion, self and other, and communalism and cosmopolitanism (Chan 2006; Sandercock 2003). In so doing, they further advance social theory by developing contemporary discussions of simultaneity (Levitt and Glick Schiller 2004), relationality (Anthias 1998), and the mutual constitution of mobility, place and subjectivity (Massey 2005). This relational perspective allows our contributors to provide new insights into processes that have often been documented by scholars of migration and travel but have been under-theorised or misrepresented. Their theoretical framework for the study of both stasis and mobility offers more than the fluctuating preference of one or the other which has marked much of previous social theory. The interrelationship between and interdependency of mobility and stasis were denied by classic social theorists such as Ferdinand Tönnies (1957 [1887]), who modelled a *Gemeinschaft* and *Gesellschaft* distinction, Robert Park and Ernest Burgess (1967 [1925]), and Robert Redfield (1965 [1953]), who postulated a rural–urban dichotomy, or Emile Durkheim (1982 [1895]), who approached population as a fixed territorialised social fact. This binary opposition was then challenged by migration researchers of colonised regions (Epstein 1967; Mitchell 1974; Prothero and Chapman 1985; Roberts 1989; Skeldon 1990). More-recent migration and mobility scholarship has tended to restore the binary by either focusing on immigrant settlement and assimilation or prioritising the study of global flows of circular migration, tourism and business travel.

In contrast, the theoretical orientation of *Regimes of Mobility: Imaginaries and Relationalities of Power* neither normalises fixed relationships between people and territory nor naturalises movement, a position that can obscure the human costs of life without rights vested somewhere. The issue contributes to a historical view of the past and on-going relationship between agricultural societies and the growth and transformations of industrial capitalism. In the nineteenth and twentieth centuries, movement to cities—or urbanisation—was part of a rural–urban interdependency both in industrialising states and in colonialised territories. Then and now these connections have been marked by ever-changing relationships between mobility and immobility, as people from different localities market, trade, harvest, fish, build cities, manufacture goods, intermarry, join or flee armies and seek land, security, work and a future.

Regimes of Mobility

The insights provided by the contributors to this special issue lead us to argue that there are *regimes* of mobility that confront both the theorist and the traveller. The term 'regime' calls attention to the role both of individual states and of changing international regulatory and surveillance administrations that affect individual mobility. At the same time, the term reflects a notion of governmentality and hegemony in which there are constant struggles to understand, query, embody, celebrate and transform categories of similarity, difference, belonging and strangeness (Burchel 1991; Foucault 2000; Hall 1997). Shamir (2000: 199) sees the emergence of a 'single global mobility regime':

> Oriented to closure and to the blocking of access, premised not only on 'old' national or local grounds but on a principle of perceived universal dangerous personhoods . . . [T]he mobility regime is constructed to maintain high levels of inequality in a relatively normatively homogenized world. In practice, this means that local, national, and regional boundaries are now being rebuilt and consolidated under the increased normative pressure of, and as a counterbalance to, the universal human rights regime . . . [P]rocesses of globalization are also concerned with the prevention of movement and the blocking of access. . . . [S]uch processes should neither be theorized as a systemic malfunction nor as the unintended consequences of globalization.

The case studies in this issue lead us to join Shamir in questioning the scholarship that celebrated the 'death of distance' (Cairncross 1997), mobility as freedom and a 'mobility turn' (Urry 2007). However, we postulate that there are several different intersecting regimes of mobility that normalise the movements of some travellers while criminalising and entrapping the ventures of others. Whether globalisation is theorised solely in terms of 'processes of closure, entrapment, and containment' (Shamir 2005: 199) or pluralised as mobility regimes, the concept of regime addresses the varying ways in which human stasis and mobility have been approached in social theory.

The authors in this collection deploy a regimes-of-mobility approach to redirect the attention of mobility researchers back to the dynamic between sedentariness and movement, and explicitly critique the dichotomy between mobility and immobility that has characterised recent scholarship. **Michaela Pelican**, in her paper 'International Migration: Virtue or Vice? Perspectives from Cameroon', discusses diverse imaginaries of migration among youths in two Cameroonian cities. Public discourse and imaginaries of international migration vary considerably in these two localities. This is reflected in differences in envisioned destinations as well as in terminologies and concepts. In recent years, the generally positive consideration of international migration has given way to more critical perspectives, with a subsequent rethinking of the local as well as the migratory life. International migration is thus viewed in a broad discursive spectrum from virtue to vice, and perceptions of both mobility and immobility are influenced by regional, national and international political discourse (cf. Salazar 2011b). As Paolo Gaibazzi points out in his paper here, we need conceptual tools broad enough not only to encompass imaginaries and relationalities of migration, but also of sedentariness and the right to settlement.

As the articles demonstrate, a regimes-of-mobility approach must move beyond the ready equation of mobility with freedom by examining not only movement as connection but also as an aspect of new confinements and modes of exploitation (Salazar and Smart 2011). Refugees and asylum-seekers are forced to flee and yet, when granted some form of legal status, may find themselves restricted to settling in specific cities, towns or rural areas (Lubkemann 2008). Meanwhile 'illegals', who live or work without documents, may have to move from residence to residence, their mobility compelled by their need to avoid surveillance (Bloch *et al.* 2009). In this situation, mobility produces entrapments (see Barak Kalir's paper in this issue) since, at each stop in their furtive journeys, these migrants may spend any non-working time confined to their living spaces, afraid to venture forth. Meanwhile, a growing cohort of the global workforce, including domestic workers and computer technicians, migrate with fixed work contracts that confine them to a specific employer and perhaps residence as a condition of their 'mobility' (Anderson 2000; Biao 2007). However, it is not only the current moment of neoliberal global capital that has produced precarious labour. Rather, each historic restructuring of modes and spaces of accumulation creates new and dynamic relationships between mobility and immobility that empower the few and create conditions of spatialised but connected contestation among the many (Massey 2005; Sassen 1999; Wolf 1982).

As can be seen, the perceptions of the connections between stasis and mobility offered by *Regimes of Mobility: Imaginaries and Relationalities of Power* are more than an iteration of past insights into the construction of locality through migration. The various contributors examine the subjectivities and reflective sensibilities within which local people reflect upon and incorporate migratory experiences into their sense of the fixity of place and the concept of 'home'. For example, in his article 'Cultivating Hustlers: The Agrarian Ethos of Soninke Migration', **Paolo Gaibazzi** offers an ethnography that documents the life path and outlook of rural young men in The Gambia who are aware of their location within both agrarian ethos and on-going circuits of exploitative labour migration. He notes that 'an agrarian ethos pervades and actually sustains Soninke migration'; the villagers invest in the agrarian upbringing of young men, the most mobile section of society, to instil particular dispositions, skills and ethical orientations in them in view of sedentary as well as migratory livelihoods. That is to say, rural Soninke, in educating their next generation of young men, have stepped beyond the various regimes of mobility with their competing narratives about the virtues or evils of migration. Similarly, in her article in this collection—'The Great Departure: Rethinking National(ist) Common Sense'—**Dace Dzenovska** argues that, through their recent collective experience of mobile practices and transversals, which they refer to as 'the great departure', Latvians have developed a collective reappraisal of a dichotomous value system that linked the good life with home territory and cast mobility in negative terms. A regimes-of-mobility approach will allow researchers to identify forms of sociability that create both forms of commonness extending across space and difference, and shared identities of place (Glick Schiller *et al.* 2011).

At the same time, as Dzenovska argues, such an approach moves past the 'blind spot' that allows us to misperceive what we observe, think beyond the descriptive tracing of 'flows and relations' and build on Massey's (2005) approach to the mutual constitution of place and subject. This 'double articulation' results in a coherent narrative of place and of self in relation to it (Dzenovska, this issue). To analyse the changing dynamics of mobility and immobility, the contributors in this special issue theorise power within multiple intersecting geographic scales. They make it clear that, when we speak of mobility and interconnection, we cannot dismiss the significance of territory nor of governmental powers that are based in territory. As Pelican argues, both global and national power differences play a crucial role in shaping migration and its imaginaries. The challenge therefore in a regimes-of-mobility approach is the same one faced by all scholars who research social processes: how to take into account forms of organised relations of power, many of which are territorially based if not bounded and, at the same time, do not deploy a container theory of society. How can we develop a theory of society in which mobility is normalised and seen as integral, rather than in opposition, to territorially based social relationships?

Some work has been done in this direction by those who have critiqued methodological nationalism and its bounded approaches to social science (Amelina *et al.* 2012). A growing number of social theorists have argued that methodological nationalism has been central to much of Western social science (Beck 2000; Martins 1974; Smith 1983; Wimmer and Glick Schiller 2002, 2003). Methodological nationalists confine the concept of society to the boundaries of nation-states and the members of those states are assumed to share a common history and set of values, norms, social customs and institutions. Some writers label this orientation the 'container' theory of society to highlight that most social theorists, including Emile Durkheim, Max Weber and Talcott Parsons, have contained their concept of society within the territorial and institutional boundaries of the nation-state (Basch *et al.* 1994; Urry 2000; Wolf 1982).

There are a number of reasons why methodological nationalism came to be so pervasive in migration scholarship, a topic addressed at length elsewhere by Andreas Wimmer and Nina Glick Schiller (2002, 2003). Migration scholars in the US and in Europe have been strongly influenced by periods of intense concern for national security, national economy and the national social fabric. Their scholarship often reflects funding streams that stress national priorities, with nation-states used as units of analysis. Statistics about migration are organised by, and in the interests of, national governments. Recent iterations of a methodological nationalist perspective in migration scholarship has led to the separation of internal and international migration, which ignores many similarities in the migration process, whether or not the migrant crosses national borders. It has also meant the negation of the previous body of migration scholarship that was influenced by global and regional perspectives on issues of underdevelopment, colonialism, urbanisation, the centrality of mobility in different cultural contexts, and issues of mobility and power in pre-capitalist contexts (Kosinski and Prothero 1975; McGee 1973, 1982; Prothero and Chapman 1985; Skeldon 1986).[2] Methodological nationalism has also led to the curious inability of migration scholars to sufficiently address instances in which states such as China inhibit internal migration. As Glick Schiller (2010) has noted, studies of transnational migration and diasporic nationalism have generally retained as the unit of analysis a national, ethnic or ethno-religious community that is thought to share history, culture and language

To reject methodological nationalism requires migration scholars to recover an approach to migration that does not use nation-states as units of analysis but rather studies the movement of people across space in relationship to forces that structure political economy. These forces include, but are not confined to, states and their policies. Furthermore, national and international policies are considered within the same analytical framework. It is the methodological nationalism of contemporary migration scholarship, reflecting the tendency of researchers to think like a nation-state, which led them to only study movement that crosses borders and to label as mobile only those who move to or settle in another state (Glick Schiller 2010).

It is important to note that to critique methodological nationalism is not to discount the nation-state as an actor in questions of international migration or to endorse the contemporary silences about internal migration. Nation-states *do* participate in the formation and legitimation of globe-spanning regimes of mobility by imposing barriers on the emigration and immigration of some individuals and facilitating the movement of others and by using national identities and nationalist ideologies to justify the exclusion or inclusion of those who cross state borders. As this special issue illustrates, to adequately theorise mobility, scholars must examine the role of nation-states and the influence of national identities in shaping the experience of migrants without confining their study and analysis within the parameters of the nation-state. Dzenovska's contribution here furthers this perspective by arguing that the...

...practices of mobility are shaped by the material reality of the national order of things and that the national order of things also lends meaning to mobility in collective and individual narratives. At the same time, the experiences of mobility— and the associated emplacement and displacement—exceed their co-optation by national(ist) common sense. I suggest that identifying national(ist) common sense as an animating discourse about mobility often overlooks this excess. To unleash the analytical and political potential of this excess, one needs to undertake the work of excavation. This, in turn, requires the bracketing of facile diagnoses of nationalism.

The critique of methodological nationalism and discussions of the limits of nation-states as units of study and analysis highlight the current challenge within the growth of 'mobilities studies', a challenge taken on by the presenters of the articles in this special issue. The challenge is as follows: What do we see if we do not think about mobility like a nation-state? The conceptual terrain we can envision when we think beyond the lens of the nation-state allows us to build a regimes-of-mobility approach that sees movement and settlement in constant and reconstituting interrelationships.

In her contribution, 'Development Mobilities: Identity and Authority in an Angolan Development Programme', **Rebecca Peters** offers just such an analysis. She describes globe-circulating narratives that differentially construct, evaluate and empower local, national and global identities. Peters focuses on international NGO workers to illustrate ethnographically the production and negotiation of locality and internationality. These imaginaries are produced within efforts to position Angolans who work in international development organisations. They become a point of contention as they simultaneously appear to be 'locals' in development and transnational, cosmopolitan professionals. Peters joins Gaudette and Vasantkumar (all in this issue) in making it clear that stepping out of methodological nationalism allows us to better understand the way in which the global, national and local are simultaneously and differentially constructed. At the same time, Vasantkumar, deploying the term 'methodological belongingism', uses the case of 'proliferating varieties of post-1959 Tibetan imagined communities' to emphasise that methodo-logical nationalism 'obscured how others have thought of the nation beyond the nation-state'.

As they critique methodological nationalist perspectives, the authors also make clear that this critique cannot be equated with the position that all mobility is equal. Mobility clearly benefits different sets of actors in very different ways. This point is forcibly made by **Barak Kalir** in his article 'Moving Subjects, Stagnant Paradigms: Can the "Mobilities Paradigm" Transcend Methodological Nationalism?'. Kalir also makes clear that the narrative of migration as physical mobility has been integrally linked with the promise of social mobility. His interest in mobility is not only geographic—from small home village in China to village with more employment and opportunity, to Tel Aviv, to Shanghai—but also across class lines. Pelican makes a very similar point in her article here about the complex and, importantly, changing interrelations of physical and social mobility. These two kinds of mobility have often come together in US immigrant rags-to-riches tales. In US and contemporary global migration narratives, the unspoken, unacknowledged underpinnings of migrant success are the processes of capitalist accumulation, which are always emplaced. Taken together, Kalir's and Pelican's articles make clear that the two forms of mobility are linked because the structures of capital accumulation are always situated in time and space.

As Kalir shows, the exploitation of Chinese workers in Israel and in China should not be dismissed within a rhetoric of global flows of people and ideas. There are a few winners and many losers. This is not to validate stasis but to argue for a regimes-of-mobility approach that constantly theorises the relationships of unequal power within which relative stasis and different forms of mobility are constructed and negotiated. To move beyond methodological nationalism, we need a global perspective on mobility—physical and social, upward and downward (Glick Schiller 2010). David Harvey's (2006) theorisation of the movement, flexible accumulation and destruction of capital within globe-spanning but emplaced networks of power is more useful here than Appadurai's (1996) talk of flows. It is not that it would have been better to focus on internal rather than cross-border migration. Rather, it is important to look at how the relative backwardness of China made it a prime competitor globally and provided opportunities for a handful in new emplacements of wealth.

By defining movement and stasis within social and economic relationships rather than in relation to geographic borders, a regimes-of-mobility approach can facilitate a scholarship that is neither confined by nor ignores nation and territory (Jansen and Löfving 2009). Whilst not seeing like a nation-state, we must be aware of the role of national mythscapes that confine our ability to analyse the dynamic relationship between stasis and movement. Bell defines the concept of mythscape as: 'the discursive realm, constituted by and through temporal and spatial dimensions, in which the myths of the nation are forgotten, transmitted, reconstructed and negotiated constantly' (2003: 75).[3] Mythscapes tend to be rooted in constructions of 'an idealized bounded territory, for example... pastoral English villages, [or] rugged American frontiers or bucolic German forests' (Bell 2003: 76). These are the mythscapes that propel a constant sense of the inauthenticity of the present and a search for the scapegoat that has destroyed the sanctity of the homeland. In contrast, as the papers in this special issue so clearly illustrate, there is actually no place like the imagined home. These papers share a critical perspective on the narrative and romance of the nation-state by querying its mythscapes.

The imaginaries of mobility that complement national mythscapes (Carling and Åkesson 2009; Ferro 2006; Salazar 2011b) are also a subject in *Regimes of Mobility across the Globe*. In the cultural logics of migration, imaginaries play a predominant role in envisioning both the (often-mythologised) green pastures of the new land and the nostalgic memories of the homeland (Jackson 2008). Migration is about these imaginaries as well as about actual physical movement from one locality to another and back (Salazar 2012b). The images and ideas of other (read as better) possible places to live—often misrepresented through popular media—circulate in a very unequal global space (Englund 2002) and are ultimately filtered through migrants' personal aspirations. Migration thus always presupposes some knowledge or, at least, rumours of 'the other side'. Imaginaries of such movements play out in uneven and even contradictory ways.

Finally, in his article 'Tibetan Peregri-nations: Mobility, Incommensurable Nationalisms and (Un)belonging Athwart the Himalayas', **Christopher Vasantkumar** provides an illustration of the dynamic tensions between migration and the national imaginary. His research indicates that those Tibetans who fled to India from China see the life of the refugee Tibetan community as inauthentic, degraded, commercialised Tibetan culture, even as they gain skills and education through migration. Meanwhile, those who stay in Tibet see national culture as degraded, feeling that the best Tibetans have fled. They, too, experience a sense of loss. It is important to note that Vasantkumar describes a plurality of national forms at play, one of which reflects the global modernist narrative of the nation as it is played out and replayed within the constitution of a space of refuge. The mythscape of the nation (and of what is seen as 'home') is one of the romance of nostalgia—a longing for a lost past and a projection of a restored future purity, which plays off the binaries of past and future and here or there, without acknowledging global connectivity. Vasantkumar, in his querying of nationalism through an optic of mobility, faces the challenge of speaking about and locating the contingencies of differential power that mark all mobility experiences and practices.

Although their ethnographies are situated in disparate geographic locations ranging from Africa (Gaudette, Peters, Gaibazzi and Pelican), Asia (Kalir and Vasantkumar) and Europe (Dzenovska), each author contributes to a relational approach to the study of mobility that theorises place-making, spatiality and borders as part of networks of social relationships and circuits of movement (King 1996; Massey 2005). Each author also illustrates the conceptual and political dilemmas of the people amongst whom they worked.

Conclusions

As more people are on the move, states attempt to maintain their authority, not only over mobilities but also over their meaning (Nyíri 2010). In a world that is perceived to be in constant flux, control over people's movement and mobility potential, sometimes termed *motility* (Kaufmann *et al.* 2004), has become a central concern for projects of biopolitics and governmentality. The papers in *Regimes of Mobility: Imaginaries and Relationalities of Power* make important contributions to the formulation of six key ideas that can set the direction for mobility studies. First, the relationship between mobility and immobility, which always define each other, must be highlighted. Secondly, to understand the relative and changing definition of mobility and immobility, we need to place these concepts within a theory of unequal globe-spanning relationships of power. In the third place, within the contemporary moment, these unequal relationalities are shaped by the social, political, cultural and economic relations of capital production as they play out within specific local contexts. Fourth, rather than a mobility studies that speaks of the general category of travelling or movement, we need a regimes-of-mobility approach that addresses the range of actors within specific situations, including, but not exclusively, state actors. Such state actors define key categories such as legal, undocumented, territory, space and border, which shape the ways in which we conceptualise mobility and stasis. We need to interrogate the situations in which certain kinds of mobility, or certain types of mobile individuals, become the subjects of praise or condemnation, desire, suppression or fear. The fifth point continues the discussion about categories to contest our received notions of class. A long-standing definition of class in historical anthropology spoke of class differences being based on differential access to a range of resources. A regimes-of-mobility approach can challenge us to expand this understanding so that the ability and legal right to travel become one of the criteria by which class is defined and class privilege upheld. The sixth and final point is about history. The discussion of mobility and immobility reflects and shapes our understanding of time as well as space.

Acknowledgements

Earlier versions of the articles in this special issue of *JEMS* were presented at a panel entitled 'A New Virtue? Imaginaries and Regimes of Mobility Across the Globe', organised by Noel B. Salazar and Pál Nyíri at the 11th EASA Biennial Conference in Maynooth, Ireland, in 2010. We would like to thank the audience, and all the session participants for their comments and suggestions. We also want to show our gratitude to Pál Nyíri for his valuable input to this special issue.

Notes

[1]   There is an interesting parallel during colonial times when pastoralists such as the Maasai in East Africa were revered but also demonised. Colonial migrants were sometimes similarly sought as a key to modernisation and urbanisation and feared as deculturated (Epstein 1967). Today, the glamorisation and criminalisation of those who move may also happen at the same time, so that temporary tourists are sought while those who come to work or settle more permanently are rejected.

[2]   In making this point, we acknowledge and thank an anonymous *JEMS* reviewer.

[3]   Bell's concept of mythscape has been applied to migration studies by anthropologist Garbi Schmidt (2012).

References

Amelina, A., Faist, T., Glick Schiller, N. and Nergiz, D.D. (2012) 'Methodological predicaments of cross-border studies', in Amelina, A., Faist, T., Glick Schiller, N. and Nergiz, D. (eds) *Comparative Studies in Methodological Nationalism*. London: Routledge, 1–31.

Anderson, B. (2000) *Doing the Dirty Work? The Global Politics of Domestic Labour*. London: Zed.

Anthias, F. (1998) 'Evaluating "diaspora": beyond ethnicity', *Sociology, 32*(3): 557–80.

Appadurai, A. (1996) *Modernity at Large: Cultural Dimensions of Globalization*. Minneapolis: University of Minnesota Press.

Appiah, A. (2006) *Cosmopolitanism: Ethics in a World of Strangers*. New York: W.W. Norton.

Basch, L.G., Glick Schiller, N. and Szanton Blanc, C. (1994) *Nations Unbound: Transnational Projects, Postcolonial Predicaments, and Deterritorialized Nation-States*. Langhorne: Gordon and Breach.

Bauman, Z. (2000) *Liquid Modernity*. Cambridge: Polity Press.

Bauman, Z. (2002) *Society Under Siege*. Cambridge: Polity Press.

Bauman, Z. (2007) *Liquid Times: Living in an Age of Uncertainty*. Cambridge: Polity Press.

Beck, U. (2000) 'The cosmopolitan perspective: sociology of the second age of modernity', *British Journal of Sociology*, *51*(1): 79–105.

Beck, U. (2002) 'The cosmopolitan society and its enemies', *Theory, Culture and Society*, *19*(1/2): 17–44.

Bell, D. (2003) 'Mythscapes: memory, mythology, and national identity', *British Journal of Sociology*, *54*(1): 63–81.

Bell, M. and Ward, G. (2000) 'Comparing temporary mobility with permanent migration', *Tourism Geographies*, *2*(1): 87–107.

Biao, X. (2007) *Global 'Body Shopping': An Indian Labor System in Information Technology*. Princeton: Princeton University Press.

Bloch, A., Sigona, N. and Zetter, R. (2009) *No Right to Dream*. London: Paul Hamlyn Foundation.

Burchel, G. (1991) *The Foucault Effect: Studies in Governmentality*. Chicago: University of Chicago Press.

Cairncross, F. (1997) *The Death of Distance: How the Communications Revolution will Change our Lives*. Cambridge: Harvard Business School Press.

Calhoun, C. (2002) 'The class consciousness of frequent travelers: toward a critique of actually existing cosmopolitanism', *South Atlantic Quarterly*, *101*(4): 869–97.

Canzler, W., Kaufmann, V. and Kesselring, S. (eds) (2008) *Tracing Mobilities: Towards a Cosmopolitan Perspective*. Aldershot: Ashgate.

Carling, J. and Åkesson, L. (2009) 'Mobility at the heart of a nation: patterns and meanings of Cape Verdean migration', *International Migration*, *47*(3): 123–55.

Castells, M. (1996) *The Rise of the Network Society*. Cambridge, MA: Blackwell.

Chan, W.F. (2006) 'Planning Birmingham as a cosmopolitan city: recovering the dept of its diversity?', in Binnie, J., Holloway, J., Millington, S. and Young, C. (eds) *Cosmopolitan Urbanism*. Milton Park: Routledge, 204–19.

Chapman, M. and Prothero, R.M. (eds) (1985) *Circulation in Population Movement: Substance and Concepts from the Melanesian Case*. London: Routledge.

Cunningham, H. and Heyman, J. (2004) 'Introduction: mobilities and enclosures at borders', *Identities: Global Studies in Culture and Power*, *11*(3): 289–302.

Deleuze, G. and Guattari, F. (1987) *A Thousand Plateaus: Capitalism and Schizophrenia*. Minneapolis: University of Minnesota Press.

Durkheim, E. (1982 [1895]) *The Rules of Sociological Method*. New York: Free Press.

Englund, H. (2002) 'Ethnography after globalism: migration and emplacement in Malawi', *American Ethnologist*, *29*(2): 261–86.

Epstein, A.L. (1967) 'Urbanization and social change in Africa', *Current Anthropology*, *8*(4): 275–95.

Ferro, A. (2006) 'Desired mobility or satisfied immobility? Migratory aspirations among knowledge workers', *Journal of Education and Work*, *19*(2): 171–200.

Foucault, M. (2000) 'Truth and power', in Faubion, J. (ed.) *Essential Works of Foucault 1954–1984*. New York: The New Press, Vol. 3, 111–33.

Frändberg, L. (2008) 'Paths in transnational time-space: representing mobility biographies of young Swedes', *Geografiska Annaler*, *90B*(1): 17–28.

Franquesa, J. (2011) "'We've lost our bearings": place, tourism, and the limits of the "mobility turn"', *Antipode*, *43*(4): 1012–33.

Freitag, U. and von Oppen, A. (eds) (2010) *Translocality: The Study of Globalising Processes from a Southern Perspective*. Leiden: Brill.

Geertz, C. (1973) *The Interpretation of Cultures: Selected Essays*. New York: Basic Books.

Glick Schiller, N. (1999) 'Transmigrants and nation-states: something old and something new in the US immigrant experience', in Hirschman, C., DeWind, J. and Kasinitz, P. (eds) *Handbook of International Migration: The American Experience*. New York: Russell Sage, 94–119.

Glick Schiller, N. (2003) 'The centrality of ethnography in the study of transnational migration: seeing the wetland instead of the swamp', in Foner, N. (ed.) *American Arrivals*. Santa Fe: School of American Research, 99–128.

Glick Schiller, N. (2010) 'A global perspective on transnational migration: theorizing migration without methodological nationalism', in Bauböck, R. and Faist, T. (eds) *Diaspora and Transnationalism: Concepts, Theories and Methods*. Amsterdam: Amsterdam University Press, 109–29.

Glick Schiller, N. (forthcoming) 'Diasporic cosmopolitanism: migrants, sociabilities and city-making', in Irving, I. and Glick Schiller, N. (eds) *Whose Cosmopolitanism? Critical Cosmopolitanism, Relationalities and Discontents*. New York: Berghahn.

Glick Schiller, N., Darieva, T. and Gruner-Domic, S. (2011) 'Defining cosmopolitan sociability in a transnational age: an introduction', *Ethnic and Racial Studies*, *34*(3): 399–418.

Greenblatt, S. (ed.) (2009) *Cultural Mobility: A Manifesto*. Cambridge: Cambridge University Press.

Gupta, A. and Ferguson, J. (1992) 'Beyond "culture": space, identity, and the politics of difference', *Cultural Anthropology*, *7*(1): 6–23.

Hall, S. (ed.) (1997) *Representation: Cultural Representations and Signifying Practices*. London: Sage.

Hall, C.M. and Williams, A.M. (eds) (2002) *Tourism and Migration: New Relationships Between Production and Consumption*. Boston: Kluwer.

Hannam, K., Sheller, M. and Urry, J. (2006) 'Editorial: mobilities, immobilities and moorings', *Mobilities*, *1*(1): 1–22.

Hannerz, U. (1990) 'Cosmopolitans and locals in world culture', *Theory, Culture, and Society*, *7*(2/3): 237–52.

Harvey, D. (2006) *Spaces of Global Capitalism*. London: Verso.

Held, D., McGrew, A., Goldblatt, D. and Perraton, J. (eds) (1999) *Global Transformations: Politics, Economics and Culture*. Stanford: Stanford University Press.

Isotalo, R. (2009) 'Politicizing the transnational: on implications for migrants, refugees, and scholarship', *Social Analysis*, *53*(3): 60–84.

Jackson, M. (2008) 'The shock of the new: on migrant imaginaries and critical transitions', *Ethnos*, *73*(1): 57–72.

Jansen, S. and Löfving, S. (2009) 'Towards an anthropology of violence, hope, and the movement of peoples', in Jansen, S. and Löfving, S. (eds) *Struggles for Home: Violence, Hope and the Movement of People*. Oxford: Berghahn, 1–24.

Kaufmann, V., Bergman, M.M. and Joye, D. (2004) 'Motility: mobility as capital', *International Journal of Urban and Regional Research*, *28*(4): 745–56.

Kesselring, S. (2006) 'Pioneering mobilities: new patterns of movement and motility in a mobile world', *Environment and Planning A*, *38*(2): 269–79.

King, A.D. (1996) 'Introduction: cities, texts and paradigms', in King, A.D. (ed.) *Re-Presenting the City: Ethnicity, Capital and Culture in the 21st Century*. New York: New York University Press, 1–22.

King, R. and Ruiz-Gelices, E. (2003) 'International student migration and the European "year abroad": effects on European identity and subsequent migration behaviour', *International Journal of Population Geography*, *9*(3): 229–52.

King, R. and Skeldon, R. (2010) 'Mind the gap! Integrating approaches to internal and international migration', *Journal of Ethnic and Migration Studies*, 36(10): 1619–46.

King, R., Warnes, A.M. and Williams, A.M. (1998) 'International retirement migration in Europe', *International Journal of Population Geography*, 4(2): 91–111.

Kosinski, L.A. and Prothero, R.M. (eds) (1975) *People on the Move: Studies on Internal Migration*. London: Methuen.

Latour, B. (2005) *Reassembling the Social: An Introduction to Actor-Network Theory*. Oxford: Oxford University Press.

Levitt, P. and Glick Schiller, N. (2004) 'Conceptualizing simultaneity: a transnational social field perspective on society', *International Migration Review*, 38(3): 1002–39.

Lindquist, J.A. (2009) *The Anxieties of Mobility: Migration and Tourism in the Indonesian Borderlands*. Honolulu: University of Hawai'i Press.

Lubkemann, S.C. (2008) 'Involuntary immobility: on a theoretical invisibility in forced migration studies', *Journal of Refugee Studies*, 21(4): 454–75.

Malkki, L.H. (1992) 'National Geographic: the rooting of peoples and the territorialization of national identity among scholars and refugees', *Cultural Anthropology*, 7(1): 24–44.

Martins, H. (1974) 'Time and theory in sociology', in Rex, J. (ed.) *Approaches to Sociology: An Introduction to Major Trends in British Sociology*. London: Routledge and Kegan Paul, 248–94.

Maryanski, A. and Turner, J.H. (1992) *The Social Cage: Human Nature and the Evolution of Society*. Stanford: Stanford University Press.

Massey, D.B. (2005) *For Space*. London: Sage.

McGee, T.G. (1973) 'Peasants in the cities: a paradox, a paradox, a most ingenious paradox', *Human Organization*, 32(2): 135–42.

McGee, T.G. (1982) 'Labour mobility in fragmented labour markets: the role of circulatory migration in rural-urban relations in Asia', in Safa, H.I. (ed.) *Towards a Political Economy of Urbanization in Third World Countries*. Delhi: Oxford University Press, 47–66.

Mitchell, J.C. (1974) 'Social networks', *Annual Review of Anthropology*, 3: 279–99.

Nowicka, M. (2007) 'Mobile locations: construction of home in a group of mobile transnational professionals', *Global Networks*, 7(1): 69–86.

Nowicka, M. and Rovisco, M. (eds) (2009) *Cosmopolitanism in Practice*. Farnham: Ashgate.

Nyíri, P. (2010) *Mobility and Cultural Authority in Contemporary China*. Seattle: University of Washington Press.

Park, R. and Burgess, E. (1967 [1925]) *The City*. Chicago: University of Chicago Press.

Prothero, R.M. and Chapman, M. (eds) (1985) *Circulation in Third World Countries*. London: Routledge.

Redfield, R. (1965 [1953]) *The Primitive World and its Transformations*. Ithaca: Cornell University Press.

Rees, M.W. and Smart, J. (eds) (2001) *Plural Globalities in Multiple Localities: New World Borders*. Lanham: University Press of America.

Roberts, B. (1989) *Urbanization, Migration, and Development*. Austin: University of Texas.

Rockefeller, S.A. (2011) '"Flow"', *Current Anthropology*, 52(4): 557–78.

Salazar, N.B. (2010a) *Envisioning Eden: Mobilizing Imaginaries in Tourism and Beyond*. Oxford: Berghahn.

Salazar, N.B. (2010b) 'Towards an anthropology of cultural mobilities', *Crossings: Journal of Migration and Culture*, 1(1): 53–68.

Salazar, N.B. (2011a) 'The power of the imagination in transnational mobilities', *Identities: Global Studies in Culture and Power*, 18(6): 576–98.

Salazar, N.B. (2011b) 'Tanzanian migration imaginaries', in Cohen, R. and Jónsson, G. (eds) *Migration and Culture*. Cheltenham: Edward Elgar, 673–87.

Salazar, N.B. (2012a) 'The anthropology of mobility', in Adey, P., Bissell, D., Hannam, K., Merriman, P. and Sheller, M. (eds) *The Routledge Handbook of Mobilities*. London: Routledge, in press.

Salazar, N.B. (2012b) 'Imagining (im)mobility at the "end of the world"', in Vannini, P., Jiron, P., Jensen, O.B., Budd, L. and Fisker, C. (eds) *Technologies of Mobility in the Americas.* New York: Peter Lang, 237–54.

Salazar, N.B. and Smart, A. (eds) (2011) 'Anthropological takes on (im)mobility'. Special issue, *Identities: Global Studies in Culture and Power, 18*(6).

Sandercock, L. (2003) *Cosmopolis II: Mongrel Cities of the 21st Century.* London: Continuum.

Sassen, S. (1999) *Globalization and its Discontents.* New York: New Press.

Schmidt, G. (2012) 'A neighbourhood caught between national mythscapes and local engagement', in Nielsen, J. (ed.) *Islam in Denmark: The Challenge of Diversity.* New York: Lexington Books, 95–114.

Shamir, R. (2005) 'Without borders? Notes on globalization as a mobility regime', *Sociological Theory, 23*(2): 197–217.

Sheller, M. and Urry, J. (2006) 'The new mobilities paradigm', *Environment and Planning A, 38*(2): 207–26.

Skeldon, R. (1986) 'On migration patterns in India during the 1970s', *Population and Development Review, 12*(4): 759–79.

Skeldon, R. (1990) *Population Mobility in Developing Countries: A Reinterpretation.* London: Belhaven Press.

Smith, A. (1983) 'Nationalism and social theory', *British Journal of Sociology, 34*(1): 19–38.

Tönnies, F. (1957[1887]) *Community and Society (Gemeinschaft und Gesellschaft).* East Lansing: Michigan State University Press.

Tsing, A.L. (2005) *Friction: An Ethnography of Global Connection.* Princeton: Princeton University Press.

Turner, B.S. (2007) 'The enclave society: towards a sociology of immobility', *European Journal of Social Theory, 10*(2): 287–303.

Urry, J. (2000) *Sociology Beyond Societies: Mobilities for the Twenty-First Century.* London: Routledge.

Urry, J. (2007) *Mobilities.* Cambridge: Polity Press.

Vertovec, S. (2009) *Cosmopolitanism in Attitude, Practice and Competence.* www.mmg.mpg.de/workingpapers.

Vertovec, S. and Cohen, R. (2002) 'Introduction', in Vertovec, S. and Cohen, R. (eds) *Conceiving Cosmopolitanism: Theory, Context and Practice.* Oxford: Oxford University Press, 1–23.

Werbner, P. (2006) 'Vernacular cosmopolitanism', *Theory, Culture and Society, 23*(2–3): 496–98.

Werbner, P. (ed.) (2008) *Anthropology and the New Cosmopolitanism: Rooted, Feminist and Vernacular Perspectives.* Oxford: Berg.

Wimmer, A. and Glick Schiller, N. (2002) 'Methodological nationalism and beyond: nation-state building, migration and the social sciences', *Global Networks, 2*(4): 301–34.

Wimmer, A. and Glick Schiller, N. (2003) 'Methodological nationalism, the social sciences, and the study of migration: an essay in historical epistemology', *International Migration Review, 37*(7): 576–610.

Wolf, E.R. (1982) *Europe and the People Without History.* Berkeley: University of California Press.

The Great Departure: Rethinking National(ist) Common Sense

Dace Dzenovska

This article argues that, in order to overcome the national(ist) common sense that continues to haunt everyday political and scholarly interpretations of mobility, scholars need not diagnose nationalism with greater vigour, but should rather move beyond facile diagnoses of nationalism. The article calls for a meticulous tracing of relations and practices of emplacement and displacement that ubiquitous national(ist) interpretive frames both co-opt and exceed simultaneously. The argument is elaborated on the basis of an analysis of historical articulations of emplacement and displacement in Latvian understandings of 'the good life'. The article pays particular attention to the ways in which the figure of the migrant has emerged historically as an aberration to Latvian understandings of the good life. It also considers how this ethical configuration is being unsettled through massive labour migration to Western Europe—or 'the Great Departure'.

The Great Departure as a Site of Possibility

In December 2009 I was standing in line at the gate of the Ryanair flight from London to Riga. I was moving to Riga—after many years of back and forth between there, New York and San Francisco—to take up a three-year research position affiliated with the University of Latvia. Financed by the European Social Fund, my employment was conceived as 'bringing back the human resources' who had left the Latvian nation-state to study or work elsewhere. I was thus a prime subject of a policy articulated in the spirit of 'the national order of things', that is, a policy that posited a necessary link between particular bodies and territories, and that took the system of nation-states as a natural formation within which life, including mobility, is organised (Balibar 2010; Gupta and Ferguson 1992; Malkki 1992, 1995; Torpey 1998; Wimmer and Glick

19

Schiller 2002). Within this national order of things, people who had left their 'country of origin' and were thought to possess skills and knowledge were best returned to it rather than constituting a burden on the social budget.

On that winter day, I was not the only one in the Ryanair queue who could have been marked as returning in one or another sense of the term. Most people in the line and later on the plane identified each other as fellow travellers through their shared experiences of working and living away from home or of crafting home between two or more places (Lulle 2010). People asked one another from which part of Great Britain, Ireland or elsewhere in Europe they had travelled to board this Ryanair flight from London to Riga. After assessing the length of travel to the airport, the conversation turned to the town or village to which each was going. Two women sat on either side of me. We quickly established that both women came from Daugavpils—a city in south-east Latvia—and now lived in London. One of them, the woman travelling with a 15-month-old baby, arrived in London seven years ago, got married and was now hoping to have another child. She was going to visit her 70-year-old mother who refused to move, and to purchase a washing machine. The other woman—in her 60s—had lived in London for four years with her whole family and was travelling to Daugavpils to oversee the renovation of the apartment she owned there, and to visit friends. She said they worked hard and lived well in London and that her son did not want to go back for a visit, because he did not want to be upset by his friends' poverty. In recognising each other as fellow travellers, we did not form bonds on the basis of national belonging; this would have been differentiated in Latvia, since I spoke Latvian while the other two women spoke Russian. Rather, we found solidarity in our shared experiences of movement, labour and the long absence from home.

My travel companions' and my traversals were profoundly shaped by the national order of things. My moving to Riga was made possible by patterns of resource distribution that attempted to re-establish links between particular bodies and territories, even as I hardly saw myself as a returning national. In turn, my travel companions' mobile practices were made possible by particular relationships between states and their citizens, formed within the uneven configuration of power relations that is the European Union. Most of the older EU member-states instituted temporary restrictions on the movement of the labour force from the new Eastern European member-states when the latter joined in 2004, thus rendering freedom of movement a right accessible only to those deemed mature enough to make good use of it. Britain and Ireland became favourite destinations for Latvia's residents seeking work abroad because these states, along with Sweden, did not institute such restrictions.

In Latvian public discourse, the massive labour flow to London, Dublin and other Irish and British cities, towns and villages tends to be talked about as 'the Great Departure'.[1] The lives of most people—whether those who stay or those who move—are shaped by the Great Departure. Knowledge about the phenomenon is largely produced through people's situated reflections about their surroundings.

For example, when suggesting that the scale of departure is noteworthy, people count how many of their peers (usually taken to be a person's cohort at university or high school as far back as 20 years ago) are still around and how many are known to have left. People note that houses and apartments in the areas they live in stand empty, that schools lack children, and that there are considerably fewer people in the streets than there were 10 or 20 years ago. Media reports contribute to the shared sense that something consequential is under way. Social media sites circulate cynical jokes calling for the last person at the airport to turn off the light, as one would when leaving one's home.

Parallel to the commentary on the reconfiguration of the social fabric and the material environment, there is also public concern with the consequences of the Great Departure for the nation. Policy-makers, politicians and intellectuals have begun to articulate this concern through a discourse on 'the problem of emigration' (Hazans 2005, 2011; SAK 2006). When talking about the problem of emigration as a matter of policy and political concern, the focus shifts from tangible social and material relations to ever-elusive statistical enumerations of the extent of emigration and to debates about the effects of emigration on the economy, the demographic situation and other matters pertaining to the life of the nation. For example, economist Mihails Hazans (2011) has estimated that about 250,000 people have left Latvia over the last decade. The latest population census suggests that the population has dropped from 2.38 million in 2000 to 2.07 million in 2011.[2] Economists, geographers and demographers prognosticate that the population might drop further to well below 2 million by 2030, which would mean a severe shortage of the working-age population to support the non-productive segments of society, and a serious threat to the reproduction of the cultural nation.[3] Yet, while rendered 'real' through statistics, prognoses and scientific language, the problem of emigration is not simply out there. It is constituted through a number of historically formed discursive repertoires, including the pervasive power of the national order of things, modern scientific discourse and modern practices of governing, which aim to cultivate a healthy and plentiful body whether conceived of as the nation or as the population (Foucault 2003; Hacking 2007).[4]

In this article, I take the experiences of and commentaries about the Great Departure as a site for critical reflection on national(ist) common sense. In her seminal piece on the national order of things, Liisa Malkki (1992) speaks of national common sense to mark the ways in which the national order of things is not just something that exists in the realm of politics but also something that orients people's understandings of the world and their place in it. I borrow from her, yet I speak of *national(ist)* common sense to emphasise the ways in which the national order of things permeates ordinary worldviews, politics, practices of governance, and scholarship. Thus, I combine Malkki's concern with the national order of things with Ulrich Beck's (2004) concern with 'methodological nationalism' in the social sciences (see also Wimmer and Glick Schiller 2002). As argued by Nina Glick Schiller and Noel Salazar in their introduction to this special issue, the production of knowledge and academic perspectives about the movement of people continue to be affected by methodological nationalism, which they urge scholars to overcome. However, how is national(ist) common sense to be overcome? Moreover, how is it to be overcome in conditions when it is not just an artificial interpretive frame imposed upon social reality, but is also a worldview that structures people's understandings of the world and the self, as well as forms individuals as particular agentful subjects? I argue here that it is the very same practices and discourses that are shaped by the national order of things and enframed by national(ist) common sense that should be excavated for alternative ways of seeing and conceptualising mobility. To put it another way, I argue that revisiting discourses and practices that seem to be saturated by nationalism, methodological or otherwise, might produce analytical and political possibilities for loosening the grip of nationalism that shapes how ordinary people, policy-makers and academics alike understand and assess mobility.

This is an interpretive exercise of excavating or brushing away layers of national(ist) common sense that have pervaded popular discourse and critical scholarship. For example, it means reconsidering how people, including scholars, make sense of the relationship between people and place or people and land. While there is a strand of anthropology that has renewed attention to concrete relationships to land and place as sites of agency and possibility rather than of tradition and backward nationalism (e.g. Candea 2010; Escobar 2001; Gibson-Graham 2006), many scholars have taken the well-founded anthropological critique of place and culture as bounded entities to the extreme, by engaging in a fast-track identification of nationalism in any mention of people's relationship with place or land. This is especially so in Eastern European contexts, which already enjoy the stereotype of being mired in backward cultural nationalism of the Herderian kind.

In undertaking this exercise, I draw on J.K. Gibson-Graham's critique of the tendency in left-oriented scholarship to write with the 'affect and attitude of entrenched opposition' (2006: xxv), namely the tendency to identify oppressive power structures offering little space for alternatives. Perhaps this is because alternatives are hard to see if one has been cultivated as a scholar in the tradition of leftist critique. In re-orienting scholarly affects and capabilities, Gibson-Graham urges a cultivation of the capacity 'to linger with the object and process of thought in a ruminative space of not knowing' and suggests that, in so doing, 'we might see that we possess the capability (and ever-present option) of opening to what is novel rather than familiar in situations' (2006: xxviii). A number of techniques for cultivating oneself as 'a thinking subject within a politics of (economic) possibility' are outlined—'ontological reframing (to produce ground of possibility), rereading (to uncover or excavate the possible) and creativity (to generate actual possibilities where none formerly existed)' (2006: xxx).

Inspired by these affective and analytical orientations, I turn to re-reading the discourses and practices of mobility that seem to be saturated by national(ist) common sense in search of that which might be 'novel in familiar situations'. In this small project of excavation, drawing on feminist geographer Doreen Massey (1994,

2005), I invite attention to practices and relations of emplacement. I think of emplacement as a partaking in tangible social and material relations and trajectories that make up particular places, subjects and lives. I also think of emplacement as a site of analytical and political possibilities.

My argument draws on ethnographic data gathered during fieldwork in rural villages in Latvia. It is elaborated on the basis of an analysis of the historical articulation of mobility and ethics in the Latvian social and political imaginary. Within this imaginary, the figure of the migrant emerges as an aberration to relations of emplacement that are constitutive of Latvian understandings of the good life. However, rather than diagnosing this ethical configuration as grounded in common-sense ideas about national rootedness (Malkki 1992), I suggest that it emerges from local understandings of emplacement which can be co-opted by national(ist) common sense, but are not in a necessary relationship to it.[5]

To summarise, then, I argue that practices of mobility are shaped by the material reality of the national order of things and that the national order of things also lends meaning to mobility in collective and individual narratives. At the same time, the experiences of mobility—and the associated emplacement and displacement— exceed their co-optation by national(ist) common sense. I suggest that identifying national(ist) common sense as an animating discourse about mobility often overlooks this excess. To unleash the analytical and political potential of this excess, one needs to undertake the work of excavation. This, in turn, requires the bracketing of facile diagnoses of nationalism.

Emplacement and Displacement

A documentary film produced by Laila Freimane and Ivars Zviedrs in 2007 invites comparison between the departure to Ireland today and the deportation of many of Latvia's residents to Siberia in the 1940s and 1950s after the Soviet state marked them as enemies of the newly established regime. The opening cadre features an imagined border with Ireland marked by a sign that says *Īrija* (Ireland); only the sign is altered by adding three letters in front, to read *SibĪrija* (Siberia).

The reference to Siberia suggests that the displacement entailed in the mass departure for Ireland is comparable in its violence to the displacement that resulted from the forced movement of people by the Soviet administration. At the end of the 1950s, when the Soviet administration was done with the deportations, many families had been destroyed or separated. Many homes remained empty and were later settled by incoming Soviet military officers or workers in the new Soviet factories and collective farms who came from other parts of the Soviet Union (Bunkše 2007; Riekstiņš 2004).[6] For the deportees sent to Siberia, contrary to the workers relocating to Soviet Latvia, displacement was not followed by a bright socialist future, but rather by the arduous construction of a new life in the often physically and socially challenging, if not outright hostile, environment of the new settlement (e. g. Kalniņa 2001; Manfelde 2010).

Deportations to Siberia in the twentieth century and the Great Departure of the twenty-first are widely thought of as consequential for the life of the cultural nation as a result of their displacing of Latvians from their national territory. Most importantly, however, the deportations and the Great Departure also reconfigured tangible social and material relations constitutive of a particular kind of emplaced life. Consequently, an alternative way to think of the Great Departure is not in terms of migration, but in terms of the relationships and practices of both the people on the move and those who have remained behind. Instead of reading the rhetorical comparison between Siberia and Ireland as a tale of migration conceived in relation to the nation, it is possible to read it as a tale of severed and reworked relations. An important element of analysis that aims to loosen the grip of the national(ist) common sense is tracing when and how these relations and practices become articulated as matters of migration and as matters of concern to the nation. For example, even as the film focused on the severance of relationships with relatives, homes and surroundings that resulted from the move to Ireland or England, the comparison with Siberia invited reflection on the collective aspects of the departure. Such comparison was made possible by an assumed historical continuity between the collective subject affected by the Soviet deportations and the collective subject affected by the Great Departure. In both cases this collective subject was the Latvian cultural nation. This comparison posits the national subject as a privileged historical subject which both suffers from the deportations and is affected by the Great Departure. Given the hegemony of the national(ist) common sense in Latvian public and political life, there are hardly any other options available for how to think about migration on the collective register. Other collective identifications—such as those based on socio-economic inequalities—have either been discredited due to wide-spread aversion to leftist politics after the collapse of the Soviet Union or do not have a sufficient popular base. Thus, the filmmakers' engagement with the Great Departure oscillates between the experiences of concrete people and the fate of the nation. While they suggest that, once again, the nation is being scattered across geographical space, the filmmakers also provide a glimpse of the relations and practices that make up concrete journeys. The hard work of constructing alternatives to national(ist) common sense requires the building upon of the tangible relations of displacement and emplacement that these journeys make visible.

The deportations carried out by the Soviet administration ruptured families and separated people from their homes and their lifeworlds. All in all, deportations affected not only those who were deported, but also those who stayed behind and were faced with missing family members and neighbours and empty homes—in other words, who found themselves amidst unravelled social fabric. The departures of today also sever family relations, leave behind empty homes, and radically remake life in concrete localities. One woman in a town near the Russian border told me how painful and abnormal it is that she is not able to have an unmediated relationship with her son, who lives in Ireland. She said: 'If he only lived in Riga [the capital city of Latvia], I could at least bring him potatoes or something, but now, nothing.

Now only moral support'. She was not satisfied with providing only moral support through email or on the telephone; she longed for a tangible relationship.

At the same time, some of those who return home for a visit note that they cannot reconstruct the relationships they had before leaving. In a recent interview with me, a young man from a small town on the west coast of Latvia who has been working in Ireland initially narrated his visit home as a return to the national homeland, where even the air feels special. 'You can feel it in the air when you disembark at Riga airport', he said. And yet, even after recounting the difficult working life on Irish fishing boats, he remarked that he is planning to leave again, because the social relations that made up his town as a place of living have disintegrated. There are fewer people around, and he cannot find a common language with his friends. He feels propelled to leave. He experiences this as a burden. He has even advised a friend not to leave, if at all possible, otherwise he will not find a path of return.

This is to say that practices of mobility—even those shaped by national(ist) common sense—displace people from the concrete social and material relations that make up life and place. Doreen Massey argues that 'to travel between places is to move between collections of trajectories and to reinsert yourself in the ones to which you relate' (2005: 131). That is, it means establishing or severing the relationships with 'collections of trajectories' that make up a coherent sense of place. Massey describes how going or returning to a place entails joining or rejoining concrete debates, picking up on practices that may have been left behind, finding out what has been happening in one's absence. In other words, it is a weaving together of stories and embodied habitual practices which make something 'here and now' (2005: 131). Thus, 'what is special about place is not some romance of a pre-given collective identity', but rather a 'throwntogetherness, the unavoidable challenge of negotiation of a here-and-now (itself drawing on a history and a geography of thens and theres); and a negotiation which must take place within and between both human and non-human' (Massey 2005: 140).

Moreover, Massey's analytic of relationality as applied to place is not simply an argument for tracing flows and relations, but rather, as I read it, an invitation to trace the ways in which relations are articulated between trajectories that make up a place and those that make up a subject, thus constituting both the place and the subject in the process. This 'double articulation' results in a coherent narrative of place, and of self in relation to it (Massey 1994). The young man above was not able to reinsert himself in the set of trajectories that made up his town as a particular place in relation to him as a particular subject, because the relations and trajectories that constituted both had changed. In other words, the double articulation of subject and place had been substantively altered; so much so that he was inclined to leave.

I have argued thus far that emplacement amounts to inserting oneself or being inserted into trajectories that make up place, whereas displacement means removing oneself or being removed from them. In that sense, one can be displaced even if physically present, as in the case of the young man above. Moreover, particular configurations of emplacement and displacement can be co-opted by national(ist) common sense, but they also exceed it. In order to trace this excess, it is imperative to put a hold on a facile diagnosis of nationalism. I now turn to tracing one historical instance of displacement and emplacement through which I would like to further illustrate the point.

Peasants, Land and the Nation

In the second half of the nineteenth century, the freeing of Latvian peasants from indentured servitude to Baltic German land-owners went hand-in-hand with an expansion of capitalism in the Russian provinces. As part of what Karl Marx called 'primitive accumulation' and David Harvey has expanded upon as 'accumulation by dispossession' (Harvey 2010), Baltic German landlords freed the serfs not only from indentured service, but also from land (Dunsdorfs 1937; Plakans 2006; Šķilters 1928; Spekke 2008; Strods 1987). Thus, the peasants, whose existence until then had been tied to land, were freed, dispossessed and displaced all at once. Hearing of cheap land in Russia, many peasants set off on the road. Historian Vita Zelče (1999) describes one episode in this historical instance of departure whereby Krišjānis Valdemārs, a prominent Latvian intellectual studying and working in St Petersburg, had purchased some land 70 km from there. He was planning to sell off some plots to other Latvians and settle on the rest himself. After great initial interest from the peasants, Valdemārs purchased more land and thus set into motion what became a chaotic emigration campaign. Trying to curtail the flow of too many ill-informed peasants unprepared for life on the new land, Valdemārs wrote to a priest in one of the parishes in Kurzeme, asking him to inform his and the neighbouring parishes that there was not enough land for everyone and that the first year would be very difficult until the harvest came in (Zelče 1997: 111). Valdemārs also wrote that such a mass exodus was of concern from the perspective of the Latvian nation-in-formation. Prior to the second half of the nineteenth century, ethnicity and class overlapped insofar as Baltic German landed elites dominated Latvian peasants. After being freed from servitude to land and German lords, the peasants did not act in a particularly Latvian manner in their search for their own piece of land. However, this was also a time of 'national awakening', when Latvian intellectuals—educated in Tērbata and St Petersburg—actively worked on the consolidation of the cultural nation of Latvians within the political boundaries of the Russian Empire. In his letter to the priest, Valdemārs already thought in national categories. He expressed concern that the mass departure of peasants might have negative consequences for the nation-in-formation. The peasants were, after all, its popular base.

The national elites emerging in the late-nineteenth and early-twentieth centuries (much before the establishment of the Latvian state in 1918) subsequently rendered this historical departure as animated by a 'desire for departure' (*izceļošanas kāre*) stemming from an unenlightened worldview and lack of concern for the nation (see Šķilters 1928: 5). The forming of the national(ist) common sense was underway. As the national frame was filled with content over the next century, the relations that the peasants established with land and through which they emplaced themselves in their new settlements came to be seen as features of a particularly Latvian modality of life which differentiated them from other local inhabitants (Sovina 2012).[7] By the end of the twentieth century, when the Soviet Union was crumbling, the descendants of the Latvian peasants residing in Russia were co-opted by the national(ist) common sense and their portrayal as a diaspora that has always struggled to maintain Latvianness far away from their homeland (Sovina 2012). The social and material relations of emplacement through which Latvian peasants and their descendants crafted their lives—even if not in their rightful national territory—became articulated as ethical practices constitutive of the Latvian way of life. Subsequently, people who lived their relationship with place differently were thought of as inhabiting a different ethical lifeworld.

In the context of the population transfers and movement that transpired during the Soviet period, many people from other parts of the Soviet Union went to reside in Latvia. Thus the population movement not only entailed the displacement of Latvia's residents, but also the emplacement of a large number of newcomers. The particular contours of this emplacement were shaped by the Soviet state's attempts to dilute Latvian nationalism, which meant that the newcomers were not encouraged to learn the Latvian language or to respect the local ways (Dzenovska nd; Pabriks 2003). As a result, the figure of the migrant emerged as an especially stark aberration to Latvian understandings of the good life. This figure, however, was not just someone who had crossed a national boundary and did not belong in the national space. It was someone who inhabited place differently.[8]

The Figure of the Migrant

Returning to Latvia for the first time in the late 1980s after decades of living in Canada as a post-World War Two refugee, geographer Edmunds Bunkše (2007) describes how he rode the train from Leningrad to Riga, longing to see a rural landscape consisting of the single farmsteads which he remembered from his childhood during the war. After having crossed the unmarked border of Soviet Latvia, Bunkše set out to visit the single farmstead that had been his childhood refuge in times of war and where the extended family of his grandmother had resided:

> Driving on the Riga–Pleskava highway—it was as empty as I remembered it; only once in a while punctuated by some truck with large, white plates with Cyrillic letters in the back—I was very anxious. [...] When we got closer to the area, the landscape became hilly and the road wove up and down. The view included pine and birch trees, as well as some single farmsteads. When we came to the right place, I slowly recognized the contours of the landscape. That's how you feel when you meet a person whom you have known as a healthy and whole being, but who has been seriously crippled by some accident or hard life.

> The road leading up to the house over a hill was no longer straight; it now hugged a large pond, which had developed from a dirty and over-grown drainage ditch stretching along the highway. When we reached the muddy and uneven road, I saw

that the animal barn and the thrashing barn no longer stood in their place. The horse barn was still standing, its stone walls like before, but the roof had many holes in it. The residential building was in its place, but its long roofline had bent inward on both ends. The house was surrounded by chaotically demarcated vegetable gardens (though it was still winter). [...]

A bony, yellow-brown dog with low hanging ears barked at us viciously. An older man and a woman, both in worn out clothing, came out the door to meet us. They were both Russian. My companions, who spoke Russian, decided that we should ask to be let in. I objected, but they asked nevertheless. And we were invited into the room, which once was the main living room (the house was now divided into four family apartments). The walls and the ceiling were covered with soot and smelled like soot too. There was a bucket in the middle of the room to collect the rainwater, which was seeping through the roof. (Later I was told that migrants have a characteristically indifferent attitude towards up-keeping homes.) It was painful to see it, but the biggest shock came when my companions told the Russian couple that I belong to the former owner's family. The woman began to weep and, gesticulating with her arms, circled the room. She thought I had come to reclaim the house and to put her out; weeping endlessly, she tried to show me how they had improved the house. Her screams and the bucket of water was more than I could take. I ran outside, behind the home, and bent over to throw up. But I only gagged (2007: 53–4).[9]

Bunkše's narrative invokes the figure of the migrant. Historians attribute the emergence of this figure to the Soviet state's policies, that is, to a concerted effort to relocate large numbers of residents from other Soviet republics to Latvia in order to dilute the nationalist sentiment of the population and to create material conditions for the cultivation of a Soviet people (Riekstiņš 2004). However, Bunkše's narrative shows that the figure of the migrant is not only a state-based category marking people who came or were recruited as part of the Soviet state's population politics. In the social imaginary, the migrant is also someone who has a qualitatively different mode of inhabiting place from those who are understood as having and taking the proper care of their surroundings. At the same time, given the Soviet and post-Soviet political legacies, Bunkše's narrative also maps ethical difference onto ethnic by emphasising that the current inhabitants of his grandmother's house are both Russians and migrants. And yet, his concern takes on concrete contours not through a focus on the fact that the new residents are Russians, but rather through a detailed description of how they do not seem to care for the space they inhabit.

On the one hand, the emphasis on the relationship with place as central to national identity and thus to an ethical way of life resonates with Malkki's (1992) argument that national(ist) discourses moralise rootedness or, more precisely, pathologise uprootedness. On the other hand, as Bunkše's narrative indicates, it is important to ask what kind of conduct is taken to be indicative of a proper relationship to place rather than simply stating that a relationship to place is important. In other words, the 'migrant' is othered not because she or he is of different blood, but rather because she or he does not care for place in a proper way. The details of emplacement and displacement get overlooked when nationalism is used as shorthand for explaining the figure of the migrant.

A case from a rural municipality in the Western part of Latvia will help to illustrate this further. In a conversation about the Great Departure, the head of the municipality told me that he thought that the local cultural identity was under threat due to emigration. 'Over the course of the last 70 years, three out of four people have disappeared', he noted, 'only patriotism and economy can save us'. In his view, this amounted to the need for proactive cultivation of the local cultural identity not only as a communal or ideological project, but also as an economic one. In recent years, the municipality had obtained UNESCO funding for the preservation of their unique cultural space. The development vision of 'patriotism and economy' had proved to be viable thus far. Yet not all the residents of the municipality supported it:

> We see that there is a big difference between people who have local roots, those who have the local feeling, and those who have come here as migrants from elsewhere. We have some incomers here who are very negative towards what we do here. We have a similar situation to what Latvians have in Riga with the Russians who do not care about all this and would rather be part of Russia. Here we have the same thing. They [incomers] are from another place, and they think that the local culture is not necessary, that there are not many of us, and that therefore there is no need for further distinctions [between the specifically local identification and identification with Latvians more generally].

However, through my extended presence in the township I was able to observe that many of those who were deeply involved in furthering local identity in this municipality identified themselves as *ienācēji* (incomers). This term usually came up when we had reached a point in the conversation where the person felt the extent of their knowledge about local history or politics had reached some limit or when they began to feel that they sounded too patriotic. It was rarely in response to a direct question about personal history and was almost always brought up by the person him- or herself. When I spoke of this with the head of the municipality, our conversation complicated the seemingly simplistic juxtaposition between locals and incomers:

> *DD*: But you have incomers—people from other places, other municipalities—who are strong supporters and cultivators of local identity.
> *Head of Municipality*: Thank God, we have them. Some of them are very good people. For example, Liene is not a local. Her husband is. We have some very good examples. Some of the members of the local women's folklore group are not locals. It's called integration. We don't have anything against incomers, but if the incomer comes and starts dictating his or her rules …
> *DD*: So does that mean that people become incomers because of the way they behave? Does that mean that those who have integrated are not incomers?
> *Head of Municipality*: No, I would not consider them such. There are some purists who would, but I disagree.

Our conversation seemed to be strongly coloured by national(ist) common sense about migration and integration insofar as the head of the municipality drew a comparison between the local–incomer relationship in his municipality with the nationally recognisable juxtaposition between locals (Latvians) and migrants (Russians). Moreover, he used the notion of integration—the politically instituted model of regulating the relationship between Latvians and Russians in public space— to describe the desired state of affairs with regard to incomers and locals. The metaphoric equation of locals with Latvians and incomers with Soviet-Russian migrants missed the daily practices of living, which made one local—the crafting of relations of locality through participation in community projects. And it is precisely the tracing of these practices and relations—the same ones that the head of the municipality represented through the juxtaposition between the locals and the incomers or between Latvians and Soviet-Russian migrants—that might also entail the possibility of loosening the national(ist) interpretations of mobility and proceeding with analysis of the tangible relations of emplacement and displacement.

My approach here resonates with Matei Candea's (2010) analysis of place in Corsica. In his book *Corsican Fragments: Difference, Knowledge and Fieldwork*, Candea deploys a relational analytic to show how the allegedly essential relationship between people and land in Corsica is 'put together, … [and] how it emerges from connections which are themselves contingent and shifting' (2010: 81). Candea does this by describing how the residents and visitors live a fire that breaks out in forests adjacent to a Corsican village, that is, how locality is constituted through watching a fire. In so doing, Candea puts forth a critique of the metaphorisation of the people–land relationship, which quickly leads down the well-trodden road of positing references to a relationship between people and land as nationalist. To push the idea further, it can be said that the historical tradition of treating references to the relationship between land and people (or place and people) as nationalist leads to a reduction of thick networks of relations that are quickly abstracted or fold into national(ist) common sense. Yet, Candea is also careful not to assert radical difference as a way to counter such diagnostics. Instead, he suggests that what is needed is a meticulous tracing of shifting relations through which place and locality are constituted. However, Candea asks: 'If watching a fire is one of the many ways of becoming local, then whence does the boundary making between locals as related to land and foreigners as not related to the land arise? How are shifting and contingent relations fixed as juxtapositions between locals and foreigners?'. From Candea's text, one can conclude that it happens when the locals, the foreigners, and their anthropologists turn to available framing devices to locate themselves in relation to their surroundings and 'to manipulate scale and context' (2010: 83). It is what the Corsicans do when they depict tourists as disconnected from the locality. It is what the head of the municipality in Latvia did when he drew a comparison between local incomers and national migrants.

The implication of this for the scholarly analysis of mobility is that the search for alternative analytics to nationali(ist) common sense is not to be found in new objects of study, but rather in the bracketing of hegemonic interpretive frames—including the one that allows an identification of particular practices as being tainted by nationalism, methodological or otherwise. Consequently, the figure of the migrant emerges as a historically constituted character who acts in a way that demonstrates the relationships which Latvians inhabit and the consequential differences which they fix within the network of these relationships in particular historical moments. Rather than (or in addition to) a sociological category, it is a kind of heuristic device that has emerged through conceptual work done by ordinary human beings to make sense of the world, to organize the world ethically in relation to emplacement and displacement.

Ethics in the Context of the Great Departure

The extent of the Great Departure is challenging the historically formed ethical configuration within which the migrant—as someone merely searching for a better life—is an aberration. The stories of concrete individuals both departing (and staying) exhibit a great degree of variety and cannot be easily subsumed under stable ethical configurations. Some people leave because they cannot find work, others because they cannot make ends meet with the salary they receive. Many leave because they cannot make mortgage payments or repay consumer credits as a result of having indulged in the credit orgy literally pushed upon Latvia's residents by banks and businesses before the crisis hit in 2008 (Beliaev and Dzenovska 2009).[10] Some people leave because their friends and relatives are already 'there' and convey information that it is possible to live rather than merely exist on the money that one earns, even for manual labour. In one small township in Latgale, people were telling me how one young man from the township went to Ireland, found work, and then returned to take all his friends with him. Finally, some people articulate their decision to go to Ireland or England as arising from dissatisfaction with particular features of Latvian society, such as excessive bureaucracy, oppressive and unfriendly public sociality, or corrupt politics (SAK 2006). Even among those who stay, departure is ever-present not only because their relatives and friends have left, but also because they themselves continuously think about leaving and almost daily justify to themselves why they have not left. Most of my informants regularly comment upon why they are still in their village, some explaining that they have to take care of elderly parents while others think themselves too old or too ill to set off. There are those who also say that they could never leave their home or leave Latvia. All in all, those who stay are either not capable or do not wish to sever their relations of emplacement, which are always complex articulations of multiple trajectories. In conditions of massive departure and reconfiguration of the social fabric, their staying seems to require continuous reflection and justification. They, too, inhabit what Glick Schiller and her colleagues have called a 'transnational social field' (Basch *et al.* 1994, Levitt and Glick Schiller 2004).

In the rural areas that I work in, departure is mostly perceived as unfortunate, but inevitable. However, in Latvian public and political life, departure is often negatively evaluated as an unjustified striving for a better life—dangerous for the collective life of the nation. A conversation that ensued during one of my field trips is a good example of such an attitude. Upon finding out that I, too, was leaving after the end of the project that brought me to Latvia, a man who was visiting one of my informants, and whom I had not met before, urged me to explain why I was leaving. Sensing that a lesson in ethics was underway, I meekly suggested that it is literally impossible to live on the salary that awaits me at the end of the project. Having received the answer he expected, the man instantly and rhetorically asked me: 'But you are dressed, right? You are warm?'. He implied that my desires and expectations probably exceed my basic necessities, thus my departure is ethically questionable. I proceeded to add that it was not only about financial survival—that I also felt constrained by bureaucratic obstacles and structural shortcomings and needed to reinvigorate my intellectual capacities and motivations. He had an answer to that as well, suggesting that nothing prevents me from reading here, in Latvia, so why do I strive to leave? The man wanted to make the point that there simply was no good reason for my departure other than an ethically unjustifiable desire for more than I needed for basic survival.

While the conversation was unfolding, I was observing the man, who seemed to enjoy more than just the basic necessities of life and was wondering to myself about the kind of subject position one must inhabit to be able to suggest that other people should be content with the kind of life they have. I later found out in an unrelated conversation with my informants that he owned a wood-cutting facility and was apparently known for trying to pay his employees as little as possible. Thus, while it may have seemed that the man was a patriot who wanted to keep Latvians in Latvia, it turned out that he also wanted cheap labour and thought that his employees, as well as me, were unjustified in our striving to alter our conditions of existence. Evidently, the dilemma of whether it is ethically acceptable to move in search of a better life is always already entangled with the materiality of life, and discussions of mobility and stasis must be situated within an analysis of unequal power (Glick Schiller and Salazar, this issue).

The argument about whether it is justified to leave in conditions where life may be difficult, but not physically unlivable, saturates public discourse and everyday conversations. While many of those who stay insist that those leaving want to have an easy life for themselves rather than work hard at home to make the collective life better, this argument is increasingly undermined by more and more people setting out on the road. In conditions where so many people traverse a transnational social field, attention is increasingly paid to the kind of ties they maintain or establish with home. Many of those who have left frequently return home for a variety of services. As one woman told me, she comes back to Latvia for a 'technical check-up'—she visits a gynaecologist, a dentist and a hairdresser. Others come back to attend festivities in their home villages, to monitor the renovation of their property—as did the woman I met on the Ryanair flight—or simply for a holiday. Many government and non-government institutions and organisations try to understand these ties and cultivate those that are thought to be beneficial for the state and the nation. For example, the Ministry of Foreign Affairs of Latvia is actively working on the development of diaspora politics which, at the present moment, requires an effort to convince the public that it is advantageous for everyone that the government spends money on cultivating ties with the Latvian diaspora. Other states, such as Lithuania and Ireland, are invoked as exemplary in having understood the value of the diaspora for national well-being.

Overall, the extensive reconfiguration of the social fabric brought about by the Great Departure is demanding a rethinking of ethics and of the nature of the hegemonic collective subject—of the nation. It seems that the long-assumed stable foundation of the nation as the articulation of national subjects with national territory is being unsettled. As demonstrated by scholars working on diasporic nationalism (e.g. Bernal 2004; Glick Schiller and Fouron 1999), this does not necessarily mean doing away with national(ist) common sense. In fact, it might even mean a strengthening of the national sentiment. However, even if this is so, the severance of the articulation between the nation and the territory through tangible relations of displacement and emplacement cannot but remake the collective subject. Whether and how this will happen remains an ethnographic question which requires a careful tracing of the ties that link people to each other and to particular places—a careful study of the relations of displacement and emplacement and of the double articulation between subjective and spatial trajectories. The difference between the nation 'as we know it' and the formation of a new collective subject lies in the sociality formed by particular relations of displacement and emplacement, as well as in the ability to see novel possibilities in seemingly familiar configurations of politics, ethics and analytics.

Acknowledgments

I would like to thank the editors of this special issue of *JEMS* for inviting me to participate in this collective project. I would also like to thank Iván Arenas for reading and commenting on several versions of this article. Acknowledgment also goes to the European Social Fund project 'Changing Development Strategies and Cultural Spaces of Latvia's Rural Inhabitants', (2009/0222/1DP/1.1.1.2.0/09/APIA/VIAA/087) for providing research funding.

Notes

[1]   A local TV station (TV3) produced a documentary series entitled 'The Great Departure' where they interviewed people as they were preparing to leave and subsequently followed them as they were trying to make a new life in England, Ireland and, later, in Germany.

[2]   See www.csb.gov.lv.

[3]   For example, such prognoses were put forth by the Minister of the Economy during the conference 'Migration and Identity: Strengthening the Role of Diaspora', organised by the

Ministry of Foreign Affairs and the Jean Monnet Centre for Excellence of the University of Latvia, in March 2012.

[4]   It is important to note that the conception of the nation operative in Latvia is that of a cultural nation which is linked to, but also separable from, the political entity—the Latvian state—that is supposed to ensure its existence. See Verdery (1994) on the specificity of the conception of the nation in Eastern Europe and its implications for theorising transnationalism. It should also be noted here that much of the scholarship on migration that works Foucault's analytic is mostly concerned with the ways in which states regulate migration and treat migrant bodies as expendable rather than as integral to the living body of the nation or society and thus subject to the disciplinary and exclusionary politics of the state (De Genova and Peutz 2010; Hyndman 2000; Mandel 2008; McDowell 2005; Mountz 2010). Scholarship that focuses on the cultivation of the social body through work upon the body itself (rather than through the exclusion of those who do not belong to it), is usually concerned with pro-natal politics (Greenhalgh and Winckler 2005; Paxson 2004), though concern with migration appears in Taussig's (2009) study of genomics in the Netherlands.

[5]   In her work on the metaphysics of sedentarism, Malkki has argued that the naturalised articulation of place and identity in nationalist discourses has produced the pathological figure of the refugee which is thought to lose its moral bearings as a result of losing its bodily relationship to the homeland (1992: 32).

[6]   It should be noted that many people also set out as refugees before the Soviet regime was re-established in 1945. They did so largely due to the experience of the repressions of the first Soviet government in 1940. The refugee life is described in works such as McDowell (2005), Zaķe (2010) and Žīgure (2009). Like deportees, refugees also experienced a violent rupture of their network of relations.

[7]   See Sovina's (2012) MA thesis. Sovina describes how particular practices of land cultivation and inhabiting of place, such as growing flowers, came to be seen as particularly Latvian features that distinguished the descendants of Latvian peasants from Russians and Baskhirs.

[8]   Analytically, I think of this figure as a combination of Max Weber's ideal-types and Alasdair MacIntyre's characters. On the one hand, it is akin to the figures Weber uses in his historical work to illustrate ideal-typical conduct, such as how Benjamin Franklin is used to illustrate specific ideas about work as a religious calling in Weber's *The Protestant Ethic and the Spirit of Capitalism* (2003). On other hand, it resonates with MacIntyre's characters—for example, the manager—who define the possibilities of plot and action. They are not simply social roles; rather, 'they are a very special type of social role which places a certain kind of moral constraint on the personality of those who inhabit them' (1984: 27).

[9]   Author's translation.

[10]   Several bank employees confidentially told me about the internal policies during the period before the crisis whereby credit departments were encouraged to push credits in all possible ways and bank employees received bonuses for selling more and more credit.

References

Balibar, E. (2010) 'At the borders of citizenship: a democracy in translation?', *European Journal of Social Theory*, 13(3): 315–22.

Basch, L., Glick Schiller, N. and Szanton Blanc, C. (1994) *Nations Unbound: Transnational Projects, Postcolonial Predicaments, and Deterritorialized Nation-States*. New York: Gordon and Breach.

Beck, U. (2004) *The Cosmopolitan Vision*. Cambridge: Polity Press.

Beliaev, A. and Dzenovska, D. (2009) 'Some reflections on the "global" crisis in Latvia', *Newsletter of the Institute of the Slavic, East European, and East Asian Studies*, 26(2): 3–6.

Bernal, V. (2004) 'Eritrea goes global: reflections on nationalism in a transnational era', *Cultural Anthropology*, *19*(1): 3–25.

Bunkše, E. (2007) *Intīmā Bezgalība*. Riga: Norden AB.

Candea, M. (2010) *Corsican Fragments: Difference, Knowledge, and Fieldwork*. Bloomington: Indiana University Press.

De Genova, N. and Peutz, N. (2010) *The Deportation Regime: Sovereignty, Space, and the Freedom of Movement*. Durham: Duke University Press.

Dunsdorfs, E. (1937) *Klaušu Beigu Cēliens Kurzemē*. Riga: Latvijas Vēstures Institūts.

Dzenovska, D. (nd) 'How to be a minority: the politics of conduct and difference in the new Europe', in Gille, Z. (ed.) *What Was Post-Socialism and What Comes Next? Whiteness, Transparency, and the Politics of Care in a Global Context*.

Escobar, A. (2001) 'Culture sits in places: reflections on globalism and subaltern strategies of localization', *Political Geography*, *20*(2): 139–74.

Foucault, M. (2003) *Society Must Be Defended: Lectures at the College de France*. New York: Picador.

Gibson-Graham, J.K. (2006) *A Post-Capitalist Politics*. Minneapolis: University of Minnesota Press.

Glick Schiller, N. and Fouron, G.E. (1999) 'Terrains of blood and nation: Haitian transnational social fields', *Ethnic and Racial Studies*, *22*(2): 340–66.

Greenhalgh, S. and Winkler, E. (2005) *Governing China's Population: From Leninist to Neoliberal Biopolitics*. Stanford: Stanford University Press.

Gupta, A. and Ferguson, J. (1992) 'Space, identity and the politics of difference', *Cultural Anthropology*, *7*(1): 6–23.

Hacking, I. (2007) 'Kinds of people: moving targets', *Proceedings of the British Academy, 151*: 285–318.

Harvey, D. (2010) *The Enigma of Capital and the Crises of Capitalism*. Oxford: Oxford University Press.

Hazans, M. (2005) *Ekonomiskās Migrācijas Cēloņu Izpēte un Monitoringa Sistēmas Izveide Ekonomiskās Migrācijas Ietekmes Noteikšanai uz LR Tautsaimniecību*. Riga: Report to the Ministry of Economy of the Republic of Latvia.

Hazans, M. (2011) 'Latvijas emigrācijas mainīgā seja 2000–2010', in SPPI (ed.) *Latvija. Pārskats par tautas attīstību. 2010./2011. Nacionālā Identitāte, Mobilitāte, Rīcībspēja*. Riga: Latvijas Universitātes Sociālo un politisko pētījumu institūts, 79–91.

Hyndman, J. (2000) *Managing Displacement: Refugees and the Politics of Humanitarianism*. Minneapolis: University of Minnesota Press.

Kalniņa, S. (2001) *Ar Balles Kurpēm Sibīrijas Sniegos*. Riga: Atēna.

Levitt, P. and Glick Schiller, N. (2004) 'Conceptualizing simultaneity: a transnational social field perspective on society', *International Migration Review*, *38*(3): 1002–39.

Lulle, A. (2010) *New Others: Identity Construction and Transnational Belonging Among Latvian Migrants to Guernsay*. Manchester: University of Manchester, EastBordNet Working Paper No.78.

MacIntyre, A. (1984) *After Virtue: A Study in Moral Theory*. Notre Dame: University of Notre Dame Press.

Malkki, L. (1992) 'National Geographic: the rooting of peoples and the territorialization of national identity among scholars and refugees', *Cultural Anthropology*, *7*(1): 24–44.

Malkki, L. (1995) *Purity and Exile: Violence, Memory, and National Cosmology among Hutu Refugees in Tanzania*. Chicago: University of Chicago Press.

Mandel, R. (2008) *Cosmopolitian Anxieties: Turkish Challenges to Citizenship and Belonging in Germany*. Durham: Duke University Press.

Manfelde, A. (2010) *Zemnīcas Bērni*. Riga: Autora Izdevums.

Massey, D. (1994) 'Double articulation: a place in the world', in Bammer, A. (ed.) *Displacements: Cultural Identities in Question*. Bloomington: Indiana University Press, 110–19.

Massey, D. (2005) *For Space*. London: Sage.

McDowell, L. (2005) *Hard Labour: The Forgotten Voices of Latvian Migrant Volunteer Workers*. London: UCL Press.

Mountz, A. (2010) *Seeking Asylum: Human Smuggling and Bureaucracy at the Border*. Minneapolis: University of Minnesota Press.

Pabriks, A. (2003) *In Defiance of Fate: Ethnic Structure, Inequality, and Governance of the Public Sector in Latvia*. Riga: United Nations Research Institute for Social Development.

Paxson, H. (2004) *Making Modern Mothers: Ethics and Family Planning in Urban Greece*. Berkeley: University of California Press.

Plakans, A. (2006) 'Migration, households and agrarian reform in the Baltic provinces of Russia: 19th and 20th centuries', *History of the Family*, *11*(3): 151–9.

Riekstiņš, J. (2004) *Migranti Latvijā. 1944–1989. Dokumenti*. Riga: Latvijas Valsts Arhīvs.

Šķilters, K. (1928) *Latkoloniju Vēsture*. Maskava: Prometejs.

Sovina, A. (2012) '"Bashkirians" and "Bashkirian Latvians": Tension between the Social Register and the National Register'. Riga: University of Latvia, unpublished MA thesis.

Spekke, A. (2008) *Latvijas Vēsture*. Riga: Jumava.

SAK (2006) *Latvija un Brīva Darbaspēka Kustība: Īrijas Piemērs*. Riga: Stratēģiskās Analīzes Komisija.

Strods, H. (1987) *Kurzemes Kroņa Zemes un Zemnieki, 1795–1861*. Riga: Zinātne.

Tausig, K.-S. (2009) *Ordinary Genomics: Science, Citizenship, and Genetic Identities*. Durham: Duke University Press.

Torpey, J. (1998) 'Coming and going: on the state monopolization of the legitimate "means of movement"', *Sociological Theory*, *16*(3): 239–59.

Verdery, K. (1994) 'Beyond the nation in Eastern Europe', *Social Text*, *38*(Spring): 1–19.

Weber, M. (2003) [1904–05] *The Protestant Ethic and the Spirit of Capitalism*. Minneapolis: Dover Publications.

Wimmer, A. and Glick Schiller, N. (2002) 'Methodological nationalism and beyond: nation-state building, migration, and the social sciences', *Global Neworks*, *2*(4): 301–34.

Zaķe, I. (2010) *American Latvians: Politics of a Refugee Community*. New Brunswick: Transaction.

Zelče, V. (ed.) (1997) *Krišjānis Valdemārs: Lietišķā un Privātā Sarakste. Pirmais Sējums: Krišjāņa Valdemāra Vēstules*. Riga: Latvijas Valsts Vēstures Arhīvs.

Zelče, V. (1999) 'Pirmā latviešu emigrācijas kampaņa', *Latvijas Arhīvi*, *3*: 76–88.

Žīgure, A. (2009) *Viņi. Ceļā*. Riga: Jumava.

Tibetan Peregri-nations: Mobility, Incommensurable Nationalisms and (Un)belonging Athwart the Himalayas

Chris Vasantkumar

Putting into context the sentiment expressed by Tibetans on both sides of the Himalayas that true Tibet is located elsewhere, this essay focuses on an under-commented-upon consequence of Tibetan trans-Himalayan mobilities since 1959: the creation of two incommensurable modes of nationalism. One of these is territorial, the other embodied in the form of the Dalai Lama himself. The result of this dual nationalism has not been mutual compatibility and an increase in potential modes of Tibetan belonging, but mutual interference and a broadened scope for unbelonging. As such, the dispersed spatiality of community it enacts is reminiscent not so much of the romantic, organic unity of Herderian modes of (methodological) nationalism as it is of Heine's experiences of manifold unbelonging and contemporary German-Jewish articulations of a 'portable homeland'. Ultimately, to reckon with such originary unbelonging, theories of diaspora and mobility must treat concepts of both home and mobility as mixtures of stability and instability, movement and stasis.

Introduction: Scattered Belongings

Introducing this special issue of *JEMS*, Glick Schiller and Salazar ponder the question, 'What do we see if we do not think about mobility like a nation-state?' This essay is both an exemplification and a reformulation of their response: 'The conceptual terrain we can envision when we think beyond the lens of the nation-state allows us to build a regimes-of-mobility approach that sees movement and settlement in constant and reconstituting interrelationships'. On the one hand, I argue below that a close attention to the realities of originary unbelonging in the Tibetan diaspora, both within and beyond Tibet, highlights the co-mobility of homeland and diaspora. This insight is fundamentally consonant with the editors' exhortation to 'redirect the attention of mobility researchers back to the dynamic between sedentariness and movement and explicitly critique the dichotomy between mobility and immobility that has characterised recent scholarship'.

On the other hand, my argument moves past a critique of methodological nationalism writ large to focus on a sub-variant thereof that I term 'methodological belongingism'. In so doing, I attempt to rescue the nation from methodological nationalism, highlighting how the proliferating varieties of post-1959 Tibetan imagined communities neither respect national borders nor neatly conform to the Herderian vision that underpins both methodological nationalism and its critiques. In addition to contributing to a rethinking of binary logics of movement and stasis, I also suggest a key corollary to Glick Schiller and Salazar's question: How has methodological belongingism obscured how others have thought the nation beyond the nation-state?

Since the flight into exile in India of the fourteenth Dalai Lama and much of the religious and cultural elite of old Tibet in 1959, Tibetans on both sides of the Himalayas have traced a complex skein of journeys across that range's high passes. In the West, understandings of such movements have been dominated by the figure of the refugee. Indeed, the first wave of Tibetans moving south across the ranges largely comprised refugees from the region of Ü-Tsang in central Tibet. Since the 1980s, however, a second wave of migrants, hailing mostly from the eastern regions of Kham and Amdo,[1] has made the arduous journey across the mountains to north India. Prior to 2008, when Tibetan unrest across the PRC led to a clampdown on trans-border flows, upwards of several thousand migrants a year travelled to and, in many cases, from Dharamsala and other refugee Tibetan centres on the subcontinent.[2]

The effects of such peregrinations have been manifold. Notions of national belonging in the exile community have been complicated by the ambivalent reception of 'sinicised' Tibetans fresh off the path from Tibet itself (see Diehl 2002; Falcone and Wangchuk 2008; on broader circuits of Tibetan travel, see Hess 2009; Yeh 2007). Many of these 'new arrivals' ultimately return to China, taking with them both a critical consciousness of Chinese nationalism and English-language skills that, prior to 2008, enabled them to get ahead in the rapidly developing tourism industry back 'home'. In any event, Tibetans on both sides of the Himalayas today are acutely aware of how the other half lives. Despite the many dangers of the illicit border crossings and recrossings involved, there has been significant cultural and affective cross-pollination. Ideas of Tibetan nation, culture and community are on the move.

This paper addresses some significant aspects of this movement by tracing the links between migration, nationalism and a widespread sense of homelessness amongst Tibetans on both sides of the Himalayas. In the course of conducting ethnographic research amongst Tibetans and their neighbours—in China from 2003–04 and again in 2006, 2007 and 2009, with shorter stays in Dharamsala in 2006 and 2007—I was surprised to discover that, in both places, many Tibetans I talked to felt out of place. In both Amdo and Dharamsala, I was struck by the degree to which Tibetans thought of the true Tibet as a keenly felt, but absent, elsewhere, existing at spatial or ethical remove from the contexts of our interactions. Three brief ethnographic examples can serve to highlight the tenor of these conversations.

Visiting a friend's house near the town of Xiahe in Gansu Province's Gannan Tibetan Autonomous Prefecture over Tibetan New Year 2004, I met Phuntsok, a monk from a nearby monastery. As we relaxed on the *kang* (a raised, heated seating area common in rural Chinese houses) enjoying the abundance of the holiday season, he passionately described (in Chinese) the plight of his people:

> On the outside, Tibetans look happy and beautiful, but inside, in their hearts, their situation is very difficult. All our best people (*women zui hao de ren*) have gone: to India, or America or England, and the only ones who are left are stupid (*naozi ben de ren*) like me. The best folks have all gone or been forced out, and those who are left have no solution to our problems (*xiang buchu yige banfa*). In China today, people's brains are good, but their hearts are bad. If a Tibetan person makes friends with you, they will give you their whole heart, but our brains are not good. The current situation of the Tibetans is so different than it was in the past. We used to have gold and nice things, but they were all spoiled (*nongzaole*) by the Chinese and today even rich people have things like this [points to a plastic fruit bowl]. Tibetans have to stay well behaved. Otherwise it will cause problems for the monastery and for the Living Buddha. We are constrained [he makes a ring with his hands]. We have to live within this [ring]: if we go outside of it we'll be shot.

Phuntsok, who, it should be noted, had not been to India, locates the true Tibet, or at the very least the best Tibetans, in places outside Tibet itself. According to him, the situation in Xiahe is much better than it once was. Yet, he still maps it primarily in terms of absence: of important personages, of the dead, of looted treasures and of the ability of Tibetans to make futures on their own terms.

By contrast, my conversations with young migrant Amdowas in India highlighted the perils of freedom. One evening at Nick's Italian Café in the Tibetan centre of McLeod Ganj, I was talking with a self-styled poet named Dhonjub and his friend Tsering Dawa when the latter remarked that, in his opinion, people are much more religious in Amdo than in India. There the percentage of believers might reach 90 per cent while, in India, it is more like 10 per cent. Tibetans in China, even though they might drink, play cards and video games, and hang out in bars, in their hearts are religious—'more simple and innocent'. With them, a friend is a friend, they give from the heart. 'Here', he says, 'religion is moving away from us'. In Tibet, the Chinese have introduced bars, computer games and other distractions but, because people are 'somewhat trapped', this keeps their thinking similarly constrained so there hasn't been much change. In India, people are not forced to imitate the Chinese so they imitate Indian or American things. Access to a much broader scope of ideas might make religion not seem so appealing in light of more modern alternatives. In contrast to Phuntsok's assessment, Tsering Dawa cites constraint itself as productive of religious Tibetan subjects. Yet he, too, locates true Tibet somewhere other than in his current location.

This sense of the elsewhere-ness of proper Tibetan-ness in India cropped up in many other conversations (on both sides of the border) with Tibetans who had been to Dharamsala. When I mentioned to Pema, another friend of Dhonjub's, that a monk I knew in Xiahe who had studied in Dharamsala had told me that the quality of religious instruction is better in China, to my surprise he agreed. He said:

> Well, here you can see several famous personages—the Dalai Lama, the Karmapa and some others—but the rest of the religious practitioners are all surface. They are always proclaiming their own skills a little too loudly and trying to convince or seduce folks regarding their abilities. I mean, here you even have [monks as] Tibetan massage and Kung Fu teachers—how can they teach that? In China, religious teachers are more 'sincere' and less self-aggrandising; they are not always singing their own praises. Even if they are greatly skilled, they keep it to themselves. Life in Dharamsala is hard away from family, with angry and discriminatory locals, strange food, awful weather and other problems.

In response to all this, I asked what he would say to a young Amdowa who was thinking about coming to India. He replied that, if they were poor, he would tell them to come because, at the TCV (Tibetan Children's Villages), for example, food, lodging, clothing, etc. are all taken care of by the Dalai Lama. But if they were reasonably well off, he would tell them to stay home.

These examples indicate that a strange sort of bifocality conditioned by the possibility of movement across the Himalayas colours perceptions of Tibetan-ness in communities on both sides of the mountains. In this bifocality, life inside China is alternately perceived as repressive and spiritually stifling or as productive of simplicity and religious commitment. Life in India is mapped as alternately a fondly-hoped-for release from political and spiritual repression or as a context for secular distractions and cultural dissolution (cf. Lau 2010). In both cases, actual understandings of place are considerably more ambivalent than the received scheme that maps China as a negative space—repressive of Tibetan culture—and India, by contrast, as the locus of freedom, religiosity and true Tibetanness. In both cases, the real Tibet is thought to be elsewhere.

This elsewhere-ness of Tibet points to a surprising consequence of the movements of exile, migration and return since 1959: a proliferation of modes of imagining what it means to be Tibetan. This proliferation has produced, in turn, not so much an augmented sense of Tibetan belonging but a generalised sense of unbelonging. This widespread sense of alienation from true Tibet is less a phenomenon readily intelligible in terms of a general notion of 'nostalgia' (Boym 1996; Smith 2000; Stewart 1988) that accompanies all would-be national imaginings of communities, than a phenomenon specific to the particular historical and spatial vicissitudes of what one might call the Tibetan diaspora. Further, the particularities of the Tibetan case suggest potential avenues for deepening the critical force of recent work on mobilities.

New Mobilities, New Impediments

Over the last two decades, anthropologists, sociologists, critical human geographers and others have become increasingly cognisant of the crucial role played by migration and other journeying practices in the creation of even the most apparently sedentary communities. From Anderson's (1991) discussion of the role of 'administrative pilgrimages' in the inculcation of a sense of national identity in the functionaries of the state, to Malkki's (1997 [1992]) influential highlighting of the importance of both roots and routes to the imagining of community, and to recent work on 'new mobilities' (e.g. Sheller and Urry 2006), the movement in social theory has been decidedly away from imaginaries of fixed, rooted or isolated communities and towards what has become almost an ethos of interconnection and mobility. It is a mark of the growing maturity of work in this vein that early appeals to mobility as an always already liberatory domain of freedom and cultural creativity (e.g. Appadurai 1990) have been superseded by a chastened awareness that, even in motion, some people and some communities are more equal than others.

Yet, despite this on the whole salutary move towards putting routes alongside roots in the theoretical pantheon, there has arguably also been a more insidious move toward reifying the border between the mobile and the immobile. In this reification, as in an older anthropological model of clearly bounded cultural forms, difference between the categories is heightened while internal difference is elided. In that older anthropology, the result was a map of cultures and nations with the clear boundaries and tile-like colour scheme of a child's atlas (see Gupta and Ferguson 1992) that did little justice to the complex interconnections and intra-alterities of the realities on the ground. Current work on mobilities helpfully acknowledges the interdependence of the mobile and the immobile—often in a vaguely structural-Marxist allusion to an immobile infrastructure serving as the basic 'moorings' (Hannam *et al.* 2006) of an implicitly superstructural set of mobilities. Yet, less helpfully, it treats both these two terms and the boundary between them as relatively commonsensical.

This is to say, justly influential work such as Cresswell's (2010) on the relationship between raw movement and what one might term cultural constructions of mobility placed thereupon, does not really grapple with the idea that the boundary between mobility and immobility and the cultural sense placed upon that boundary might differ radically from context to context. The analysis of mobility and its opposite(s) are thus are treated as proceeding from the level of a human universal, 'the fact of physical movement' (Cresswell 2010: 19). This apparently unproblematic naturalisation of movement parallels, perhaps, the way in which anthropologists conceptualised kinship before Schneider (1984) revealed it to be a Western folk theory. As a result, there is a somewhat perplexing lack of attention to 'Where?'[3] in much of the 'new mobilities' work, even as there is an almost super-abundance of attention to 'How?'.

The focus of the new-mobilities turn on 'the fact of physical movement', the 'representations that give it meaning' and its embodied practice (Cresswell 2010: 19), has produced fascinating and innovative work on the unexpected symbolic lives of various modes of transit. The latter have included everything from the unexpectedly provocative social dynamics of 'aerostatic flight' (McCormack 2009) to the banal aesthetics of post-privatisation British Railways (Bissel 2008). It is unclear, however, whether the new-mobilities turn has also grounded such studies of embodied experience and its representation in a full reckoning of the relationship between familiar and non-Euro-American modes of mobility (e.g. Flower 2004). Further, and here more significantly, in commonly starting from 'the fact of physical movement', much work on mobility treats the boundaries between mobile and non-mobile, home and away as givens, the starting-points for, rather than objects of, analysis.

To remedy this oversight, work on im/mobilities, new and old, must be brought into productive articulation with recent critical approaches to concepts of home (e.g. Blunt 2003; Ralph and Staeheli 2011; Tolia-Kelly 2004). Linking theorisation of movement and homing practices may enable scholars to focus less on reified boundaries between mobile and immobile than on the significant traffic across these bounds that colours imaginings of belonging and unbelonging alike. Such an approach might also push us to reconceptualise the relationship between territoriality, movement, national belonging, home and displacement as contingent and contextual rather than as pre-given. As Ralph and Staeheli write in a recent review article on the subject, 'The challenge . . . is to conceptualise the simultaneity of home as sedentarist and mobile' (2011: 518). They note perspicaciously 'how home is already inflected with mobility—and conversely, [how] mobility is inflected with gestures of attachment' (2011: 519). Ultimately they suggest that 'recognizing home as at once grounded and uprooted highlights the often-overlooked dissonances between the lived and the desired meanings with which people imbue the notion' (2011: 525).

This is all well and good, yet it does not quite go far enough in problematising what one might call the methodological belongingism of much work on mobility, diaspora and the spatial politics of community. A subspecies of the methodological nationalism critiqued by Wimmer and Glick Schiller (2002), methodological belongingism builds on a romantic, implicitly Herderian (see Patten 2010) emphasis on the world as divided into nations conceptualised as organic entities whose peoples, unified by language and culture, express their political will over the national territories that are their birthright. Specifically, it assumes that, if all of these factors are arranged properly, everyone has a place in which they will fit. If people are out of place, it is because of aberrant circumstances that have disordered their present situation rather than a result of the nature of the world. In a Herderian or, for that matter, Westphalian, framework, every nation, in theory, has its proper place. The goal of many subsequent nationalist movements—especially of those whose conceptualisation of the issue has taken rather more procrustean form than Herder's own—has been to reshape territorial and political entities so that culture, language, territory and the *volk* might correspond.

In some instances this has been remarkably successful (as with the creation of the German nation or of the Han as a pan-regional and pan-dialectical exemplar of the nascent Chinese nation in the nineteenth century; see Chow 2001). In other cases—such as the massive transmigrations of ethnic and religiously defined populations to and from Turkey and Greece, or India and Pakistan—conformity with the Herderian ideal was purchased only with tremendous human suffering. Yet the idea that unbelonging might be as common or more common than belonging in the negotiation of self, home and (dis)place(ment) has not been commonly entertained. In recent years, however, critical human geographers, in particular, have increasingly sought to think through notions of originary unbelongings. Their efforts have resulted in some compelling work on 'ruined' Benjaminian (Dubrow 2010; Edensor 2005), loosely Derridean 'spectral' (Wylie 2007, 2009), and even more loosely Freudian 'uncanny' (Della Dora 2006; Gelder and Jacobs 1992) geographies of the nexus of im/mobility, in/stability and processes of identity formation. These in turn have added a particularly spatial element to the critique of Herderian visions of territorial nationalism.

Portable Fatherlands

Such literatures deserve a fuller discussion than present space allows but, as an abbreviated gesture towards their significance, I signal an alternative figure to Herder and the methodological belongingism that has been his legacy for contemporary studies of mobility. Heinrich Heine (1797–1856), the noted poet, was born into a Jewish family but converted to Christianity age 28. Of the generation following Herder's, he was both acquainted with and enamoured of the older man's theories (see Barnard 1981 for details). Yet the Herderian narrative of national belonging and organic unity is belied by Heine's own itinerant life. As discussed by Feinberg (1997) in her essay on unbelonging and homeland-lessness amongst contemporary German Jewish thinkers, Heine's travails emerge as a prototype for a kind of nomadic, belonging-less, extra-territorial existence. Sammons highlights most clearly the complexity of Heine's engagements with home, belonging and their opposites:

> As for his nationality, it is not easy to see under the legalities of the time what that was. He was born theoretically under Palatine sovereignty but in fact under French occupation. He was briefly a subject of Bavaria and for a longer time of that Napoleonic contraption, the Grand Duchy of Berg. His hometown was shifted under his feet from Dusseldorf to Luneburg to Hamburg. Eventually he probably became a Prussian *de jure*, and on occasion he liked so to identify himself, though not without an underlying irony, for his allegiance to Prussia was, to say the least, restrained. For nearly half his life he was a permanent resident of France, but he declined to become a French citizen. He was a voluntary, then an involuntary exile, yet he was never very far from home; he was both at home in Paris and a stranger there (1986: 615).

In place of (or alongside) Herderian territorial nationalism and its innate belongings, we have Heine and his *portatives Vaterland* (portable fatherland) wherein belonging, where possible, is not natural or grounded but the result of situationally constrained *bricolage*. Feinberg notes the account of literary critic Marcel Reich-Ranicki, who

> rejects his native Poland and his adopted country, Germany as his *Heimat* [affective or territorial home]: 'I have no *Heimat* and no fatherland, but I don't complain. In the end, I'm not *Heimat*-less, and certainly not a person without roots... I have a country of my own, a portable fatherland, a *Heimat* not of the worst kind: literature, more precisely stated, German literature' (1997: 165).

The ultimate referent of both this comment and Heine's more famous reference to the Bible as itself a *portatives Vaterland* is, as Safran reminds us, the creation, after the destruction of the second temple, of a 'form of Judaism in which the Torah became a "portable Temple" and a "portable fatherland". In this context, the maintenance of this portable fatherland, i.e., of the diaspora itself became a religious obligation' (2005: 44).

Uncanny Parallels

At this point in the discussion, caught with contemporary German Jews between their '"uncanny" [Central European] homelands' (Feinberg 1997: 168) and Israel, we might seem very far indeed from the lives of trans-Himalayan-ly mobile Tibetans poised between the Scylla of China and the Charybdis of external exile. Yet, there are particularly uncanny parallels between the Jewish and Tibetan cases, not least in their framings of the tense relationship between territorial (unportable) and extra-territorial (portable) imaginings of national (un)belonging. This suggestion stems from a particularly close resemblance in many aspects (apart from temporal duration of exile) of the processes by which the two communities were scattered.[4]

Anand perspicaciously highlights the similarities between Tibet and the Jewish historical prototype of scattered belonging.[5]

> Remarkably, the Tibetan case fits such a definition of Diaspora quite closely. Perception as well as evidence of coercion was the root cause of the dispersion of thousands of Tibetans from Tibet to South Asia. Like the watershed of the 586 BCE exile within Jewish diasporic consciousness, the Lhasa Uprising of 10 March 1959 (which led to the flight of the Dalai Lama, who took refuge in India) plays an important role in Tibetans' discourse about themselves, pinpointing a particular date as *the* moment of exile of the Tibetan nation. To a significant extent, the crucial elements of Tibetan identity—religion, language, folk memories—were already in place well before the dispersion, and so the exile leadership saw itself as the custodian of an ancient culture. In fact, this ethos of preserving the culture from possible extinction permeates the entire material and performative domain of Tibetan Diaspora (2003: 214).

Yet, as useful and wittily engaging as Anand's account of 'Tibetan culture-in-displacement' (2003: 223) is, it has two significant flaws. First, he replicates some of the unthinking conceptual separations of most work on diaspora. Further, he underplays the similarity between Tibetan and Jewish cases that is most crucial to understanding the generalised sense of homelessness amongst Tibetans on both sides of the Himalayas. On the first count, he seems to conclude that only diasporic Tibetans (in interaction with Westerners) produce diasporic consciousness. 'It is fruitful to look at Tibetanness', he writes,

> as a product of the creative negotiations conducted by diasporic Tibetans with the dominant representational regime and as a process of selective resistance to and appropriation of dominant identity concepts, including (trans)nationalism, sovereignty, indigeneity, universal human rights, and Diaspora (2003: 222).

What of those Tibetans who, while not exiles themselves, circulate through the exile communities of north India and in turn affect Tibetan self-conceptions on both sides of the Himalayas? Further, what of those Tibetans who stay behind in China but maintain actual or affective connections with wider communities (cf. Yeh 2009)? Surely diasporic Tibetan-ness(es) must be produced at the intersection of what Beck (2000) might call a geographically polygamous set of Tibetan communities and their multiply positioned interlocutors. Diaspora is not just about those who move.

A generous reading of Anand's argument would attribute his focus on diasporic Tibetans as particularly important in the process of collective identity formation to the fact that, in the Tibetan case, nationalism is clearly a product of the process of forming the diaspora. Anand argues, as have many other scholars (e.g. Dreyfus 2005; Kapstein 1998; Yeh 2007, to name but a few) that exile itself was responsible for the formation of a recognisably 'modern' Tibetan national consciousness. Yet his suggestion that, since 'imagining Tibet as a nation is, to a large extent, a post-exilic phenomenon', and that it 'therefore ... comes as no surprise that the most sophisticated articulation of Tibetan national identity comes from the more radical sections of Tibetan Diaspora' (2003: 224), is rather more problematic.

The problems with this assertion stem from the duality at the heart of contemporary Tibetan nationalism. Upon closer inspection, the dynamics of Tibetan exile have produced not a single nationalism on a modern, secular, territorial model, but at least two. While one would be recognisable to Anderson, Thongchai and other theorists of nations as territorial geobodies, the other looks like nothing so much as Heine's *portatives Vaterland*. This latter nationalism is a sacred cultural nationalism associated not with geobodily representations of national territories but with what Ramaswamy has called the idiom of 'the anthropomorphic sacred' (2010: 9).

The 'True Body of Tibet'

The object of this latter set of nationalist desires is not the territory of the nation. Rather, its object is the (more-than-)human body of the fourteenth Dalai Lama as, in Kolås' words, 'a personification of the protector deity of Tibet ... [and] the primary symbol of Tibetan unity. As a reincarnation of the deity Chenrezig', she notes, 'the Dalai Lama is the only unquestioned leader of the Tibetan people. Chenrezig not only provides continuity to the history of Tibet, but epitomises the community of Tibetans itself' (1996: 57; also see Klieger 1992).[6] In this mode of enacting the Tibetan nation, true Tibet lies not in a territorial homeland, but in a body of religious and cultural practice that has travelled with the Dalai Lama and other members of the Tibetan religious and cultural elite into India and even, perhaps, beyond territory itself into putatively universal salience.

In her work on Tibetan migrants to Western countries, Hess notes that,

> The utopian ideal of Tibet stands in opposition to the evils of modernity as a reason why the entire world should care about its fate: because Tibet's cultural ideals can help save an imperiled humanity. In this way one can argue that the community of Tibet has been imagined as inherently limitless primarily by non-Tibetans. . . . Tibetans themselves tend to be a little less grandiose, but suggest that Tibetan culture, particularly Buddhism might have something to offer others. But for this hypothesis to work, one must equate nation with culture. And in fact, Tibetans do this (2009: 57).

In its incipient transformation of a territorialised ethno-national category into a cultural or religious resource of potentially universal availability, 'the' Tibetan case again uncannily parallels 'the' Jewish one. Anand acknowledges this, noting that, 'there is some tension between "Tibet" as an ideal religious practice and "Tibet" as an exile nation with necessary links to territory' (2003: 221), but he does not fully pursue the consequences of this similarity, preferring to emphasise the 'highly political act' of 'presenting oneself as [a displaced member] of *a* bounded territory of Tibet' (2003: 222).

From a perspective informed as much by Heine as by Herder, it is harder to dismiss these parallels. The evolution of Tibetan Buddhism into a utopian ideal seems substantially consonant with Safran's observation that 'the Jewish Diaspora lasted for such a long time without a permanent hinterland . . . and without any territorial backup that Jews could no longer be imagined as a *Staatsnation* [state-nation] and were thought of only in religious terms' (Safran 2005: 43). Thus, alongside historical references to the Torah as portable Temple and recent German-Jewish references to German literature as a portable *Heimat* in contrast to the unhomeliness (*unheimlichkeit*) of territorial origins, we can see a particular version of sacred, if putatively post-sectarian, Tibetan religious culture as also coming to constitute a *portatives Vaterland*. As such it is a form of mobile nationalism that operates across boundaries of traditional and modern, secular and sacred. The unwillingness of the nation itself in this instance to respect national boundaries casts the elisions of methodological nationalism into even bolder relief (cf. Vasantkumar 2012).

The point is not that Tibetan nationalism is really ungrounded and has been done injustices by the methodological sendentarisms of scholars of nationalism and diaspora alike. Instead, as Dreyfus (2005) notes, 'Tibetan nationalism is not a unified discourse, but a site of contention, where conflicting visions compete for the allegiance of Tibetans' (2005: 14; see also Misra 2003: 192). Specifically, as mentioned above, the present situation is characterised by the mutual interference[7] of at least two incommensurable nationalisms. The first is territorial and largely, if not entirely, secular. It is grounded in the soil of Tibet, defined as 'the tradition[al] three provinces of Ü-Tsang, Do-toe, and Do-med'.[8] These form the locus of Tibet as a 'moral destination' (cf. Malkki 1997 [1992]), whether conceived of as independent state (in the envisionings of the Tibetan Youth Congress) or as a 'zone of peace' under the nominal control of the Chinese nation-state (as embodied in the Tibetan constitution).[9] The second incommensurable nationalism locates the 'true body of Tibet' in the person of the Dalai Lama (Falcone and Wangchuk 2008: 179–80). It thus argues that, as the Tibetan nation is embodied in culture rather than territory, in the words of Kasur Lodi Gyari, the Dalai Lama's Special Representative in Washington, 'Today Tibet lives, not within Tibet but outside Tibet. Everything that is Tibet—the culture, the religion, every aspect of Tibet lives outside Tibet' (2008: 197 fn. 45).

Tibetan Nationalisms and Unbelonging

At one time, it was possible to associate each of these incommensurable nationalisms with populations on one side of the mountains—the situated, territorial version with Tibetans from Tibet (and with official Chinese pronouncements on the subject), the portable, cultural version with the exile community. Hess cites Calkowski's (1997) work on

> the controversy that has arisen on multiple occasions when Tibetan cultural groups from the Tibetan Autonomous Region and from India each represent themselves as the true emissaries of Tibetan culture. Tibetans in exile have positioned themselves as maintaining a bastion of cultural purity in the face of Chinese practices in Tibet . . . whereas the Tibetan troupes from China link their authenticity to the physical location of Tibet (2009: 65).

Yet, increasingly, there is no longer any simple connection between geographic location and the territorial and religio-cultural modes of Tibetan nationalism. As the ethnographic vignettes with which I began this essay demonstrate, in addition to the oppositions Calkowski describes, one may encounter territorial nationalists in India, mourning their separation from the homeland, and cultural nationalists in China, bemoaning the flight of 'all our best and brightest' into exile.

That territorial and cultural modes of Tibetan nationalism now exist in uneasy proximity on both sides of the Himalayas is no doubt in part attributable to the changing dynamics of Tibetan peregrinations across the mountains since the 1980s. One-way journeys premised on the taking of refuge have been supplemented and to some degree superseded by return migrations and, especially, tarrying circulations of Amdo and Kham Tibetans through the largely Lhasa-centric (see Diehl 2002) cultural forms of the diaspora. Thus, a classical model of diaspora as comprising a spatially and temporally (cf. Axel 2001) distinct homeland and its dispersed populations only imperfectly captures contemporary Tibetan reality. For Tibetans, homeland and diaspora are *both* in motion, and understandings of self and of political possibility are coloured at least in part by the traffic between the two.

Perhaps the most surprising element of this entire picture is the conundrum this complexly spatialised plurality at the heart of Tibetan nationalist imaginings poses for concepts of belonging. One might expect a dual conception of Tibet as longed-for territory and jealously guarded cultural possession—as both grounded and portable fatherlands—to result in an expanded compass of national belonging. Yet, for the most part, just the opposite has been the case. While recasting Tibetan Buddhism as a universal soteriological and political resource has had some success in rallying Westerners to the Tibetan cause (see Prost 2006), in general, amongst Tibetans, the mutual interference between the two most prominent modes of imagining possible Tibetan nations has resulted in an augmented field of possible unbelongings—in more ways, that is, not to fit.

Tibetans in China who might otherwise see themselves as belonging to true Tibet by virtue of their territorial location are now, perhaps, just as liable to see themselves as degraded or out of place by virtue of their separation from Tibetan culture as embodied in the Dalai Lama. Similarly, many Tibetans who have passed through Dharamsala since the intensification of the second wave of migration from Amdo in the 1980s find their proximity to the traditional religious and cultural elite in India small compensation for their distance from the cuisine, kin, climate and sincere religiosity of territorial Tibet. While trans-Himalayan migration may have knit the two sides of the mountains more closely together than the communities of most diasporas, it has also opened a widening zone of homelessness at the centre of Tibetan community. Given the Dalai Lama's centrality to cultural nationalism in particular and his efforts to set up an effective secular political structure in preparation for his passing, only time will tell whether territorial and religio-cultural versions of Tibetan nationalism will move closer together or farther apart.

Conclusion: The Co-Mobility of Home and Diaspora

I conclude with some reflections on the resonances between the double-ness at the heart of Tibetan nationalism(s) and Malkki's classic article (1997 [1992])[10] on the place of refugees in the 'national order of things'. Malkki described the differing responses to exile amongst two groups of Hutu refugees in Tanzania. The first group had lived in a refugee camp in rural western Tanzania since escaping the 1972 genocide in their native Burundi. The second group had spent the intervening years 'in and around the township of Kigoma on Lake Tanganyika' (Malkki 1997 [1992]: 54). The 'camp refugees', she suggests, 'saw themselves as a nation in exile and defined exile, in turn, as a moral trajectory of trials and tribulations that would ultimately empower them to reclaim (or create anew) the "Homeland" in Burundi' (1997 [1992]: 66). In their case, 'displacement had become a form of moral purity', and this purity, based centrally on their status as refugees, had become intimately bound up with a collective sense of essential Hutu-ness. The 'town refugees', by contrast, 'were not *essentially* "Hutu" or "refugees" or "Tanzanians" or "Burundians", but rather just "broad persons"'. They pursued, 'not a heroized national identity but a lively cosmopolitanism' that prompted the camp refugees to see them as 'impure' or 'problematic' (1997 [1992]: 67, 68).

The parallels between the Tibetan contexts I have described above and Malkki's case should be clear enough. In both, alternatively nationalist and cosmopolitan visions of community are in circulation. Yet where Malkki casts both sets of Hutu refugees as relating primarily to a geographically defined homeland that has stayed put while they have travelled away from it, in the Tibetan case the homeland has *itself* been in motion. Both groups of refugees in Malkki's account, '[invent] homes and homelands in the absence of territorial national bases—not *in situ* but through memories of and claims on places that they can or will no longer corporeally inhabit' (1997 [1992]: 52). By contrast, both migrant and *non-migrant* Tibetans imagine their relationship to an absent homeland in a context of both chronic mobility and the mutual interference of incompatible nationalisms. Phuntsok and others like him, after all, never went to India, and live to this day *in Tibet*. Unlike their refugee and returnee compatriots and unlike both sets of migrants in Malkki's article, they stayed put while their homeland moved away from them. Their example, more Heine than Herder, pushes us to attend to the central role of displacement to imagining homelands *in situ*. Amdowa migrants to and from India, as well as their non-migrant co-nationals, invent homes and homelands, both at a distance *and in situ*, through, around and in idioms shaped but not exhausted by 'territorial national bases' that are themselves both compelling moral destinations and significant elsewheres.

I began this essay with a discussion of the creeping reification of the boundary between mobility and immobility in some of the most innovative work on 'new mobilities'. Here, it also bears noting that similar sorts of reification can also be observed in much recent work on diaspora as a more-than-national social formation. In particular, even thinkers attuned to the complexities of 'home' as a category freighted with ambiguous and gendered political and cultural content have tended to see diaspora as always already referring back to a fact of physical movement.[11] The stories we commonly read of diasporic identity are almost entirely those of making home in the aftermath of a spatial movement away; reflections on how, in Tolia-Kelly's words, 'the experience of a past home resides with you as you traverse toward your next' (2004: 316).[12]

In this mapping, home is the fixed or the desire to fix, and movement is that which unfixes or refixes, even if such binaries are no longer approached in terms of a purely sedentarist ethics that would mark displacement or uprooting as aberrant. Diasporic consciousness is approached via a dialectic of movement and stability, but the story told about it is over-determined by what has become an almost universal set of genre expectations—people who move have, as a result, had their notions of home reshaped. These genre expectations have rendered it surprisingly difficult for the anthropology of diaspora (and, perhaps, of mobility more broadly) to reckon with people who are displaced *in place*, as in Stewart's evocative phrase, 'exiles in their own homelands' (1988: 235).

Thus, it seems clear that placing a common-sense notion of movement alongside a common-sense notion of stasis in one's analytic scheme is insufficient to gain critical purchase on the co-mobility of home and diaspora. Placing routes alongside roots is certainly an improvement on an exclusive focus on static or grounded social forms. Yet a focus on a dialectic of stability and mobility wherein we assume we know what each of these are ahead of time is likely to be ultimately as rigid and constraining an analytic frame as the methodological nationalism it has been intended to supersede. In place of stark contrasts between stable homes and mobile aways, proximate securities and distant risks, scholars would be better served by treating both home and the unhomely, those who move and those who stay, not as neatly mappable onto either the mobile or the stable but as complex *mixtures* of movement and stability. Further, the particular contours of these mixtures must be studied *in vivo* rather than assumed *a priori*. Such studies will undoubtedly make substantive contributions to emergent work on regimes of mobility across the globe. Further, work in this vein can play a central role in producing, in Glick Schiller and Salazar's words in their introduction to this special issue of *JEMS*, 'narratives of movement' that 'normalis[e] neither mobility or stasis'.

Notes

[1] These areas, historically two of the three regions of cultural (but not political) Tibet, are not part of the contemporary Tibetan Autonomous Region but are parcelled out between the Chinese provinces of Gansu, Qinghai, Sichuan and Yunnan.

[2] A useful source of information on such movements is the International Campaign for Tibet's annual publication entitled *Refugee Report: Dangerous Crossing*. The 2011 version is accessible at: http://www.savetibet.org/documents/reports/refugee-report-dangerous-crossing-2011

[3] Cresswell alludes to this only in passing: 'and it matters where walking happens the walk in 19th-century Paris is very different from the walk in rural Mali or the walk in the contemporary British countryside' (2010: 20).

[4] In other words, were made into diasporas; see Safran (2005) for an eye-opening reappraisal of the relationship between the Jewish case and scholarly work on diasporas more broadly construed, and Yeh (2009) for a contrasting list of Tibetan similarities to the Palestinian diaspora.

[5] The Jewish model of diaspora, he suggests, incorporates 'coercion as a causative factor of out-migration of people with a well-defined identity from their homeland; conscious cultivation of collective memory of the homeland, with a strong emphasis on ultimate return (this is more about "re-turn", a repeated turning to the concept and/or reality of the homeland, than a physical return); preservation of culture through a patrolling of communal boundaries as the defining feature of the dispersal; and maintenance of communication and solidarity through institutionalized practices' (Anand 2003: 214).

[6] Dreyfus (2005: 11) confirms the central importance of Chenrezig/Avalokitesvara to both historic and contemporary imaginings of Tibetan nationalism.

[7] The term is Donna Haraway's; see Law and Hetherington (2003) for a fuller contextualisation.

[8] http://tibetanyouthcongress.org/about-tyc/.

[9]   http://www.savetibet.org/resource-center/dalai-lama/guidelines-future-tibet-policy.
[10]   Moran (2004: 189) argues compellingly that the Tibetan example stands Malkki's argument about the place of the refugee in the 'national order of things' on its head.
[11]   See, for example, Safran's assertion that 'It [is] difficult to refer to the Québécois, Spanish Basques, or Tamil Sri Lankans as diasporas: they have not been dispersed, but they wish political independence in the land in which they have remained' (2005: 38–9).
[12]   The unquestioned focus on movement as the sole source of displacement in Tolia-Kelly's essay is in contrast to her critical feminist sensibility towards 'home'.

References

Anand, D. (2003) 'A contemporary story of "diaspora": the Tibetan version', *Diaspora*, *12*(2): 211–29.

Anderson, B. (1991) *Imagined Communities*. New York: Verso.

Appadurai, A. (1990) 'Disjuncture and difference in the global cultural economy', *Public Culture*, *2*(2): 1–24.

Axel, B.K. (2001) *The Nation's Tortured Body*. Durham, NC: Duke University Press.

Barnard, M. (1981) 'Particularity, universality, and the Hebraic spirit: Heine and Herder', *Jewish Social Studies*, *43*(2): 121–36.

Beck, U. (2000) *What is Globalization?*. Oxford: Polity.

Bissell, D. (2008) 'Visualising everyday geographies: practices of vision through travel-time', *Transactions of the Institute of British Geographers*, *33*(1): 42–60.

Blunt, A. (2003) 'Collective memory and productive nostalgia: Anglo-Indian homemaking at McCluskieganj', *Environment and Planning D: Society and Space*, *21*(6): 717–38.

Boym, S. (1996) 'Estrangement as a lifestyle: Shklovsky and Brodsky', *Poetics Today*, *17*(4): 511–30.

Calkowski, M. (1997) 'The Tibetan diaspora and the politics of performance', in Korom, F. (ed.) *Tibetan Culture in the Diaspora*. Vienna: Österreichischen Akademie der Wissenschaften, 51–9.

Chow, K.W. (2001) 'Narrating nation, race, and national culture: imagining the Hanzu identity in modern China', in Chow, K.W., Doak, K.M. and Fu, P.S. (eds) *Constructing Nationhood in Modern East Asia*. Ann Arbor: University of Michigan Press, 47–83.

Cresswell, T. (2010) 'Towards a politics of mobility', *Environment and Planning D: Society and Space*, *28*(1): 17–31.

Della Dora, V. (2006) 'The rhetoric of nostalgia: postcolonial Alexandria between uncanny memories and global geographies', *Cultural Geographies*, *13*(2): 207–38.

Diehl, K. (2002) *Echoes from Dharamsala*. Berkeley: University of California Press.

Dreyfus, G. (2005) 'Are we prisoners of Shangri-la? Orientalism, nationalism and the study of Tibet', *Journal of the International Association of Tibetan Studies*, *1*: 1–21.

Dubrow, J. (2010) 'The mobility of thought: reflections on Blanchot and Benjamin', *Interventions*, *6*(2): 216–28.

Edensor, T. (2005) 'The ghosts of industrial ruins: ordering and disordering memory in excessive space', *Environment and Planning D: Society and Space*, *23*(6): 829–49.

Falcone, J. and Wangchuk, T. (2008) '"We're not home": Tibetan refugees in India in the twenty-first century', *India Review*, *7*(3): 164–99.

Feinberg, A. (1997) 'Abiding in a haunted land: the issue of *Heimat* in contemporary German-Jewish writing', *New German Critique*, *S70*: 161–81.

Flower, J.M. (2004) 'A road is made: roads, temples, and historical memory in Ya'an County, Sichuan', *Journal of Asian Studies*, *63*(3): 649–85.

Gelder, K. and Jacobs, J. (1992) 'Uncanny Australia', *Ecumene*, *2*: 171–83.

Gupta, A. and Ferguson, J. (1992) 'Beyond "culture": space, identity and the politics of difference', *Cultural Anthropology*, 7(1): 6–23.

Hannam, K., Sheller, M. and Urry, J. (2006) 'Editorial: Mobilities, immobilities and moorings', *Mobilities*, 1(1): 1–22.

Hess, J.M. (2009) *Immigrant Ambassadors*. Stanford, CA: Stanford University Press.

Kapstein, M. (1998) 'Concluding remarks', in Goldstein, M. and Kapstein, M. (eds) *Buddhism in Contemporary Tibet: Religious Revival and Cultural Identity*. Berkeley: University of California Press, 139–49.

Klieger, P.C. (1992) *Tibetan Nationalism*. Meerut: Archana Publications.

Kolås, Å. (1996) 'Tibetan nationalism: the politics of religion', *Journal of Peace Research*, 33(1): 51–66.

Lau, T. (2010) 'The Hindi film's romance and Tibetan notions of harmony: emotional attachments and personal identity in the Tibetan diaspora in India', *Journal of Ethnic and Migration Studies*, 36(6): 967–87.

Law, J. and Hetherington, K. (2003) *Allegory and Interference: Representation in Sociology*. Lancaster: University of Lancaster, Working Paper in Sociology, http://www.comp.lancs.ac.uk/sociology/papers/Law-Hetherington-Allegory-Interference.pdf.

Malkki, L. (1997 [1992]) 'National Geographic: the rooting of peoples and the territorialization of national identity among scholars and refugees', Gupta, A. and Ferguson, J. (eds) *Culture, Power, Place*. Durham: Duke University Press, 52–74.

McCormack, D.P. (2009) 'Aerostatic spacing: on things becoming lighter than air', *Transactions of the Institute of British Geographers*, 34(1): 25–41.

Misra, A. (2003) 'A nation in exile: Tibetan diaspora and the dynamics of long distance nationalism', *Asian Ethnicity*, 4(2): 189–206.

Moran, P. (2004) *Buddhism Observed*. New York: RoutledgeCurzon.

Patten, A. (2010) '"The most natural state": Herder and nationalism', *History of Political Thought*, 31(4): 657–89.

Prost, A. (2006) 'The problem with "rich refugees" sponsorship, capital and the informal economy of Tibetan refugees', *Modern Asian Studies*, 40(1): 233–53.

Ralph, D. and Staeheli, L.A. (2011) 'Home and migration: mobilities, belongings and identities', *Geography Compass*, 5(7): 517–30.

Ramaswamy, S. (2010) *The Goddess and the Nation*. Durham: Duke University Press.

Safran, W. (2005) 'The Jewish Diaspora in a comparative and theoretical perspective', *Israel Studies*, 10(1): 36–60.

Sammons, J. (1986) 'Heine as *Weltbürger*? A skeptical inquiry', *Modern Language Notes*, 101(3): 609–28.

Schneider, D. (1984) *A Critique of the Study of Kinship*. Ann Arbor: University of Michigan Press.

Sheller, M. and Urry, J. (2006) 'The new mobilities paradigm', *Environment and Planning A*, 38(2): 207–26.

Smith, K. (2000) 'Mere nostalgia: notes on a progressive paratheory', *Rhetoric and Public Affairs*, 3(4): 505–27.

Stewart, K. (1988) 'Nostalgia—a polemic', *Cultural Anthropology*, 3(3): 227–41.

Tolia-Kelly, D.P. (2004) 'Locating processes of identification: studying the precipitates of re-memory through artefacts in the British Asian home', *Transactions of the Institute of British Geographers*, 29(3): 314–29.

Vasantkumar, C. (2012) 'What is this "Chinese" in Overseas Chinese? Sojourn work and the place of China's minority nationalities in extraterritorial Chinese-ness', *Journal of Asian Studies*, 71(2): 423–46.

Wimmer, A. and Glick Schiller, N. (2002) 'Methodological nationalism and beyond: nation-state building, migration and the social sciences', *Global Networks*, 2(4): 301–34.

Wylie, J. (2007) 'The spectral geographies of W.G. Sebald', *Cultural Geographies*, 14(2): 171–88.

Wylie, J. (2009) 'Landscape, absence and the geographies of love', *Transactions of the Institute of British Geographers*, *34*(2): 275–89.

Yeh, E.T. (2007) 'Exile meets homeland: politics, performance and authenticity in the Tibetan diaspora', *Environment and Planning D: Society and Space*, *25*(4): 648–67.

Yeh, E.T. (2009) 'Tibet and the problem of radical reductionism', *Antipode*, *41*(5): 983–1010.

International Migration: Virtue or Vice? Perspectives from Cameroon

Michaela Pelican

This article argues that both global and national power differences play a crucial role in shaping local imaginaries of international migration among youths in two Cameroonian cities—Bamenda and Yaoundé. While Yaoundé is the national capital, Bamenda is the headquarters of the Anglophone north-west, an area generally opposed to the ruling regime and claiming historical as well as contemporary political marginalisation. Physical mobility has long been associated with social mobility and viewed rather positively. In both areas more critical perspectives on international migration are emerging. This is reflected in differences in envisioned destinations as well as in terminologies and concepts. Thus, in Yaoundé 'the dangers of illegal migration' have become the topic of the day—a theme publicised by international organisations in collaboration with local NGOs. Conversely, youths in Bamenda consciously compare their conceptualisations of the advantages and disadvantages of life abroad on the basis of imparted experiences of migrant family members and friends. These discourses influence not only youths' perception of different forms of migrancy but also their assessment of their future in Cameroon. International migration is thus viewed in a broad discursive spectrum from virtue to vice, and perceptions are shaped by regional, national and international political discourse.

Introduction

The recent literature on international migration from Cameroon and, more generally, from Africa, paints a relatively homogenous picture of the perceptions and aspirations of young people. Authors like de Rosny (2002), Förster (2010), Jua (2003), Nyamnjoh and Page (2002) and Pelican and Tatah (2009) depict the situation of Cameroonian youths as overshadowed by general feelings of disappointment and disillusionment; disappointment with the economic and political situation in Cameroon, and disillusionment about the (im)possibility of a decent future in their home country. As a result according to this narrative, aspiring Cameroonians consider migration to the US, Europe and the Near and Far East, as well as within Africa, to be a preferable alternative to social immobility and failure at home.

It is the aim of this article to refine and qualify this generalised portrayal of local perceptions of international migration by drawing attention to regional variations. As I argue, contemporary imaginaries include a broad discursive spectrum that ought to be seen in response to national and international political discourses. Furthermore, the article sheds light on the complex interrelations of physical and social mobility. On a more theoretical level, I wish to contribute to the novel approach of *regimes of mobility* proclaimed by Nina Glick Schiller and Noel Salazar in the introduction to this special issue of *JEMS*.

According to Glick Schiller and Salazar, the discipline of migration studies has been characterised by periodic shifts in orientation, defining either mobility or stasis as the original human condition. While critiquing these approaches as normative and exclusivist, they propose a new mobilities studies that transcends this dichotomy and allows for varied and varying arrangements of mobility, stasis and connection. I agree with their argument, but wish to take it further and draw attention to geographical differences in addition to temporal shifts. I have noticed a tendency in scholarly and policy discourse to formulate broad statements about countries or even continents with regard to mobility or stasis. For example, Africa has long been perceived and described as a continent of mobility, be it in terms of original human expansion, historical population movements, 'cultures of migration' (Hahn and Klute 2007) or economically, ecologically or politically driven mobility (e.g. Adepoju 2008). While undisputedly there are many historical and contemporary instances of mobility, a uniform view of Africa is problematic. I therefore wish to highlight the need to deconstruct broad generalisations about mobility or stasis on the level of a continent, a region or a country.

Cameroon is a particularly good example with which to illustrate my point, as historical, political and economic factors have contributed to substantial internal differentiation. Moreover, international connections on the level both of organisations and individuals impact significantly but variedly on local actors' perceptions and abilities of movement. The Cameroonian case study thus illustrates the significance of theorising internal and international conditions in the same framework; an approach that supports the plea of Glick Schiller and Salazar (this issue; see also Wimmer and Glick Schiller 2002, 2003) to overcome methodological nationalism. In this context, they also draw attention to the fact that researchers have prioritised some forms of mobility over others. For example, there has been a remarkable division between internal and international migration in the study of mobility in Africa. While this article does not fully bridge this gap, I believe that, by embedding local views of international migration in a historical context of mobility, I can point out some of the various connections and transitions between internal, international and intercontinental migration.

Finally, in their introduction, Glick Schiller and Salazar point out the neglect of the concept of power in much previous research. They propose the idea of *regimes of mobility* to account for both national and international modes of regulation as well as the ability to sanction specific types of movement, while criminalising others. Understanding the role of power in shaping physical and social mobilities in Cameroon is a key interest of this article. Massey's (1993) concept of 'power geometry' here proves helpful. As she argues, individuals and groups are placed differently in relation to their movements and connections. This not only influences who moves or who does not, but who is in charge of mobility or benefits from it. As the Cameroonian case study suggests, international development organisations play a crucial role in this power geometry, as they provide not only locally situated resources but also narratives that frame mobility and stasis. The findings of this article advance the need to examine differential regional, national and international power and networks of connection in theorising regimes of mobility.

Historical Dimensions of Mobility in Cameroon

Cameroon is widely known as a peaceful country that is politically stable and relatively well off. Furthermore, large parts of the population see themselves as sedentary rather than mobile, and attach much meaning to their rural home village as constitutive of their identity. Against this background it may come as a surprise that so many Cameroonians aspire to go abroad.

On closer inspection we may notice that this portrayal of Cameroon has been informed by state interests and policies that emphasise stability over mobility. For example, identification with the home village has been reinforced by governmental policies of the 1990s that have promoted the creation of ethnic and regional elite associations (Nyamnjoh and Rowlands 1998). At the same time, struggles over natural and political resources have been conflated with discourses of autochthony that privilege stasis over mobility, and that have engendered new dynamics of inclusion and exclusion (Geschiere 2009).

As in many parts of Africa, mobility is not a new phenomenon in Cameroon. Rather, the country has an extended history of mobility both within and across its national borders. Since the pre-colonial period, participation in trade networks, as well as pastoral mobility, have characterised the lives of several of its peoples (Boutrais 1995/96; Warnier 1993). At the same time, there have been instances of involuntary mobility engendered by the domestic and transatlantic slave trade as well as by the colonial practice of forced labour (Argenti 2006, 2009; Röschenthaler 2006; Warnier 2006). Subsequently, the coastal plantations—instituted in the colonial period—attracted a large labour force mostly from the country's populous north-west (Ardener *et al.* 1960). Concurrently, rural-to-urban migration became a consistent phenomenon which, today, is again gaining momentum in a chain of movement from village to town to city to abroad.

Much of Cameroon's international or transnational mobility takes place within the continent. It often relates to informal cross-border activities, such as illustrated by Roitman (2004) for the Chad Basin and Niger-Thomas (2000) for the Cross-River Area bordering Nigeria and Cameroon. Similarly, there have been established networks of trade and labour migration linking Cameroon with Gabon and Equatorial Guinea, both countries with a higher income level and a demand for foodstuffs and labour (Bennafla 2002; Chouala 2004). Besides economically motivated mobility, we may also consider religious networks that, for a long time, have linked Cameroon with centres of Islamic pilgrimage and scholarship, such as in Nigeria, Egypt and Sudan. On the other hand, Cameroon has been an attractive destination for Nigerian entrepreneurs and Islamic clerics and, in recent years, has seen a considerable influx of refugees mainly from Chad and the Central African Republic (IOM 2009).

Cameroon's transcontinental mobility has mainly been linked to the country's colonial history, which involved Germany, France and Britain. Several Cameroonians have travelled or lived in Europe, benefitting from religious, educational and professional networks. In recent years, however, with increasing restrictions on migration to Europe, many have turned to alternative destinations. Top of the list is the US, whose diversity visa lottery programme has attracted wide interest (Hugentobler 2009; Makuchi 1999).[1] Others have ventured to the Near and Far East, pursuing a variety of economic, educational and religious opportunities (Pelican and Tatah 2009). Among those determined to reach Europe by any means, several have tried to stow away or embark on the dangerous passage through the desert.[2]

Movement and connection have thus been part and parcel of Cameroon's history, and most communities have been exposed to mobility in one way or another. As Geschiere and Gugler (1998) have noted with regard to rural-urban migration, there has been a continuing commitment among migrants to 'the village' or home community. This includes a variety of translocal practices, such as the transfer of money, goods, services and ideas, as well as the participation in migrant or hometown associations. The same applies to international migrants. Moreover, their investments and involvement have become increasingly evident in both changing landscapes and community development (Fleischer 2007; Malaquais 2002; Mercer *et al.* 2008; Ndjio 2009).

We have to note, however, that some peoples and regions have participated in networks of mobility more than others, and have developed different perspectives and experiences. It is the aim of this contribution to analyse such divergences by focusing on two locales that occupy disparate positions in Cameroon's history and political hierarchy.

Regional Variations

The regional focus of this paper is on Yaoundé, the country's capital in the Francophone south, and Bamenda, the headquarters of the Anglophone north-west. Here it is important to remember that Cameroon has a triple colonial legacy, of which I name only the most significant facts. Initially administered by the Germans, it was split in 1919 and placed under the mandate of the French and British colonial powers. While the larger part went to France, the Western region came under British mandate. Subsequently, yet not without grievances, Francophone and Anglophone Cameroon were integrated into a single country with co-existing administrative systems. As Cameroonian scholars argue, this colonial history considerably impacted on the political culture and identity of Cameroonians in the two parts of the country (e.g. Awasom 2003; Chiabi 1997; Fanso 2009). Moreover, the Anglophone minority, which comprises two out of ten administrative regions, has long been at pains to reassert its political parity. This situation was aggravated during Cameroon's democratisation process, which culminated in the upsurge of secession movements and became known as 'the Anglophone problem' (Eyoh 1998; Konings and Nyamnjoh 1997, 2003).

As I argue, Cameroon's political history, with its regional variations, has impacted on the political self-understanding and commitment of its citizens and, in consequence, on their views of mobility and stasis. Anglophone Cameroonians assess their chances of a decent future in their home country in a different light to their Francophone compatriots in Yaoundé, and associate considerable hope and expectation with migration as a viable alternative. This argument is illustrated here by analysing local imaginaries of international migration both in terms of terminology and media representation. Furthermore, I show that, in Yaoundé, migration is seen in a more critical light, a perspective influenced by recent discourse in national and international migration policy.[3]

Bamenda: The Peripheries

Bamenda is the largest town in Anglophone Cameroon and has approximately 270,000 inhabitants (INS Cameroun 2010: 20). It is the capital of the North-West Region, and the headquarters of the main political opposition party. The north-west is mostly an agricultural region and provides food to urban centres in the south, including the capital Yaoundé. In addition, this region is renowned for its high-quality educational and medical facilities, which are the result of considerable colonial and post-colonial mission investment (Bowie 1985; Dah 1982; de Vries 1998; Weber 1993; Winterberger 2009).

North-westerners are generally proud of their agricultural productivity and, inspired by the missionaries' emphasis on literacy and professional training, attribute much value to education. For several decades, individuals benefited from academic and mission networks spanning Cameroon, Britain, Germany and Switzerland.

Besides furthering their education, many were able to establish business relations and invest back home, thus setting an example for later generations.

At the same time, most north-westerners are convinced that, as Anglophones, they are politically marginalised and thus largely excluded from government positions. They contend that, while Cameroon is supposedly a bilingual country, the language of administration is French, thus disadvantaging Anglophones. In addition, they criticise that the region in general, and Bamenda in particular, lacks strong industrial and service sectors where the abilities and knowledge of their young people could effectively be put to use. Similarly, they complain about heavy taxes imposed on private businesses, thus daunting individual initiatives. For example, the Anglophone magazine for aspiring migrants, entitled *Bushfallers*, reports that the yearly taxes and mandatory contributions add up to 51.4 per cent of business profit (*BFM* 2008). Against this background it is not surprising that many Anglophones look to international migration as an alternative, as they perceive no valid future within their country.[4]

'Bushfalling': Travelling Abroad in Search of Opportunities

The *lingua franca* of Anglophone Cameroon is Pidgin English. The Pidgin term popularly used to denote an international migrant is *bushfaller*—as in the title of the above-mentioned magazine and in a wall-painting in a bar in south-west Cameroon (see Figure 1).[5] A similar expression, yet with wider application, is the search for 'greener pastures' which may refer to internal as well as international migration (see also Förster 2010).

A *bushfaller* is 'someone who made it', i.e. who left Cameroon and now leads a good life in the West. As the etymology of the term shows, *bushfalling* implies going to the bush to hunt, gather or harvest; i.e. one never returns from the bush with empty hands (Alpes 2011; Jua 2003; Nyamnjoh 2011). But *bush* has a double connotation: on the one hand it is associated with wilderness and backwardness, on the other with places of enrichment—thus the US and Europe also qualify as *bush*. Similarly, a distinction is made between the *black bush*, referring to one's home village in the African countryside, and the *white bush*, denoting the West. However, not all migration destinations are seen as *bush*. Within the continent, only South Africa may count as such, as it is often considered as the African US. Besides the West, destinations in the Near and Far East may equally qualify as *bush*, as long as they signify modernity and prosperity (Pelican and Tatah 2009).[6]

While *bushfaller* is a relatively novel term, there have been earlier concepts. *Been to*, for example, refers to elite members of the post-colonial era who, with the help of mission networks or personal connections, studied abroad, and subsequently returned to Cameroon to take up white-collar jobs with the government or international corporations.[7] *America Wanda*, on the other hand, denotes the first generation of Cameroonian migrants to the United States, most of whom left for studies but eventually decided to stay on and integrate into US society (Nyamnjoh

Figure 1. Wall-painting in a bar in Idenao, South-West Cameroon, named 'Lasvega's Bush-Faller Creeck'.
Photo: M. Pelican (2009).

2011). In comparing these two notions with the concept of *bushfalling*, a shift in ideals of personal success is evident. Whereas *America Wanda* and *been to* imply mainly educational achievement, *bushfaller* is associated with adventure and self-enrichment. Moreover, *bushfaller* entails a strong transnational connotation, largely absent in the earlier concepts. It is associated with a continuous flow of remittances as well as migrants' regular home visits as a demonstration of their belonging and success.

As a Cameroonian friend explained, the term *bushfalling* has also been used in criminal jargon:

> The first time I heard the phrase 'fall bush' was in the late 1990s. Someone was telling an interesting encounter with khaki boys [meaning uniformed officers]. He built up his story and left a suspended pause at the end. Someone then said 'What happened next?'. He said 'Ma man, weti you go do? I fall bush'[8] and everyone exploded with laughter. I was probably the only one who missed the joke, so I inquired further and was 'educated' that. in the criminals' encounter with the law, the last resort is to 'fall bush'. This clearly meant—you ran. It was said with a lot of bravado which probably remains true for [the contemporary] bush-falling (migrate—for good?) phenomenon. It was much later (2000s) that I became aware of the use of the phrase [bush faller] for going abroad (NS, e-mail communication, 29 March 2010).

The connections, both imagined and real, between migration and illicit activities are manifold. Fraudulent practices, such as the use of false documents for visa applications or the fabrication of stories to make an asylum case, are widely known and have engendered controversial discussions in the media (Nyamnjoh 2011). Yet, as Alpes (2011) convincingly argues, the distinction of real and fake, legal and illegal is elusive and of little relevance to aspiring Anglophone migrants.

Moreover, migration is often associated with *feymania* (con artistry). As outlined by de Rosny (2002) and Jua (2003), both avenues have become popular imaginaries of making a successful future, particularly among disillusioned youths determined to counter their condition of social immobility. *Feymania* falls into the realm of criminal activities and refers to a phenomenon that gained prominence in the 1990s—namely individuals making a fortune through large-scale fraudulence, cons and scams such as money-doubling and pretended investments (Malaquais 2001a, 2001b; Ndjio 2006, 2008). *Feymania* is interlinked with migration, as most successful *feymen* (professional swindlers) operate on an international level. Thus, in popular understanding, migration and *feymania* go together, and migrants' or *bushfallers'* economic success may well be attributed to fraudulent dealings. It is important to note, however, that the moral judgement entailed in such allegations is not obvious but complex and subtle, as discourses of morality have changed in the context of increasing deprivation, poverty and abjection (Ndjio 2008; Nyamnjoh 2011).

The connection between *bushfalling* and *feymania* was brought home to me during fieldwork in Dubai (United Arab Emirates). Most Cameroonians here engage in informal activities, many of which—due to the city state's Islamic rules—verge on illegality (Pelican and Tatah 2009). Moreover, several individuals had successfully tricked Arab clients, thus negatively affecting the name of Cameroonians in Dubai. Criticism was raised by members of the Cameroonian expatriate community who, reflecting the Anglophone–Francophone divide, accused each other of spoiling their national reputation. In consequence, several individuals decided to disassociate themselves from the Cameroonian expatriate association, and to avoid contact with individuals whom they suspected of shady dealings.

The Dubai material also illuminates some of the key features of the Anglophone concept of *bushfalling*. As outlined above, countries considered *bush* are those associated with modernity and prosperity. Dubai is one of the destinations that, at first glance, seem to offer abundant opportunities to get rich and partake in global consumerism. However, as it soon transpires, Cameroonians find themselves at the lower end of the economic and social scale where they have to cope with overcrowded housing conditions, low salaries and precarious legal status. Thus, *bushfalling*, initially viewed as adventure and an opportunity to work for money for the family back home, proves to be a temporary deadlock. However, most Anglophone Cameroonians I met in Dubai are committed to saving whatever they can, so that, in the long run, they can make their way to Europe or the US, where they dream of finding a suitable job and furthering their education. Thus, their ultimate dream is to achieve a secure financial position and to advance their knowledge and status. The high esteem attributed to education, however, seems a particularity of Anglophone Cameroonians, and shapes their expectations of migration.

International Migration in the Anglophone and Francophone Media

To give an idea of the different perceptions and discourses on international migration in Bamenda and Yaoundé, I will now juxtapose recent book publications and film productions from Anglophone and Francophone Cameroon.

In Bamenda, international migration or *bushfalling* is generally viewed favourably. Of course, individuals may have different preferences and opinions may vary depending on imparted experiences of migrant family members and friends (see also Frei 2011; Nyamnjoh 2011). In public discourse, however, positive perspectives prevail. Anglophone media representations tend to emphasise economic and educational success, while dealing with the problems encountered in a humorous way. For example, a book entitled *From Dust to Snow: Bush-Faller* (Ngwa and Ngwa 2006) was released and sold in Anglophone bookstores, in which migrants (predominantly Cameroonian students) told of their positive and negative experiences of living and studying in the West. With regard to visual media, Anglophone Cameroon is flooded with Nigerian home-movie productions. Two Nigerian movies very popular in Bamenda, which deal with the subject of international migration, are the comedies entitled *Osuofia in London* and *Mama G in America*. Both films depict, in a humorous way, the difficulties which the Nigerian protagonists face in adapting to Western life.

Two recent Anglophone Cameroonian movie productions that address the topic of international migration are *China Wahala* and *Berlin Icon*. Both focus less on Cameroonians' encounter with Chinese or German society, but more on exploitative and adultery practices within the respective Cameroonian expat communities. *China Wahala* is a comedy that deals with the potentially abusive practices of Cameroonians in China who offer their services as migration-brokers and local conduits. The movie was so successful that a sequel (*China Wahala 2*, 2009) was produced, expanding on the same subject. The fate of Cameroonians in China is also a topic repeatedly dealt with in the Cameroonian press. Most articles focus on Cameroonians involved in illegal activities, such as money-doubling (*feymania*), and their prosecution by the Chinese government (*The Herald* 2009)

In contrast to the rather humorous character of Anglophone media representations of international migration, their Francophone counterparts produced and consumed in Yaoundé have much more critical and ambivalent undertones. Here it is important to note that media representations in Yaoundé have been shaped by international discourse as promoted by the Cameroonian government, European embassies and the International Organization for Migration (IOM).

For example, in 2007 Jean-Emmanuel Pondi (Professor of International Relations, University of Yaoundé) published an edited volume entitled *Immigration et Diaspora: Un Regard Africain* which takes up subjects central to international migration policy from the perspective of Cameroonian academics—such as the involvement of African diasporas in the development of their countries, the protection of migrants' rights and the fight against illegal migration. The same year, the Cameroonian director and television actress Josephine Ndagnou released her cinema production *Paris à Tout Prix* which tells the story of a young woman in Europe faced with prostitution, failure and deportation.

Both Pendi's book and Ndagnou's feature film provide an informed but critical perspective which highlights the potentially negative and dangerous aspects of the migration enterprise—both for Cameroon society and for the individual migrant.

Similarly, the Francophone terminology for international migration differs from its Anglophone equivalent. Here they use the expression *aller au front, aller se battre,* i.e. to go to the front, to go into battle. These terms are borrowed from military vocabulary and refer to the challenges and dangers which migrants may encounter as well as the audacity and vigour required for being successful abroad. In her study on Cameroonian women in the region of Paris, Bouly de Lesdain (1999: 28) mentions that, at the time of her research, the terms popularly used to describe international migration in Cameroon were *faire l'aventure, être en aventure, se debrouiller* (i.e. to go on an adventure, to manage/cope). While these terms come closer to the meaning implied in *bushfalling,* the contemporary terminology in Yaoundé has a much more vigorous connotation, speaking of the many obstacles and risks that characterise the current migration enterprise.

This ambivalent perception of international migration is also reflected in Figure 2 in the drawing by the Cameroonian artist Ediem, whose workshop is located in Bastos, the upper-class quarter of Yaoundé where embassies and international organisations have their offices. This is the explanation Ediem provided with the drawing:

> The painting represents Europe and America as a light that shines across the ocean. This light or sun is the symbol of wealth, of everything that is good in contrast to obscurity. That is why Africans decide to travel at all cost and risk of life to find fortune. The young take with them the knowledge, culture and African wisdom that will be lost in the future. The basket contains, therefore, all the African cultural riches that the migrants take along. The parents have hope in the emigration of their daughter and son, that he or she will bring happiness to the family, but this happiness is never achieved. It is rather their lives that perish at sea; the dead, the drownings, the prisons, etc. that form part of the journey. Some migrants never return to their families and very often, it is a shoe washed ashore by the current that makes us believe that the migrant has died while crossing the desert or the sea (my translation, email communication 24 March 2010).

Yaoundé: The Political Centre

Yaoundé is the capital of Cameroon and has a population of approximately 1.8 million inhabitants (INS Cameroon 2010: 20). It is the country's second largest town after the economic centre, Douala, and benefits from the presence of a considerable

Figure 2. Drawing by Ediem, Cameroonian artist, Yaoundé 2010. Reproduced with the kind permission of the artist.

government apparatus and international institutions which provide employment and business opportunities to Yaoundé citizens. Furthermore, it is a university town and has long been the centre of higher and professional education.

Life in the capital is quite different from living in the periphery. There is money in Yaoundé, which is reflected in the living standards and buying power of government and NGO workers, as well as in the infrastructure and beautification of the city. Moreover, it is the centre of political decision-making, and citizens occasionally have the opportunity to take part in the life of politicians and celebrities.

However, life in Yaoundé is no bed of roses and there is no guarantee of employment after completing university or professional education. Nonetheless, the political spirit in Yaoundé is much different to that in Bamenda and, while many youths criticise the current government for its nepotism and corruption, they may still hope to get a decent job. Thus, in my reading, their perspective on international migration as an alternative to making a living in Cameroon is shaped more by the presence than by the absence of opportunities.[9]

At the same time, Yaoundé is the centre of national policy discourse, much of which is shaped by the international development establishment. In recent years, there has been a shift in international migration policy—spearheaded by European governments and the United Nations—which advocates collaboration between sending and receiving countries and their diasporas in order to better control migration flows, and to ensure positive effects for all parties involved or—in UN jargon—to produce a win-win-win situation (Annan 2006; de Haas 2010). This new trend in migration and development policy has also impacted on Cameroon which, since 2006, has participated in European–African negotiations (IOM 2009). Since 2008 the Cameroonian government has been in the process of revising its migration policies, an undertaking that has not been completed at the time of this article going to press. Initial steps have been aimed at facilitating the mobility of highly skilled personnel, and integrating the Cameroonian diaspora in the country's economic and political development. Moreover, in line with international policy discourse, emphasis has been placed on minimising the negative sides of migration, such as illegal migration and human trafficking.[10] In these endeavours the government is aided by international bodies such as the ILO, the UNHCR and the IOM. Furthermore, it draws on the expertise of Cameroonian academics and civil-society institutions. Among the latter are three youth organisations based in Yaoundé to which I turn in the following section.

The Fight Against Illegal Migration: Yaoundé Discourses

The three youth organisations in Yaoundé that focus on international migration are Solutions aux migrations clandestines (SMIC), l'Association de lutte contre les migrations clandestines (ALCEC) and Welcome Back Cameroon (WBC). I centre my analysis on SMIC and ALCEC.

These organisations act as brokers between Cameroonian youths and the international migration and development establishment. Their visions and activities, however, are largely shaped by current discourse in international migration policy and, in particular, focus on the fight against illegal migration.

Both SMIC and ALCEC were founded by Francophone university students, many of them the sons and daughters of well-placed families who have a good chance of realising a professional career within the country. As the founder of SMIC (an energetic and committed university graduate of sports management) explained, the idea for the association was conceived in 2003 in discussions with acquaintances and friends, some of whom had been abroad and, disappointed by the realities in Europe, had returned to work and live in Cameroon:

> They saw that life in the West was not that easy and wanted to share this knowledge with their fellow compatriots. There was, for example, a young woman who had lived in Canada for a while but decided to return to Cameroon and is now working with the Goethe Institute. There are many others who had mixed experiences in Europe and the US and wanted to share this knowledge. Also, there are those who tried to make it through the Sahara and witnessed their compatriots perish on the way. When they came back, they felt it necessary to share their experiences. So, when they came together, they saw that the topic of discussion that united them all was the issue of illegality. SMIC is not against migration in general, but against

clandestine/illegal migration (Interview notes, Yaoundé, 16 August 2009; original interview in French).

Both SMIC and ALCEC run sensitisation campaigns for Cameroonian youths, educating them on the risks involved in illegal migration—i.e. migration without valid papers (see Figure 3). For example, they regularly organise information meetings in secondary schools and during university games. Moreover, they carry out research on the migration phenomenon and disseminate their findings via reports, public presentations and the media (e.g. ALCEC 2007; Novopress 2008; Tsala 2010). They collaborate with government institutions, university departments and international organisations, and fund their activities partly through membership dues, partly through EU migration and development schemes. Accordingly, their programmes have to correspond to the aims of international funders.

SMIC and ALCEC are quite dynamic and, through their activities, influence local perceptions of international migration. For example, in 2009 SMIC was commissioned by the IOM to produce an anti-illegal-migration TV spot, funded by the Belgian Embassy and broadcast on Cameroon national television. Similarly, ALCEC received funding from the Flemish nationalist party Vlaams Belang for a sensitisation campaign against illegal migration to Europe, launched in March 2010. Apparently, ALCEC had been criticised for their political opportunism: to avoid further embarrassment, the association's president asked me about the political orientation of the Swiss Peoples' Party, a conservative populist party, which had contacted them about a similar project.

In my reading, the perspectives on international migration promoted by SMIC and ALCEC are influenced both by their members' relatively privileged backgrounds, which allow them to see migration as an option rather than a must; and by international discourse on migration in which right-wing political ideas about belonging and entitlement have gained currency (Geschiere 2009).

So far, however, this vision of international migration as an endeavour fraught with risk of life and identity (as illustrated in Figures 2 and 3) seems largely confined to Yaoundé and its surroundings. In areas politically and economically less privileged, such as Bamenda, this view has not gained ground.

Conclusion

This article has analysed local discourses and imaginaries of mobility, taking into account relations of differential power both within Cameroon and on a more global scale. My focus here has been on regional disparities but I have also suggested that differences with regard to gender and age are equally relevant. Whilst the article describes local views of international migration, I suggest that the common distinction of internal and international, intra- and intercontinental migration is somewhat arbitrary. Historically and currently, people's mobility extends in various geographical directions. As I have shown, destinations are ranked less by the criteria

L'immigration **illégale tue**

ce fleau a vu perir depuis 1990 pres de **18.500** de nos freres et soeurs.
nous jeunes africains ne devons-nous pas **inventer notre avenir differemment**?

Figure 3. Poster by ALCEC (2010): Campaign against illegal migration. Reproduced with the kind permission of ALCEC.

of location or distance than on the basis of migrants' expectations of modernity and a comfortable life. It would be misleading, however, to ignore the crucial role of economic, political and cultural power that makes mobility and home-making possible for some and not for others. As I have shown in this article, not everyone—either everywhere in Africa or even within a single country—is able or willing to be mobile. Actors suffer a variety of constraints, not least the contemporary policies of mobility and stasis adopted by African and other nation-states.

As the Cameroonian data illustrate, both mobility and stasis may be viewed as a privilege. Among many peoples of north-west and western Cameroon, mobility has long been part of their social and economic organisation, as reflected in networks of trade and labour migration. Thus, for them, physical mobility is closely related to social mobility. Moreover, under the current political and economic conditions, mobility is perceived as a precondition for individual and collective progress. By contrast, for politically and economically well-placed Francophones in Yaoundé, mobility is a matter of choice, as they enjoy the privilege of a future at home. Thus mobility and stasis each have their separate advantages and disentitlements, and each are determined according to their Anglophone or Francophone context.

In his recent article on African imaginaries of Europe, Förster (2010) considers the attractions and fictions of international migration in Anglophone Cameroon. He explains the persistence and persuasiveness of migration narratives as resulting from two intertwined processes. On the one hand, there is the oral reproduction of cognitive images that, in turn, attain the quality of common knowledge; on the other, their pictorial representations in migrants' photographs and in the media that may serve as evidence in the face of reservation and doubt. While I appreciate Förster's analysis of the dissemination and perpetuation of ideas, I believe we need to take into account the power geometry that shapes these perspectives. As I have argued, international organisations and the political regime play crucial roles in placing young people in relation to their movements and connections. From an outside perspective, the oral and pictorial engagement with international migration in Yaoundé may seem more accurate and nuanced than in Anglophone Cameroon. On a closer look, however, it transpires that the views of NGOs, artists and academics in Yaoundé are shaped by the structural and political impositions of the international development establishment. Their reflections about the advantages and disadvantages of international migration go hand-in-hand with contemporary discourse on good and bad, legal and illegal migration, as promoted by the member-states of the European Union.

As we know from widespread media campaigns, European political narratives by-and-large frame Africans as potential migrants eager to descend on a Europe that cannot sustain them. Critical voices thus read the European engagement in the development-and-migration nexus as a strategy aimed at 'keeping them [unwanted migrants] in their place' (Bakewell 2008: 1431). Researchers of Saharan transit migration outline the criminalisation and victimisation of migrants as a result of Europe's externalisation of its borders and migration policy to the Maghreb (e.g.

Bredeloup 2010; Düvell 2010). Landau and Vigneswaran (2007a, 2007b) criticise not only international organisations but also African governments for adopting policies that support European rather than African interests.

Most contemporary migration policies are based on the assumption of Africa as a continent of unwarranted movement. Considering the emphasis on mobility in much of the recent literature, I suppose, we scholars of Africa have inadvertently contributed to such inapt generalisations. These political narratives not only ignore the crucial role which colonial and post-colonial Europe have played in engendering mobility through economic and political intervention, but also overlook the varying perspectives on migration within the continent. My study, hence, reads as an attempt to place mobility, stasis and connection within a single analysis and to pay attention to variation.

Hence I have stepped back from popular generalisations about African mobility and migrant desires in order to examine the ways in which debates about migration and the possibilities of staying at home take shape differently within a single country at a particular point in time. The article calls for a contemporary discourse that both acknowledges and problematises migration, and whose power geometry involves regional, national and international dimensions. It makes apparent the need for re-theorising mobility such as the regimes-of-mobility framework, that situates the concepts of mobility, stasis, connection and power within specific locations and social relations, which jointly constitute the local, the national and the global.

Acknowledgements

This paper has resulted from a broader research project on the transnational relations of Cameroonian migrants for which anthropological fieldwork was conducted in Cameroon, Gabon, South Africa and the United Arab Emirates between 2007 and 2011 (Pelican 2010, 2011a, 2011b). Funding was provided by the University of Zurich and the Swiss National Science Foundation. I wish to thank Nina Glick Schiller, Deli Teri Tize and the anonymous *JEMS* reviewers for valuable comments on earlier drafts. My heartfelt thanks also go to the many individuals and organisations in Cameroon and abroad who shared their visions and experiences with me.

Notes

[1] For an insightful analysis of local responses to the diversity visa lottery programme in Togo, see Piot (2010).

[2] The photo-documentary *Kingsley's Crossing* by Olivier Jobard accompanies the Cameroonian protagonist on his dangerous journey across the Sahara and the sea to reach Spain and France. Ulrike Westerman's documentary *Stronger than Fear* explores the sad story of a Cameroonian adolescent who lost his life as a stowaway in a plane to Germany.

[3] Certainly, local perspectives on migration are more complex and varied than I can address within the comparative framework adopted in this article. For more in-depth analyses of discourses and practices of international migration in different parts of Cameroon, see

Alpes (2011), Bouly de Lesdain (1999), Chappart (2007), Fleischer (2012), Frei (2011) and Hugentobler (2009).

[4]   Förster (2010) describes the general feeling among youths in Bamenda as being caught in a deadlock, as living in 'a paralysed country'.

[5]   In a recent article on *bushfalling* in Cameroon, Nyamnjoh (2011) argues for enriching anthropology through a multi-vocal approach that draws on African fiction as intellectual engagement. To illustrate his case, he integrates ethnographic fiction and popular media (newspapers, magazines, blogs) in his analysis. A similar approach is followed in this contribution. While the two papers evolved independently, there are obvious congruencies. Taken together, they provide an informed understanding of the discourses and expectations associated with *bushfalling*.

[6]   The concept of *bushfalling* has also been discussed in two recent studies on international migration from Cameroon. In her research on the strategies of aspiring migrants in Cameroon's Anglophone south-west, Alpes (2011) pays attention to the role of state, market and family in regulating migration. Fleischer (2012) approaches the subject from the perspective of Cameroonians based in Germany, focusing on the interplay of transnational migration, family formation and legality. A third study that engages with contemporary ideas of mobility and success is Frei's (2011) research on the use of information and communication technology in Bamenda. All three authors provide detailed information on the varied perceptions of *bushfalling* and migration in their respective research sites.

[7]   The term *been to* and its vernacular equivalent *woyayie* (the one who 'has arrived') are also used in Ghana (Martin 2005; van Dijk 2002). A similar notion to *bushfaller*, yet with a much longer history, is *jaguar*, widely used in Western Africa (Stoller 1999, see also the docu-fiction with the same title by Jean Rouch).

[8]   This Pidgin phrase translates as: 'My friend, what would you do? I ran into the bush'.

[9]   The documentary *Europaland* by the anthropologist and filmmaker Balz Andrea Alter provides a rich repertoire of local imaginations of Europe, bringing together perspectives of Francophone and Anglophone youths living in Yaoundé.

[10]   From an anthropological perspective, the terms 'illegal migration' and 'human trafficking' are highly problematic as they engender a state-centred approach (see e.g. de Genova 2002; de Genova and Peutz 2010; Khosravi 2010; Kyle and Koslowski 2011; Kyle and Siracusa 2005; Portes 1987). At this point, however, I wish to do without a critical discussion, as the term here is used in its local policy application.

References

Adepoju, A. (2008) *Migration in Sub-Saharan Africa*. Uppsala: Nordic Africa Institute.

ALCEC (2007) *Enquête sur l'Emigration des Jeunes de la Ville de Yaoundé (Etude Exploratoire sur les Comportements Migratoires des 15–35 Ans). Rapport Principal*. Yaoundé: Association de Lutte Contre l'Émigration Clandestine.

Alpes, M.J. (2011) *Bushfalling: How Young Cameroonians Dare to Migrate*. Amsterdam: University of Amsterdam.

Annan, K. (2006) 'Address of Mr. Kofi Annan, Secretary-General, to the high-level dialogue of the United Nations General Assembly on international migration and development, New York, 14 September 2006', *International Migration Review*, 40(4): 963–72.

Ardener, E., Ardener S. and Warmington, W.A. (eds) (1960) *Plantation and Village in the Cameroons: Some Economic and Social Studies*. London: Oxford University Press.

Argenti, N. (2006) 'Remembering the future: slavery, youth and masking in the Cameroon Grassfields', *Social Anthropology*, 14(1): 49–69.

Argenti, N. (2009) *The Intestines of the State: Youth, Violence and Belated Histories in the Cameroon Grassfields.* Chicago: University of Chicago Press.

Awasom, N. (2003) 'Anglophone/Francophone identities and inter-group relations in Cameroon', in Akinyele, R.T. (ed.) *Race, Ethnicity and Nation Building in Africa: Studies in Inter-Group Relations.* Ibadan: Rex Charles, 203–38.

Bakewell, O. (2008) 'Keeping them in their place: the ambivalent relationship between development and migration in Africa', *Third World Quarterly, 29*(7): 1341–58.

Bennafla, K. (2002) *Le Commerce Transfrontalier en Afrique Centrale: Acteurs, Espaces, Pratiques.* Paris: Karthala.

BFM (2008) *Business in Cameroon.* Johannesburg: Media Africa Group, November.

Bouly de Lesdain, S. (1999) *Femmes Camerounaises en Région Parisienne: Trajectoires Migratoires et Réseaux d'Approvisionnement.* Paris: L'Harmattan.

Boutrais, J. (1995/96) *Hautes Terres d'Elevage au Cameroun.* Paris: ORSTOM.

Bowie, F. (1985) A Social and Historical Study of Christian Missions among the Bangwa of South West Cameroon. Oxford: University of Oxford, unpublished DPhil thesis.

Bredeloup, S. (2010) 'Sahara transit: times, spaces, people', *Population, Space and Place, 18*(4): 457–67.

Chappart, P. (2007) Trajectoires Migratoires de Camerounais de Retour de Force au Pays: Le Double Retour, des Souffrances de l'Immigré Expulsé aux Illusions de l'Emigré de Retour. Poitiers: Université de Poitiers, unpublished MA dissertation.

Chiabi, E. (1997) *The Making of Modern Cameroon: A History of Sub-State Nationalism and Disparate Union, 1914–1961, 1.* Lanham, MD: University Press of America.

Chouala, Y.A. (2004) 'L'installation des Camerounais au Gabon et en Guinée-Équatoriale. Les dynamiques originales d'exportation de l'état d'origine', in Sindjoun, L. (ed.) *État, Individus et Réseaux dans les Migrations Africaines.* Paris: Karthala, 93–145.

Dah, J. (1982) 'The Basel Mission in Cameroon', in Christensen, T. and Hutchison, W.R. (eds) *Missionary Ideologies in the Imperialist Era 1880–1920.* Copenhagen: Aros, 208–20.

de Genova, N. (2002) 'Migrant "illegality" and deportability in everyday life', *Annual Review of Anthropology, 31*: 419–47.

de Genova, N. and Peutz, N. (eds) (2010) *The Deportation Regime: Sovereignty, Space, and the Freedom of Movement.* Durham, NC: Duke University Press.

de Haas, H. (2010) 'Migration and development: a theoretical perspective', *International Migration Review, 44*(1): 227–64.

de Rosny, E. (2002) 'L'Afrique des migrations: les échappées de la jeunesse de Douala', *Etudes, 396*(5): 623–33.

de Vries, J. (1998) *Catholic Mission, Colonial Government and Indigenous Response in Kom (Cameroon).* Leiden: African Studies Centre, Research Report, https://openaccess.leidenuniv.nl/bitstream/handle/1887/485/01PUB0000001177.pdf?sequence = 1.

Düvell, F. (2010) 'Transit migration: a blurred and criticised concept', *Population, Space and Place, 18*(4): 415–27.

Eyoh, D. (1998) 'Conflicting narratives of Anglophone protest and the politics of identity', *Journal of Contemporary African Studies, 16*(2): 268–71.

Fanso, V. (2009) 'The latent struggle for identity and autonomy in the Southern Cameroons, 1916–1946', in Fowler, I. and Fanso, V. (eds) *Encounter, Transformation and Identity. Peoples of the Western Cameroon Borderlands 1891–2000.* New York, Oxford: Berghahn, 141–50.

Fleischer, A. (2007) *The Cameroonian Diaspora in Germany: Its Contribution to Development in Cameroon.* Eschborn: Deutsche Gesellschaft für Technische Zusammenarbeit.

Fleischer, A. (2012) *Marriage, Migration, and the Law: Making Families among Cameroonian 'Bush Fallers' in Germany.* Berlin: Regiospectra.

Förster, T. (2010) '"Greener pastures": Afrikanische Europabilder vom besseren Leben', in Kreis, G. (ed.) *Europa und Afrika: Betrachtungen zu einem Komplexen Verhältnis*. Basel: Schwabe Verlag, 59–78.

Frei, B. (2011) Sociality Revisited? Liveness, and the Use of Internet and Mobile Phone in Urban Cameroon. Basel: University of Basel, unpublished PhD thesis.

Geschiere, P. (2009) *The Perils of Belonging. Autochthony, Citizenship, and Exclusion in Africa and Europe*. Chicago, London: University of Chicago Press.

Geschiere, P. and Gugler, J. (1998) 'The urban–rural connection: changing issues of belonging and identification', *Africa*, 68(3): 309–19.

Hahn, H.P. and Klute, G. (eds) (2007) *Cultures of Migration. African Perspectives*. Münster: Lit.

Hugentobler, S. (2009) Internationale Migration bei den Hausa in Bamenda, Kamerun. Zurich: University of Zurich, unpublished MA dissertation.

INS Cameroun (2010) *Rapport de Présentation des Résultats Définitifs du 3ème RGPH*. Institut National de la Statistique du Cameroun, http://www.statistics-cameroon.org/downloads/Rapport_de_presentation_3_RGPH.pdf (last visited 16 August 2012).

IOM (2009) *Migration au Cameroun. Profil National 2009*. Geneva: International Organization for Migration.

Jua, N. (2003) 'Differential responses to disappearing transitional pathways: redefining possibility among Cameroonian youth', *African Studies Review*, 46(2): 13–36.

Khosravi, S. (2010) *The 'Illegal' Traveller: An Auto-Ethnography of Borders*. Basingstoke: Palgrave Macmillan.

Konings, P. and Nyamnjoh, F. (1997) 'The Anglophone problem in Cameroon', *Journal of Modern African Studies*, 35(2): 207–229.

Konings, P. and Nyamnjoh, F. (2003) *Negotiating an Anglophone Identity: A Study in the Politics of Recognition and Representation in Cameroon*. Leiden, Boston: Brill.

Kyle, D. and Koslowski, R. (2011) *Global Human Smuggling: Comparative Perspectives*. Baltimore: Johns Hopkins University Press.

Kyle, D. and Siracusa, C.A. (2005) 'Seeing the state like a migrant: why so many non-criminals break immigration laws', in van Schendel, W. and Abraham, I. (eds) *Illicit Flows and Criminal Things*. Bloomington: Indiana University Press, 153–76.

Landau, L. and Vigneswaran, D. (2007a) *Which Migration, What Development? Critical Perspectives on European-African Relations*. Johannesburg: University of Witswatersrand, Migration Studies Working Paper No. 37.

Landau, L. and Vigneswaran, D. (2007b) 'Shifting the focus of migration back home: perspectives from Southern Africa', *Development*, 50(4): 82–7.

Makuchi (1999) *Your Madness, Not Mine. Stories of Cameroon*. Athens: Ohio University Center for International Studies.

Malaquais, D. (2001a) 'Arts de feyre au Cameroun', *Politique Africaine*, 82: 101–18.

Malaquais, D. (2001b) *Anatomie d'une Arnaque: Feymen et Feymania au Cameroun*. Paris: Centre d'Études et de Recherches Internationales, No. 77.

Malaquais, D. (2002) *Architecture, Pouvoir et Dissidence au Cameroun*. Paris: Karthala.

Martin, J. (2005) *Been-to, Burger, Transmigranten? Zur Bildungsmigration von Ghanaern und ihrer Rückkehr aus der Bundesrepublik Deutschland*. Münster: Lit.

Massey, D. (1993) 'Power-geometry and a progressive sense of place', in Bird, J., Curtis, B., Putnam, T., Robertson, G. and Tickner, L. (eds) *Mapping the Futures: Local Cultures, Global Change*. London, New York: Routledge, 59–69.

Mercer, C., Page, B. and Evans, M. (2008) *Development and the African Diaspora: Place and the Politics of Home*. London: Zed Books.

Ndjio, B. (2006) *Feymania: New Wealth, Magic Money and Power in Contemporary Cameroon*. Amsterdam: University of Amsterdam.

Ndjio, B. (2008) 'Mokoagne moni: sorcery and new forms of wealth in Cameroon', *Past and Present*, 199(3): 271–89.

Ndjio, B. (2009) 'Migration, architecture, and the transformation of the landscape in the Bamileke Grassfields of West Cameroon', *African Diaspora*, 2(1): 73–100.

Ngwa, L. and Ngwa, W. (eds) (2006) *From Dust to Snow: Bush-Faller*. Princeton: Horeb Communications.

Niger-Thomas, M. (2000) 'Buying Futures'. The Upsurge of Female Entrepreneurship: Crossing the Formal and Informal Divide in Southwest Cameroon. Leiden: Leiden University, CNWS, unpublished PhD thesis.

Novopress (2008) *Interview d'Emile Bomba, Président de l'ALCEC*. http://www.youtube.com/watch?v = SceoFsTMFJY.

Nyamnjoh, F. (2011) 'Cameroonian bushfalling: negotiations of identity and belonging in fiction and ethnography', *American Ethnologist*, 38(4): 701–13.

Nyamnjoh, F. and Page, B. (2002) 'Whiteman kontri and the enduring allure of modernity among Cameroonian youth', *African Affairs*, 101(405): 607–34.

Nyamnjoh, F. and Rowlands, M. (1998) 'Elite associations and the politics of belonging in Cameroon', *Africa*, 68(3): 320–37.

Pelican, M. (2010) 'Local perspectives on transnational relations of Cameroonian migrants', in Grätz, T. (ed.) *Mobility, Transnationalism and Contemporary African Societies*. Newcastle: Cambridge Scholars Publishing, 178–91.

Pelican, M. (2011a) 'Researching south–south/south–east migration: transnational relations of Cameroonian Muslim migrants', *Tsantsa*, 16: 169–73.

Pelican, M. (2011b) 'Mbororo on the move: from pastoral mobility to international travel', *Journal of Contemporary African Studies*, 29(4): 427–40.

Pelican, M. and Tatah, P. (2009) 'Migration to the Gulf States and China: local perspectives from Cameroon', *African Diaspora*, 2(2): 229–45.

Piot, C. (2010) *Nostalgia for the Future: West Africa after the Cold War*. Chicago: University of Chicago Press.

Pondi, J.-E. (ed.) (2007) *Immigration et Diaspora: Un Regard Africain*. Langres: Maisonneuve and Larose.

Portes, A. (1987) 'Introduction: toward a structural analysis of illegal (undocumented) immigration', *International Migration Review*, 12(4): 469–84.

Stoller, P. (1999) *Jaguar. A Story of Africans in America*. Chicago, London: University of Chicago Press.

Röschenthaler, U. (2006) 'Translocal cultures: the slave trade and cultural transfer in the Cross River Region', *Social Anthropology*, 14(1): 71–91.

Roitman, J. (2004) *Fiscal Disobedience: An Anthropology of Economic Regulation in Central Africa*. Princeton: Princeton University Press.

The Herald (2009) 'For Duping Woman of 19m FCFA: Nine Cameroonians in Hot Waters in China!, by Ntaryike Divine Junior', *The Herald*, 2199, 30–31 March, pp. 1–3, http://www.theheraldcameroon.com/.

Tsala, Y. (2010) *Communication Solutions aux Migrations Clandestines (SMIC) Cameroun: Presentation du Rôle de la Society Civile*. Contribution to the Launching Event of the African, Caribbean and Pacific (ACP) Observatory on Migration, 25–27 October, Brussels. http://213.246.207.152/acp/sites/default/files/FR_Tsala,_SMC_-_Presentation_du_Role_de_la_Societe_Civile_au_Cameroun.pdf.

van Dijk, R. (2002) 'Religion, reciprocity and restructuring family responsibility in the Ghanaian Pentecostal movement', in Bryceson, D. and Vuorela, U. (eds) *The Transnational Family: Global European Networks and New Frontiers*. Oxford: Berg, 173–96.

Warnier, J.-P. (1993) *L'Esprit d'Entreprise au Cameroun*. Paris: Karthala.

Warnier, J.-P. (2006) 'The transfer of young people's working ethos from the Grassfields to the Atlantic Coast', *Social Anthropology, 14*(1): 93–8.

Weber, C.W. (1993) *International Influences and Baptist Mission in West Cameroon: German-American Missionary Endeavour under International Mandate and British Colonialism.* Leiden, New York: Brill.

Wimmer, A. and Glick Schiller, N. (2002) 'Methodological nationalism and beyond: nationstate building, migration and the social sciences', *Global Networks, 2*(4): 301–34.

Wimmer, A. and Glick Schiller, N. (2003) 'Methodological nationalism, the social sciences, and the study of migration: an essay in historical epistemology', *International Migration Review, 37*(7): 576–610.

Winterberger, G. (2009) Ethnographie des Spitals Manyemen. Zurich: University of Zurich, unpublished MA dissertation.

Films and Photo Documentaries

Berlin Icon (2006), directed by Terence Fomunung.

China Wahala (2007), directed by Joyce Kuchah.

China Wahala 2 (2009), directed by Joyce Kuchah.

Europaland (2010), directed by Balz Andrea Alter, http://www.fernsehworkshop.de/2011/Filme/europaland.htm.

Jaguar (1954/1976), directed by Jean Rouch.

Kingsley's Crossing (2006), directed by Olivier Jobard, http://mediastorm.com/publication/kingsleys-crossing.

Mama G in America (2004), directed by MacCollins Chidebe.

Osuofia in London (2003), directed by Kingsley Ogoro.

Paris à Tout Prix (2007), directed by Josephine Ndagnou.

Stronger than Fear (2004), directed by Ulrike Westermann, http://www.onlinefilm.org/-/film/28611.

Cultivating Hustlers: The Agrarian Ethos of Soninke Migration

Paolo Gaibazzi

Sedentariness has been disregarded in migration studies. Although recent scholarship pays greater heed to immobility, the latter is often narrowly conceptualised as the exact opposite of mobility. This article attempts to overcome such dichotomies by focusing on agrarian life and activities in one of the most migratory rural contexts in West Africa, namely the Soninke villages of the Upper Gambia River valley. It shows how young men—normally the most mobile group in Soninke society—are trained to embody an agrarian ethos in order for them to be able to pursue not only agricultural livelihoods but also migratory ones. Physical, social and moral virtues cultivated in farm fields are thought to make the young man fit and adaptable to life and work abroad. The article further suggests that this agrarian ethos is reproduced through migratory dynamics, such as the integration of West African migrants as unqualified labourers in the stratified labour market of Europe and North America. As a synthesis or symbiosis between mobile and immobile cultural practices, the Soninke agrarian ethos provides us with ways of rethinking the relation between migration and sedentariness, thus bridging the dichotomy between the two.

Introduction

Over the past decade, West African citizens have repeatedly been told that agricultural development will help to reduce emigration. In 2006, at the onset of undocumented boat migration from Senegambian shores to the Canary Islands, Senegal inaugurated the *Retour Vers l'Agriculture* plan (Willems 2008). In President Wade's words, the plan was literally aimed at reducing illegal emigration to zero (*Le Soleil* 2006), a goal which Spain has eagerly supported with generous donations. Meanwhile, in neighbouring Gambia, President Yahya Jammeh insisted that wrong attitudes, rather than simply economic factors, are the root cause of emigration: youths have grown disaffected with menial jobs and farm work, and thus daydream of migrating one day to Europe.[1] Within the last ten years, the Gambian government has launched the *Back to the Land* campaign which, in addition to alimentary self-sufficiency, aspires to shape the imaginary of migration (cf. Glick Schiller and Salazar, this issue) by making agriculture an antidote to youths' migratory yearning and idleness.

Even though scholars have revealed 'the inconvenient realities of [undocumented] African migration to Europe' within policy-makers' and media discourse (de Haas 2008), scantier attention has been paid to governance actors' efforts to reform youths ostensibly seduced by the myth of Eldorado Europe through agricultural development. During my stay in Gambia (2006–8)—which coincided with the peak period of arrivals on the Canary Islands—virtually no young man I met constructed his identity as either a farmer or as a migrant with reference to the discourse of the state on youth. Nevertheless, as this discourse is becoming more robust and consequential, I use it as my point of departure to investigate the nexus between migration, agriculture and the formation of youth dispositions in rural Gambia. I will show that, although rural dwellers attach great value to agriculture, in their view promoting an agrarian life does not necessarily prevent emigration, nor create permanence.

Drawing on ethnographic fieldwork in Soninke (or Serahuli) villages of the Upper River Region (URR) of Gambia, in this article I argue that an agrarian ethos pervades and actually sustains Soninke migration. This may seem a paradoxical argument for, in the academic literature on West African migration, the Soninke are known as a paradigmatic example of a 'culture of migration' (see Jónsson 2008). From the Gambia valley to Eastern Mali, Soninke communities have a long history of mobility, and at least a five-decade-long experience of intense intra- and inter-continental labour and commercial migration (see Manchuelle 1997; Timera 1996). Furthermore, most Soninke view migration 'as a path toward economic well-being' and deliberate over undertaking migration 'as part of their everyday experiences' (Cohen 2004: 5). Finally, young men—the most mobile group in Soninke society—readily admit that migrants' investments in their home villages give them a concern or ambition (*hanmi*) to emigrate and thus 'seek to emulate their migratory behaviour' (Kandel and Massey 2002: 983). However, my inquiries show that the ambition to emigrate gives an aim and directionality to dispositions that are instilled in the young men through other means. Adults do not base their judgements of the potential for migratory success of their juniors on how well they are socialised in a culture of migration, but rather on how hard they can work in the farm fields. In the Upper River, farm fields are not solely sites of assisted arboreal growth, but also terrains of physical, moral and social maturation, where boys and young men come to embody the competences and dispositions believed to yield an ethical and prosperous life, at home as well as abroad. By becoming good farmers, young men also become productive *hustlers*, as migrants and other off-farm workers are called in Gambia.

Far from solely resulting from a traditionalist attitude, this agrarian ethos is also imbued with mobility. After describing the virtues of the *hustler* and how rural activities are deployed to elicit them, this article demonstrates that the current political economy of labour migration, combined with migrant transnationality, has partly reinforced villagers' socio-cultural investment in agriculture. Mostly hired as unqualified labourers in advanced capitalist countries, many Soninke migrants maintain that capacity for work and the endurance acquired in farm fields are still a key to succeeding in migration. This is partially reflected in the widespread practice of transnational childrearing, whereby village kin foster the children of migrants in order to raise them according to 'their fathers' way'.

Finally, in the conclusions I expand on the theoretical implications of the present case study, suggesting ways in which we can reconsider the place of sedentariness in migration studies and, more generally, overcome dichotomous conceptualisations of mobility and immobility.

The Agrarian Ethos in a Soninke Village

I conducted most of my field research in Sabi, a village of about 5,000 inhabitants in the URR. When I asked my interlocutors about the activities of the village, many would simply reply: 'In Sabi, we farm'. This was not simply a matter-of-fact statement acknowledging that virtually all able-bodied villagers were engaged in one way or another in agriculture. Many of my interlocutors also attached great value to agriculture and praised agrarian living. This somehow came as a surprise to me. The environmental viability and the economic significance of farming had dramatically shrunk in the previous four decades. Declining and erratic rainfalls, soil exhaustion and structural adjustment programmes meant that harvests were often too poor to feed a growing number of mouths (Baker 1995). Migrant remittances had become indispensable to offset the penury of harvests. About 30 per cent of Sabi's active male population were either in Serekunda—Gambia's urban area along the Atlantic coast (23 per cent)—or abroad (58 per cent in Euro-America, 19 per cent in Africa); of those who had stayed in Sabi, 30 per cent nonetheless migrated to Serekunda to look for work during the dry season.[2] In addition to being in economic decline, food and cash-cropping were labour-intensive activities. Sabi is about eight miles south of the Gambia river, and is serviced only by an inadequately replenished stream. Crops (food: millet, maize; cash: peanuts, some horticulture) are fed by rain which falls between June and early October. Fields have to be tilled, seeded and repeatedly weeded before harvest time (October–December). When I was in Sabi, the spread of draught-animal machinery since the 1950s had significantly eased such tasks and shortened working days. Some farmers with enough money could also pay for tractor ploughing. Yet mechanisation was only partial, and most farm activities still required considerable manual-labour input in demanding weather conditions. In short, given the current circumstances, why did many Sabinko think that agriculture should still be practised and cherished?

In a review article, Bryceson (2002: 20) noticed that many African rural communities still identify themselves as farmers in spite of changing economic circumstances and livelihood strategies, including labour migration. They elevate the agrarian model to a timeless socio-moral order of society. In a similar vein, Davidson (2009) speaks of 'customary imperatives' to account for the enduring hard-work ethics among the Diola rice-cultivators of Guinea Bissau who are afflicted by worsening environmental conditions of production. As she points out: 'Diola see their agricultural work not simply as means of sustenance, but also as integrally tied to their conceptions of personhood, social relations, ritual obligations, and collective cultural identity' (Davidson 2009: 120). Therefore, Soninke villagers' granitic commitment to rural livelihoods can be seen as the product of a long-lasting agrarian civilisation, variously reinforced by a once-booming commercial agriculture and by the (post)colonial predicament of the self-reliant and hard-working peasant (cf. Saho 1979), of which the *Back to the Land* campaign is a re-run.

In contrast to the Diola studied by Davidson, however, Soninke farmers neither discourage nor undervalue alternative productive activities. Few parents expect their sons to stay in Sabi when they grow up, although some of them will eventually have to remain in the village and cultivate the household fields; on the contrary, youths are expected to go and look for the means to support their parents in their old age and to better their own lives. As these means are seldom found in crop fields, parents and relatives are often willing to mobilise resources and networks in order to help some of their sons migrate abroad or to start a business in Serekunda. Therefore, a hypostatic view of agriculture does not fully capture the ways in which this activity is integrated with other livelihoods like migration, not only at the economic level, but also at the socio-cultural one.

Cultivating Virtues

I would like to suggest that Soninke-speakers still farm not 'in spite of' migration but 'because of' it. As I was repeatedly told in Sabi: 'Before a young man can travel he must farm and learn the Quran'. In this devoutly Muslim society, Islam is a milestone in childrearing, indeed it shapes ethical conduct in most domains of life.[3] However, since farming is also at the heart of traditional Quranic education, the Sabinko's conception of rural upbringing places an emphasis on agrarian activities. In his study of a Malian Soninke village, Whitehouse (2003: 34–5) has, in fact, compared farming to a form of education:

> Time and again, informants stressed to me the positive influence of farming on young people's moral fiber [. . .] As a form of hard work, it teaches children lessons about sacrifice, duty to family, and the merits of suffering. It helps them to acquire fiscal discipline and be better able to look after their parents in their old age. Those who do not farm as children are in danger of becoming wastrels, dependent on relatives for their subsistence.

Many adults in Sabi also view farming as a tool with which to mould immature children lacking awareness of themselves into productive, ethical and compassionate subjects. What is more, these qualities are desirable in migrants as well, for it is on their capacity to work, commitment to redistribution and moral rigour that the lives of those who stay behind depend. This further directs attention to the virtues associated with agrarian toil and life, and the work of cultivation required of youngsters to incorporate them. Virtues, as anthropologist Pandian has argued, with reference to a different agrarian context,

> [...] ought to be understood not only as abstract ideals and principles of a good life but also more particularly as habits of self-conduct—as cultivable tendencies to act, think, and feel in a worthy manner, as practical elements in the ethical work of becoming a certain kind of being (2009: 223).

As with any other normative discursive practice, cultivating virtues is fraught with tension and ambivalence, and people may fail to live the way they ought (Pandian 2009). Nevertheless, while discourses on rural life contain ambiguities and dead-ends (see Gaibazzi 2010a), I argue that an appraisal of agrarian habits associated with, and inculcated through, young men's upbringing sheds light on the cultural under-pinnings of Soninke livelihoods, including migration. In what follows, I show that cultivating virtues in rural Gambia is both a disciplinary technique and a means of enabling agency (cf. Mahmood 2001): young men are shaped into obedient juniors vis-à-vis their senior kin while, at the same time, being empowered with the physical and social qualities associated with the successful *hustler*.

'His Blood Has Arrived': Strength and Toil

From about the age of five, children go with their household members to the fields and carry out tasks in accordance with their physical ability, age and gender. They learn to tell a crop from a weed and to familiarise themselves with the times and stages of agricultural activities. As they grow older, children take up more physically demanding jobs and spend longer hours on the farms, thus hardening or toughening (*tenko*) their bodies so as to endure fatigue. The ability to perform specific tasks may be used as a measure of the socio-physical maturation of the child. When a boy is able to carry out all the tasks involved in agricultural production, including the use of heavy machinery, people might say that 'the boy's blood has come/arrived' (*ke maxanbaane hooro ri*), meaning that his blood has filled and energised his body, making it able to work. As Fairhead *et al.* (2006: 1114) have observed, in Gambia, 'Red blood is associated with personal strength [...] It is the stuff of life—the vital force of living things'.

The Soninke understand work (*golle*) as an ontological principle of human life and describe most of the activities in which bodily and/or intellectual faculties are harnessed as work. Diawara has argued that this broad notion of work is widespread in the Mande cultural area and ultimately derives from agricultural labour, for 'Everything has to be prepared, caused, or at least catalysed through work, which, because of this, becomes an imperative need' (Diawara 2003: 72, my translation).

In the Soninke language, the capacity to provoke, transform and catalyse is conveyed by the word *senbe*, which can be translated as 'force' or 'strength'. *Senbe* is used for different phenomena—fertile soil, heavy rain, a powerful vehicle, etc. When young men say 'I am able to work, I have *senbe* [*n ra wa gollini, senbe wa in maxa*]', they refer to their capacity to work. To indicate their bodily strength, they often accompany their words by a clenching of the fists and a raising of the elbows. Let me emphasise here that, by virtue of its universal applicability, the capacity to labour is not restricted to farming but extends to any kind of menial job.

Given the centrality of work to the Soninke conceptualisation of the self, it is hardly surprising that toil or hard work are highly praised virtues (cf. Davidson 2009). Even though the divine will is the ultimate cause of individual success, toiling is necessary to overcome hardship and catalyse progress. A successful man (or woman) is not simply someone who is able to perform and endure heavy duties, but someone who actually does work hard. Such a person should embody a pro-active disposition, and even an entrepreneurial spirit. Eventually this becomes visible in attitudes which people capture in depictions of business and work performance. '*A ke nta taaxunu*': 'He does not sit', people may say, using the metaphor of bodily movement to emphasise his dynamism.

Living by the Sweat of One's Brow: Autonomy and Endurance

Toil is enveloped in a specific work ethic: hard work is associated with self-reliance and honesty. In contrast, laziness goes with dependency—the tendency to 'hang onto others' to fulfil one's own needs. Normally, only a child depends on others; for an adult, dependency is shameful, and the act of begging for one's own needs provokes contempt.[4] A man is someone who gives, not receives: his capacity to provide for himself and his family dependants is a foundational element of his masculinity, and the failure to meet such expectations exposes men to gossip and generates in them anxieties about their social worth.

Thus, learning to toil also means learning to live by one's own sweat (*futte*). As an embodied metaphor, sweat signifies honesty and, when talking about work, people often accompany their words by passing a finger over their foreheads as if to wipe off sweat. This is not simply a way of saying that they worked hard, but also more specifically that they relied on their own strength (see the quote from Whitehouse 2003, above). For example, S., a roughly 65-year-old elder whom I interviewed in November 2007 in Sabi, described the connection between the physical and the moral value of sweat in these terms:

> Sleeping in a hut, farming, living by the sweat [of your own brow] is better than enjoying all [comforts procured by migrants]. God said we should look for [the yields of] our sweat without cheating. You know, business is all about lies. A diamond dealer always lies. He will say '*Wallahi* [Arabic: I swear to God]! I bought this for this amount', whilst he is lying. That's why you [people] live on lies. Our former elders didn't accept that. What they bent over, weeded, and sweated over is

what they would eat. Whenever they didn't know the way something was acquired, they would not eat it. Whatever they didn't 'suffer' for, even if you gave it to them, they would not eat it.

Given that S. is both an elder and a Quranic teacher, it is not surprising that he invokes the authority of custom and religion to sanction agrarian life. By contrasting agriculture and the diamond business—which was prominent in Soninke trade migration—he gives us a glimpse into the complex local discourses about travel and permanence. In truth, few Sabinko would agree with S.'s idea that 'staying is better than travelling'. The young man who assisted me during the interview, for instance, confessed that he found this proposition idealistic and anachronistic. At the same time, he commended S.'s words about agrarian life. As a man who grew up in the village, he saw cultivation as a way of orienting oneself in life. Having also been a diamond trader in the past, he acknowledged that mores are sometimes adapted to the pragmatics of business, but he still maintained that familiarity with hard work helps one to ward off the temptation to indulge in easy, yet illicit, ways of making money: 'If you know [the value of] sweat, you will not dare to cheat or steal to make a living'.

S.'s image of sleeping in a hut (as opposed to a modern brick house) further qualifies honesty as the ability to lead a plain and humble life. These are also tenets of the rural pedagogy in domestic groups as well as in traditional Quranic schools like the one which S. ran. In such schools, the teacher usually provides some (male) pupils with full board. Teaching is compressed into the hours around dawn and dusk while, during the rest of the day the students work for their teacher, cultivating his fields, fetching firewood and hauling water. The pupils are housed in rudimentary huts and often wear ragged clothes. Spartan living conditions are thought to create a conducive environment for learning and moral maturation. This does not mean, however, that villagers are or should be satisfied with material poverty. Most people do strive for material betterment and a more comfortable life. Rather, they view the capacity to put up with suffering and hardship (*tanpiye*) as a precondition to such prosperity (cf. Lemarie 2005; Porcelli 2011). Far from being solely an abstract principle of religious conduct, endurance is seen as a desirable, practical quality of being that complements one's capacity to work and thus enables the young man to bear with adverse situations in order to find the means for his family to step out of hardship.

'He Is A Man Now': Responsibility and Empathy

Young men have an obligation to support their families. Several ethnographers have pointed out that this arrangement lies at the heart of kinship relations in West Africa and specifically stems from a logic of intergenerational reciprocity (Roth 2008): the parents and senior kin feed and care for the children until they are self-reliant; these will, in turn, feed and care for their ageing kin. Similarly, intergenerational reciprocities are the central element of the political economy of seniority and the exploitation of junior labour in Soninke domestic production (Kea 2007). Having been fed and lodged in the household during their childhood, youths have to settle their debt by growing 'subsistence food' (*biraado*) for the entire household. Thus, by going to work in the fields, youths learn not only to endure fatigue and the merit of living by their own sweat, but also to do so for the sake of their parents and household members. For instance, one day a young boy in my host compound in Sabi returned home with a bundle of freshly harvested sorghum. His grandmother joyfully welcomed him by repeating 'He is a man now!'.

Like many other Gambians, the Sabinko are rather candid about the disciplinary function of agriculture in children's upbringing (see also Kea 2007: 276). Boys and young men spend most of their time on the main field (*furubantee, tee xoore*) cultivating crops to replenish the household granary.[5] I frequently heard adults say that 'Junior men work for their *kagume*', their household head, the most senior genealogical male in the household. This is to say that becoming a man implies both becoming autonomous and submitting to authority. Intergenerational relations are further cemented by a plethora of discourses and practices which weave affection, morality, religion, politics and economy together. For instance, supporting one's parents is not only a social obligation, but also an act of devotion sanctioned by Islam. Devotion (material, moral, affective) is in turn rewarded with blessings (*barake*) which are thought to be an indispensable resource for prospering in life. The relationship between pupil and Quranic teacher described above is founded on very similar logic.

Even though the moral economy of kinship is constructed through instruction and work relations, much more is conveyed through everyday practices of relatedness, such as sharing food, living space, work and the very experience of hardship associated with an agrarian lifestyle (Gaibazzi 2010a: 108–11). The act of redistributing resources among close relatives was indeed described to me not simply as an obligation, but as the result of a compelling drive for empathy *vis-à-vis* relatives who stayed in the village. As a young man put it: 'When I have money, I cannot sit here and enjoy it all by myself, if I know my family are there in *tanpiye* [suffering/hardship]'.

Maturation thus involves more than muscular development and blind obedience to authority. From farming to partaking in village life, rural upbringing is meant to produce subjects who 'know themselves', young men capable of conducting themselves appropriately without much external guidance. Once they grow up, youths will be able to earn a leaving and cope with the many challenges that life in a context marked by hardship entails. This does not mean that, by honing their agrarian skills, young men must remain on the land for their entire life. Due to the meagre returns of cash and food cropping, many of them actually fear consuming their *senbe* in the fields over the years, without receiving an adequate counterpart for it. Few, however, complain about having been raised as farmers, for the dispositions and skills they have cultivated in the fields will accompany them in their search for better prospects outside the village.

From the 'Village Bush' to the 'Travel Bush': On the Transferability of Agrarian Virtues

Having described the virtues of farming, I now proceed to show that the agrarian ethos is understood to be exportable to other contexts, especially to off-farm, migratory occupations. A wealth of metaphors and analogies describes the linkages between agriculture and migration. For instance, Soninke-speakers sometimes refer to migration as going to the 'travel bush' (*terenden gunne*). Since people normally 'go to the bush' to either farm or make firewood, this analogy conveys the adventurous spirit of leaving home—the civilised, domestic and safe space of the village—to venture into the unknown wilderness, facing hazards (wild beasts, harsh weather, etc.) in order to secure a livelihood (cf. also Pelican, this issue). Even in places imagined as being developed and 'civilised', like Europe, migrants are known to suffer from legal insecurity, racial and religious discrimination, and heavy workloads, not to mention the risk of being seduced by the bright lights of Europe (see Gaibazzi 2010b). With their respective 'bushes', farmers and travellers have a similar mission. While farmers work hard to bring crops back from the bush, migrants endure 'exile' to earn the money with which bags of rice and sugar will be bought and parked in the granary next to the bundles of millet harvested by the farmers. Fouquet (2008: 249) has found that Wolof-speaking migrants from Senegal depict their sojourn abroad in similar terms, as 'cultivating the big (household) field'.

Far from being a mere analogy, the linkages between agriculture and migration are also forged through narratives and projections of the self. The following excerpt from my fieldnotes provides an example of the ways in which young men channel their imagination through a discourse of agrarian upbringing and the cultivation of virtue:

> Tamba [a man from my host compound] and I chatted about his boyhood years. He vividly recalled his time at the *maisi* [upper Quranic school] in Kumbija [a Soninke village near Sabi]. At that time, boys like him spent the whole day in the bush, from seven to seven. Back from the fields, he had to haul water for the senior boys. Lunch time? They would eat little, not even enough to feel satisfied. Then they would go to town and find somewhere people would offer them food. At times there was not enough room in the huts. Some boys would sleep on the veranda, shivering all night in the cold season. Tamba sighed and then concluded: 'Eh, my friend, we suffered. But it's good. Now that my body has become stronger [*tenko*], I am fit for *hustling*. I can go and find money. I can work hard, I fear no jo' (October 2007, Sabi).

In his unsolicited final passage, Tamba constructed himself as a *hustler* by linking past to future, farming to travelling. As Glick Schiller and Salazar (this issue) may put it, in Tamba's imaginary, stasis and movement are closely interrelated. In a rhetorical narrative style, he spoke in a slightly whining way about the heavy workloads, hardship, sacrifice and bullying he had to endure as a boy—thus situating himself within an agrarian upbringing—so as to legitimate his capacity to 'find something' (money/crops) and his willingness to adapt to any job and living conditions.

Adaptation to life in 'exile' requires self-discipline and moral vigilance. What Soninke parents dread the most about places like Europe is that their migrant sons might start drinking alcohol or become involved in drug-dealing. The former is a blatant violation of Islamic taboos, while the latter is the most popular example of an easy, crooked way of looking for money and avoiding toil and sweat (see Gaibazzi 2012). Some informants told me that parents refuse to eat rice bought with money obtained by sons known to be dealing drugs abroad (cf. S.'s interview, above).

Finally, the sense of responsibility and empathy acquired through farming is fundamental to ensure migrants' loyalty. Migrants are in the travel bush, away from home and outside the sphere of influence of their seniors. Yet, bags of rice, brick houses and other resources do very often materialise in Sabi.[6] Householders adopt a number of strategies to ensure migrants' compliance with their domestic duties, such as exercising pressure through senior relatives and villagers living in their proximity. Nevertheless, when I probed my informants to tell me how they could be so sure that, once abroad, the young men would send money home to them, they mostly appealed to the idiom of empathy. A standard answer was 'He will not forget us' because 'He knows the [living] conditions we are in'. In this respect, the bush is a training ground as well as an observatory of would-be migrants. Due to the costs and bureaucratic complexities of emigration, enjoying a good reputation as a hard-working farmer and devoted son is crucial to eliciting the financial and logistical support of kinsmen. Few seniors I met would be prepared to help a young man who has either shunned his household duties or protested against his parents' authority.

The Transnational Reproduction of the Agrarian Ethos

Although multiple linkages between farming and *hustling* exist, the fact that a generic agrarian ethos rather than a more specific skills training or formal education is still perceived to be a key to economic success in off-farm activities requires further explanation. One might ask why, after several decades of migratory experience, other models of upbringing and education have not substantially modified the rural training I have described. Looking at the wider political economy as well as at the specific dynamics of Soninke migration might afford some insights in this respect.

The agrarian ethos is not simply crafted in rural Gambia and exported abroad. Rural Gambia is a truly transnational context, and hence agrarian virtues are also the product of migration. There are at least two observations that support this claim. In the first place, over the last four decades, labour migration to advanced capitalist countries has become prominent among the Soninke to the detriment of trade migration, as shown by the statistics I reported above. Most of the labour migrants are employed as an unqualified workforce in labour markets where heavy menial occupations are reserved for immigrants (Piore 1979; Sassen 1991). This path of socio-economic integration might have reinforced particular attitudes to livelihoods. In his work on the Senegalese, Malian and Mauritanian Soninke in France, Timera (1996: 219) has found that the migrants' project is not linked to any particular professional career. Migrants are willing to accept *any* job: they consider the amount on the payslip more important than their occupation. This is partly an adaptation to the restructuring of the French automobile industry in the 1980s, which saw most migrants move to low-skill, and often temporary, jobs in the service economy (Timera 1996: 221). The Gambian Soninke are employed in similar economic sectors across Europe, in particular in Spain, the most popular migrant destination (Kaplan 1998). Sabi youths are familiar with Spanish terms such as *campo* (field) and *paleta* (construction worker), which index past and present migratory careers in Spain's agricultural and construction sectors. Besides this basic knowledge, however, I was often struck by observing so little discussion about the actual content of the jobs that migrants do. Indeed, all that some parents knew about their sons' occupations was that they either worked for a salary or ran a business. Given the limited hope for upward professional mobility in the Euro-American job market, the capacity to work hard and long hours thus appears to be the key to success. Like their Eastern fellows in France, most non-migrant Sabi youths like Tamba feel ready to do *any* job once they reach Europe.

I would argue that migrants' narratives further reinforce the ethics of toil and endurance. I often heard migrants who were visiting Sabi during their vacation describe the hard work and asperities they endured in Europe or North America. Emboldened by their success, some migrants complained about the local youths who preferred to spend time in their gatherings rather than work. In Sabi, I once met a migrant who, during his visit, forced his younger brothers to work with him in farm fields from 7am to 7pm, like in the old days. As he explained: 'I'm working 10, 11 hours a day in Spain. Everyday. I wake up at 6[am] and come back at 7[pm], sometimes 8[pm]. I'm working hard, while here people are sitting [idly]'.

The second indicator that migration reproduces the agrarian ethos is the widespread practice of transnational childrearing. Many migrants leave behind wife (or wives) and children; others, in contrast, take their families abroad, but foster their children to village relatives for periods of variable length, not infrequently for their entire upbringing. As clearly emerges from representations of 'exile', migrants might fear their condition of strangerhood is not suitable for raising a family, and send their children home to protect them from the negative influences of the host country (Whitehouse 2009). Exposure to agrarian life is purposely used to inculcate the discipline as well as the virtues that these children will need when they return abroad as adults. Not unlike other Soninke contexts, transnational childrearing in Sabi is premised on a 'logic of being immersed in daily practices of apprenticeship, the repetition of which trains the child' (Razy 2007: 34, my translation). Children who rebel against their parents' authority or risk following deviant paths are likely to be sent back to their villages for a period of agrarian training: 'I was stubborn [i.e. rebellious], so my father brought me here', Musa, a man (37) born in Sierra Leone and repatriated to Sabi after being in school for some years, told me.

Nowadays a number of migrant parents choose to foster their children to urban relatives and send them to school. Hometown associations in the diaspora invest in Islamic and secular schools in both cities and villages, and some migrants encourage their relatives to let their children spend more time on books than on hoes. Yet an agrarian upbringing and a formal education are not incompatible. A number of wealthy Soninke businessmen I knew in Serekunda sent their children to urban schools and planned to recruit them in their firms afterwards, where they would undergo an additional period of apprenticeship. This did not prevent them from driving their children to their native villages to spend their summer vacation with their families and to help out in the fields. Some international migrants also manage to alternate educational strategies in this fashion.

Concluding Remarks: Beyond Dichotomy, Towards Cultural (Im)mobility

In this article, I have argued that making sense of Soninke migration necessarily requires paying heed to the sedentary practices through which mobility is reproduced. In Soninke villages, farms are places for cultivating *hustlers*, both in the sense that the same people are often travellers and cultivators at different stages of their life-cycle, and that boys are trained to be farmers in order to become migrant *hustlers*. Feeding on an ancient rural tradition, this agrarian ethos of Soninke migration has also emerged as an adaptation to what Glick Schiller and Salazar (this issue) call a 'regime of mobility', in which African immigrants are literally needed as a labour force.

At present, migration theory offers inadequate tools with which to conceptualise the integration between sedentary and migratory practices observed in Soninke villages. Over the last two decades, sedentariness has become a suspicious analytical category. Scholars have learned to detect a sedentarist metaphysics in discourses and analyses of migration that assume, not unlike government officials in Gambia and Europe, that a settled life is a natural condition of being (Malkki 1992). 'Mobility', Cresswell has observed, 'has become the ironic foundation for anti-essentialism, antifoundationalism and antirepresentationalism' (2006: 46). Although it is by now evident that a nomadist perspective which posits pure movement as the foundation of society is not an ideologically neutral alternative (Cresswell 2006; Friedman 2002), mobility continues to occupy centre stage in social theory. Roots have thus become routes, place has turned out to be founded on movement, and the very concept of culture has been divorced from its etymological connection with agri-culture.

An unfortunate consequence of this 'mobility turn' in the social sciences has been the proliferation of concepts that pit movement against stasis. For instance, in an article on the uses and abuses of the term 'flow' in socio-cultural anthropology,

Rockefeller (2011) notices that terms conjuring up an idea of fluidity are often used rhetorically against territorially bounded, fixed, static notions of locality, society and culture that prevailed in anthropology in the past. Critiques of overly optimistic accounts of global unfettered movement have not always gone far enough in this respect, only invoking forced immobility insofar as it provides a counterpoint to cross-border fluidity (see, for example, Carling 2002; Turner 2007).

Endeavouring to overcome a dichotomy between migration and sedentariness, I find recent scholarly research on mobilities useful. Urry (2007) has shed light on the dialectic and symbiotic relation between mobility and immobility. His notion of 'moorings' describes infrastructures, systems (airports, service stations, etc.) or 'relative immobilities' (Adey 2006: 83) that require a certain degree of fixity to keep the flow (of people, information, vehicles, etc.) going[7] (cf. also Bissell and Fuller 2010; Cresswell 2001; Hammar and Tamas 1997). This approach is currently being applied to cultural analysis in order to single out the ways in which mobility and immobility are imbued with meaning (see, for example, Greenblatt *et al.* 2010; Salazar 2010). As an analytical project, this is progress compared to the 'culture of migration' approach in migration studies (Cohen 2004; Hahn and Klute 2008; Kandel and Massey 2002), for its object of study is broader (various kinds of mobility) and, more importantly, includes immobility. Save for terminological innovation, however, the difference between the two approaches is often minimal, especially in the context of human mobility: although such studies mention immobility, they go on to describe how various kinds of movement penetrate imaginaries and other signifying practices.

As I have shown in this article, a notion of culture/imaginary/meaning/representation of mobility alone does not cover enough physical and analytical ground in rural Gambia. We need tools with a wider conceptual compass. Since I began my inquiry from the practicalities of rural livelihoods, I chose to speak of cultivation in the old-fashioned sense, linking agricultural and cultural production. This is not a fundamentalist return to roots concepts; rather, once a sedentarist metaphysics is refuted, there is little reason not to take sedentary practices and analogies as a starting-point in the theorisation of (im)mobility. Proceeding from this analytical standpoint, one can better understand Soninke agriculture as a product of mobile as well as of immobile practices. Furthermore, while what I called an agrarian ethos of Soninke migration provides an example of relationality between mobility and immobility (see Glick Schiller and Salazar, this issue), it should not be viewed as dialectics between polar opposites; it constitutes a synthesis between the two. As such, it provides us with a concrete example of what mobilities scholars envisage at the theoretical level, but often fail to capture at the empirical one. The agrarian ethos is a synthesis forged in the furnace of culture and yet which cannot be reduced to a culture *of* mobility (or immobility), let alone to a deterritorialised culture.

Analysing sedentariness alongside migration allows for a more radical critique of governance discourse than does an exclusive focus on movement and movers.

In addition to distorted views of a rural exodus, Europe's fight against illegal immigration in West Africa seems haunted by a paradox. The harder policy-makers try to uproot youths' culture of migration by turning them into sedentary farmers, the greater the likelihood that they might reproduce an agrarian ethos that does not, in fact, presuppose a settled life. There is, however, little space for irony here. In many ways, the agrarian ethos is virtue made out of necessity in a region where earning a living implies adapting to almost any available job. Ideas and resources geared to boosting agriculture were strongly desired and solicited by Sabi farmers during my stay, possibly—this is my political opinion—without neocolonial and neoliberal tutelage attached to them. One learns from the regional history of commercial agriculture that, when favourable and fair economic conditions are in place, few exhortations or binding conditions are needed to keep people on the land (Swindell and Jeng 2006). Gambians have indeed proved to be enterprising and hard-working farmers.

Acknowledgements

Previous versions of this article were presented at the AEGIS Workshop on 'Children and Migration in Africa' (SOAS, May 2012) and at an invited lecture organised by Latvia's Association of Anthropologists (March 2011). I wish to thank the participants of these events for their comments. In particular, I am indebted to Dace Dzenovska for her insightful theoretical suggestions on cultivation and virtue. Valuable comments were also provided by Alice Bellagamba, Stephan Dünnwald and two anonymous *JEMS* reviewers. Research for this article was generously funded by the University of Milano-Bicocca with Unicredit Foundation, Italy's Ministry of Foreign Affairs via Missione Etnologica in Benin e Africa Occidentale, the European Social Fund (Exchange Visit Grant) via African Borderlands Research Network and Centro de Estudos Africanos (Lisbon), and Germany's Federal Ministry of Education and Research (BMBF).

Notes

[1] President Jammeh's speech at the Opening Ceremony of the National Assembly on 30 March 2008, broadcast by GRTS TV.

[2] Figures based on a survey carried out by the author in 2006/7 on a sample (10.9 per cent) of the village households.

[3] Some currents of Sufi Islam, like the Senegalese Muridiyya, contain explicit sanction on hard work and frugality, though this should not be mistaken for an Islamic version of the Protestant ethics of capitalism (Coulon 1981).

[4] Begging is often associated with low-ranking status groups, in particular with slave descendants (Sommerfeld 1999). Manchuelle (1997) saw the patriarchal drive for autonomy and success as a key historical reason behind Soninke migration.

[5] Women are also entitled to some of the men's labour (e.g. digging up groundnuts). Young men can also work on their own individual fields, but rarely do so these days, and mostly work to produce the grain for the whole household.

[6]   According to my household survey in Sabi, 76.9 per cent of the migrants are active remitters.
[7]   To be sure, the classic literature on circular migration has already highlighted the dynamic combination between movement and stasis (e.g. Prothero and Chapman 1985), and to some extent it has shed light on the social arrangements that have enabled such a combination. However, whereas this literature was focused on migratory models, I am interested in the very nature of mobility and immobility, and in their interrelation, from the socio-cultural point of view.

References

Adey, P. (2006) 'If mobility is everything then it is nothing: towards a relational politics of (im)mobilities', *Mobilities*, 1(1): 75–94.

Baker, K.M. (1995) 'Drought, agriculture and environment: a case study from The Gambia, West Africa', *African Affairs*, 94(374): 67–86.

Bissell, D. and Fuller, G. (eds) (2010) *Stillness in a Mobile World*. London: Routledge.

Bryceson, D.F. (2002) 'Multiplex livelihoods in rural Africa: recasting the terms and conditions of gainful employment', *Journal of Modern African Studies*, 40(1): 1–28.

Carling, J. (2002) 'Migration in the age of involuntary immobility: theoretical reflections and Cape Verdean experiences', *Journal of Ethnic and Migration Studies*, 28(1): 5–42.

Cohen, J.H. (2004) *The Culture of Migration in Southern Mexico*. Austin: University of Texas Press.

Coulon, C. (1981) *Le Marabout et le Prince: Islam et Pouvoir au Sénégal*. Paris: A. Pedone.

Cresswell, T. (2001) 'The production of mobilities', *New Formations*, 43(Spring): 11–25.

Cresswell, T. (2006) *On the Move: Mobility in the Modern Western World*. New York: Routledge.

Davidson, J. (2009) '"We work hard": customary imperatives of the Diola work regime in the context of environmental and economic change', *African Studies Review*, 52(2): 119–41.

de Haas, H. (2008) 'The myth of invasion: the inconvenient realities of African migration to Europe', *Third World Quarterly*, 29(7): 1305–22.

Diawara, M. (2003) 'Ce que veut dire travailler dans le monde Mandé', in Almeida-Topor, H.D., Lakroum, M. and Spittler, G. (eds) *Le Travail en Afrique Noire: Représentations et Pratiques à L'époque Contemporaine*. Paris: Karthala, 67–80.

Fairhead, J., Leach, M. and Small, M. (2006) 'Where techno-science meets poverty: medical research and the economy of blood in The Gambia, West Africa', *Social Science and Medicine*, 63(4): 1109–20.

Fouquet, T. (2008) 'Migrations et "glocalisation" dakaroises', in Diop, M.C. (ed.) *Le Sénégal des Migrations: Mobilités, Identités et Sociétés*. Paris, Dakar and Nairobi: Karthala; CREPOS; ONU-habitat, 241–76.

Friedman, J. (2002) 'From roots to routes: tropes for trippers', *Anthropological Theory*, 2(1): 21–36.

Gaibazzi, P. (2010a) Migration, Soninke Young Men and the Dynamics of Staying Behind (The Gambia). Milan: University of Milano-Bicocca, unpublished PhD thesis in Anthropology.

Gaibazzi, P. (2010b) 'Qui, nell'altrove: giovani, migrazione e immaginazione geo-sociale nel Gambia rurale', *Mondi Migranti*, 3: 117–29.

Gaibazzi, P. (2012) '"God's time is the best": Gambian youth and the wait for emigration in the age of immobility', in Graw, K. and Schielke, S. (eds) *The Global Horizon: Expectations of Migration in Africa and the Middle East*. Leuven: Leuven University Press, in press.

Greenblatt, S., Paul, H., Nyiri, P., Zupanov, I., Meyer-Kalkus, R. and Pannewick, F. (2010) *Cultural Mobility: A Manifesto*. Cambridge and New York: Cambridge University Press.

Hahn, H.P. and Klute, G. (eds) (2008) *Cultures of Migration: African Perspectives*. Münster and New Brunswick: Lit Verlag; Global.

Hammar, T. and Tamas, K. (1997) 'Why do people go or stay?', in Hammar, T., Brochman, G., Tamas, K. and Faist, T. (eds) *Interntional Migration, Immobility, and Development: Multi-disciplinary Perspectives*. Oxford and New York: Berg, 1–19.

Jónsson, G. (2008) *Migration Aspirations and Immobility in a Malian Soninke Village*. Oxford: International Migration Institute, Working Paper No. 10.

Kandel, W. and Massey, D.S. (2002) 'The culture of Mexican migration: a theoretical and empirical analysis', *Social Forces, 80*(3): 981–1004.

Kaplan, A. (1998) *De Senegambia a Cataluña. Procesos de Aculturación e Integración Social*. Barcelona: Fundació La Caixa.

Kea, P. (2007) 'Girl farm labour and double-shift schooling in the Gambia: the paradox of development intervention', *Canadian Journal of African Studies, 41*(2): 258–88.

Le Soleil (2006) 'Emigration clandestine zéro: le plan Retour Vers L'agriculture est la solution, estime Me Wade', *Le Soleil*, 12 September.

Lemarie, M. (2005) 'Le travail de la souffrance: parcours biographique du cultivateur sénoufo (Côte d'Ivoire)', *Systèmes de Pensée en Afrique Noire, 17*: 71–90.

Mahmood, S. (2001) 'Feminist theory, embodiment, and the docile agent: some reflections on the Egyptian Islamic revival', *Cultural Anthropology, 16*(2): 202–36.

Malkki, L.H. (1992) 'National Geographic: the rooting of peoples and the territorialization of national identity among scholars and refugees', *Cultural Anthropology, 7*(1): 24–44.

Manchuelle, F. (1997) *Willing Migrants: Soninke Labour Diasporas, 1848–1960*. London: James Currey.

Pandian, A. (2009) *Crooked Stalks: Cultivating Virtue in South India*. Durham: Duke University Press.

Piore, M.J. (1979) *Birds of Passage: Migrant Labor and Industrial Societies*. Cambridge: Cambridge University Press.

Porcelli, P. (2011) 'Fosterage et résilience: discours collectifs et trajectoires individuelles de mobilité des enfants en milieu bambara', *Journal des Africanistes, 81*(1): 119–44.

Prothero, R.M. and Chapman, M. (1985) *Circulation in Third World Countries*. London and Boston: Routledge and Kegan Paul.

Razy, E. (2007) 'Les sens contraires de la migration: la circulation des jeunes filles d'origine soninké entre la France et le Mali', *Journal des Africanistes, 77*(2): 19–43.

Rockefeller, S.A. (2011) '"Flow"', *Current Anthropology, 52*(4): 557–78.

Roth, C. (2008) '"Shameful!": the inverted intergenerational contract in Bobo-Dioulasso, Burkina Faso', in Alber, E., van der Geest, S. and Reynolds-Whyte, S. (eds) *Generations in Africa. Connections and Conflicts*. Berlin: Lit Verlag, 237–66.

Saho, L. (1979) 'TESITO: a grassroots doctrine for national development in The Gambia', Banjul: Paper presented at the Advanced Workshop on Communication for Social Development, 26 February.

Salazar, N.B. (2010) 'Towards an anthropology of cultural mobilities', *Crossings: Journal of Migration and Culture, 1*(1): 53–68.

Sassen, S. (ed.) (1991) *The Global City: New York, London, Tokyo*. Princeton: Princeton University Press.

Sommerfeld, T. (1999) *Shares and Sharing. Dynamics of Exchange, Identity and Rank in a Gambian Town*. Oslo: University of Oslo, unpublished PhD thesis in Anthropology.

Swindell, K. and Jeng, A. (2006) *Migrants, Credit and Climate: The Gambian Groundnut Trade, 1834–1934*. Leiden and Boston: Brill.

Timera, M. (1996) *Les Soninké en France: D'une Histoire à L'autre*. Paris: Karthala.

Turner, B.-S. (2007) 'The enclave society: towards a sociology of immobility', *European Journal of Social Theory, 10*(2): 287–303.

Urry, J. (2007) *Mobilities*. Cambridge: Polity.

Whitehouse, B. (2003) *Staying Soninké: migration, multilocality and identity in a Community of the West African Sahel*. Providence: Brown University, unpublished MA dissertation in Anthropology.

Whitehouse, B. (2009) 'Transnational childrearing and the preservation of transnational identity in Brazzaville, Congo', *Global Networks*, 9(1): 82–99.

Willems, R. (2008) 'Les "fous de la mer". Les migrants clandestins du Sénégal aux Îles Canaires en 2006', in Diop, M.C. (ed.) *Le Sénégal des Migrations: Mobilités, Identités et Sociétés*. Paris, Dakar and Nairobi: Karthala; CREPOS; ONU-habitat, 277–304.

Development Mobilities: Identity and Authority in an Angolan Development Programme

Rebecca Warne Peters

This ethnographic essay considers how international non-governmental organisations are able to make claims to authoritative knowledge about development work by offering the transnational mobilities of their staff members as evidence. I examine how one professional's biography—his trajectory from Angola to Britain and back again—was differentially presented to external donors and internal staff members as befitting the institutional needs of an international good governance intervention in Angola. These presentations reflect a commoditisation of the cosmopolitanism of professionals' histories in the service of development as a regime of mobility. I argue that, in this development regime, a global hierarchy prevents some individual professionals, particularly those from developing nations, from realising the same benefits of their cosmopolitan mobility as professionals from industrialised nations. While one of mobility studies' many strengths is that it highlights global interconnectedness, social scientists should not read equality in these interconnections but examine how patterns of transnational mobility may produce and reproduce global structures of inequality.

Introduction

Maximino[1] and I first met, briefly and rather disastrously, at the Angolan National Assembly. We were new to the development scene in the Angolan capital of Luanda, and were being introduced to new colleagues during a break in the Assembly's workshop on municipal development. Maximino had just been hired by an international non-governmental organisation (INGO) as the Luanda-based

95

coordinator for their portion of the Good Governance in Angola Programme (GGAP), and was so recently hired that he had not yet visited their provincial field sites.[2] I was introduced as an American doctoral student studying the GGAP for her thesis. Upon meeting, I asked Maximino if his family was of Italian extraction—his real name still sounds Italian to me—and he responded, rather affronted, 'No, I'm perfectly Angolan', walking away before I could respond. In the end, Maximino became one of my closest informants and a good friend, and we travelled widely together as he worked to shape and reshape the GGAP; I was even able to travel along on his first visits to his organisation's field sites in the far northern provinces. We got off to a bad start, though, because my question imposed an internationality that he clearly rejected as he was being introduced to new colleagues at a meeting of the National Assembly.

This ethnographic essay, using Maximino's experiences and those of other international development professionals, contributes to the theoretical explication of mobility regimes in this special issue of *JEMS*. I propose that international development is one such regime: an amalgamation of states, institutions, bureaucracies and imaginaries that differentially demands, rewards and sometimes punishes individual mobility and stasis. I argue that the development regime reproduces itself, in part, by presuming certain patterns of mobility of some of its members while presuming of others certain patterns of stasis. To emphasise how members of the development industry are constrained by these patterns, I employ the term *development cosmopolitans* to describe professionals working in development organisations, suggesting that the ways in which the development industry demands and rewards both mobility and stasis for different members of the industry—though they are all cosmopolitan—reinforces an unequal global distribution of power and opportunity that development institutions ostensibly seek to redress.

Maximino is a key figure in this ethnography of the global circulation of international development professionals, a group relatively understudied in the transnational mobilities literature (though for critical development studies, see Bornstein 2003; Coles 2007; Hilhorst 2003; Kothari 2006; Tamas 2007; Yarrow 2008). My focus on Maximino illustrates the institutional and industry-wide differential treatment of those who come from developing countries versus those who come from developed countries. His experiences are not unique, but exemplary. Born and raised in Angola, and in his mid-30s in 2008 when I met him, Maximino had recently returned from completing a Master's degree in development studies in Britain through sponsorship by his previous employer, another development organisation. While I was in Angola studying the GGAP, I knew Maximino to travel to Brazil, Morocco and South Africa, as well as extensively throughout Angola, for work.[3]

I accompanied Maximino on several domestic trips in 2008 as he settled in to his new position, and I highlight how his expertise in international development, his Angolan-ness, and his international qualifications—particularly his British graduate degree—were presented and discussed as he moved through the social milieu of international development organisations in postwar Angola. Maximino's biographical characteristics and professional experiences were co-opted as the GGAP furthered its reputation for 'global best practices' and 'deep local knowledge', simultaneously and perhaps paradoxically. Throughout my research, the GGAP alternately trumpeted or hid staff members' experiences, knowledge and backgrounds as befitted its reputational needs, and alternately rewarded the 'right' kinds of mobility or furthered a subterfuge of the 'right' kinds of stasis. I expect other development programmes and organisations engage in similar methods of reputation management through the selective presentation of staff members' global mobilities and local emplacements. I see these actions and their effects as constitutive of what Glick Schiller and Salazar (this issue) would term 'imaginaries and relationalities of power'. This reputational work supports the larger image that the development industry has of itself and its processes, wherein technologies of social and economic improvement originate in the developed world and flow through mobile and modern development experts to the developing world to be 'indigenised' by timeless, immobile locals. The self-image of the development industry relies on ideas of mobility and stasis, performed and enacted by its professionals. The cosmopolitan characteristics of international development workers—gained through travel to other developing countries, training in developed countries, and contact with other similarly mobile development professionals—are commoditised and instrumentalised: the development industry is a regime of mobility as Glick Schiller and Salazar describe in their introductory paper.

As with other mobility regimes examined in this collection, the development regime conflates identity and authority: being from a developed or a developing country, having studied in Europe, and so on are differential markers of authenticity and authoritative knowledge in international development (see also Kothari 2005). Each individual professional translates his or her experiences, education and background into 'hireable' criteria to seek employment and promotion. At a broader level, programmes and organisations commoditise their staff members to cultivate institutional reputations and compete for standing (and funding) among peer organisations. This commoditisation of cosmopolitan characteristics, however, does not level the playing field for development professionals as regards more pervasive patterns of global privilege and disenfranchisement: I observed deep cleavages between the status and opportunities available to development workers who came originally from industrialised countries and those who came from developing countries. No element of a professional life—educational achievements, programmatic responsibilities, years of experience—seemed equitable across the line of global hierarchy dividing developing- and developed-country nationals.

After discussing the performative and commoditised cosmopolitan-ness of international development workers, I consider the global movement of development cosmopolitans that both produces and limits the possibilities of these workers, constraining the promise of development itself. My examination of international development professionals working on one programme in Angola reveals how their movements both shape and are shaped by the global, social and political structures of development work—and of underdevelopment. This case study of 'mobility' moves beyond nation-states as units of analysis (though nationality is here an important 'characteristic') to global social forces, practices and perceptions that structure global political economy.

Structural Inequalities in International Development Work

Institutionalised differences between national and international staff in the GGAP consortium were among the first, most evident tensions I noted in my ethnography of the development programme. One day early in the fieldwork, as I was spending time in the GGAP headquarters (located in the main Luanda offices of the lead consortium INGO), struggling to get up to speed with the details of the complex intervention, insiders suggested that I seize an opportunity to interview the recently resigned municipal development advisor, Helena, who was considered an architect of the programme. She had participated in the predecessor programme, worked hard on the proposal that won nearly $US17 million from a donor government agency, and was instrumental in getting the field sites up and running in the GGAP's first year. Just a few months before my arrival, though, Helena had left the GGAP quite suddenly to take up a position of similar responsibility elsewhere in the same consortium organisation, but outside the auspices of the GGAP itself. She was now working in the southern provinces of Angola and was visiting Luanda briefly for personal reasons. After colleagues arranged a meeting, Helena gave me a detailed background on the GGAP's origins, orientation and activities. When I commented positively about the interview to my encouragers they seemed disappointed, though, suggesting that I had missed something important.

Weeks later I found out what they had been hinting at: Helena had delivered an ultimatum about her position, and lost. She had discovered that Julie, the GGAP's inexperienced monitoring and evaluation officer and a young European woman, was paid a larger salary than she—an Angolan woman with decades of professional experience and a founding role in the GGAP—was paid. By all accounts, Helena threatened to leave her position if she was not immediately given a raise, to be paid at least as much as Julie made. The organisation refused her request, and this was why an 'architect' of the GGAP had left the programme so suddenly, in only its second year. Helena lost because she was national staff and Julie was international: Helena had evidently reached the ceiling of what a national staff member could be paid within the structures of the INGO. In this instance, her salary was considerably less than Julie's starting salary in the same organisation. I never heard the details from Helena herself, and Julie professed ignorance about the entire incident. Coming across comparable figures and similar stories over the course of my fieldwork, though, I believe the salary differential to have been roughly triple. Given her long experience in development work, one would assume Helena to have been familiar with the discrepant pay scales between national and international staff, but this case seems to have particularly galled her. This may have been because Julie was particularly inexperienced at the time or because their working relationship was so close in the small GGAP headquarters office.

As I came to see the nuances of the dichotomy between national and international staff members, multiple cases of exception arose, such as contentious cases in which a national staff member replaced an international, or *vice versa*. The GGAP staff discussed 'hybrid' cases amongst themselves, though I contend below that the language of 'hybridity' does not adequately advance the analysis of international development professionals or the study of global mobilities. Maximino's case, for instance, complicated the INGOs' neat contradiction of local and international. After returning to Angola upon completion of his graduate degree, Maximino interviewed with several organisations and received a number of job offers. The GGAP's programme director himself made one such offer, seeking to replace Helena as the municipal development advisor for all five field sites and, several months later, still lamented the fact that they had not been able to hire him for that post. In negotiating the offer, Maximino had asked for a salary that the lead INGO of the consortium reportedly considered ridiculous for an Angolan—a local—staff person, especially one new to the organisation, regardless of his excellent education abroad and his previous work in local development. He was asking, without knowledge of the incident I describe above, for an amount roughly comparable to Julie's salary: the very amount that had precipitated Helena's resignation, and the cause of the open position search to which Maximino had responded.

In a remarkable coincidence, Julie and Maximino had graduated together from the same graduate studies programme, though with different concentrations for their Master's degrees. They remembered one another from graduate school, though they had socialised with different crowds. The lead INGO for the GGAP could not pay Maximino and Julie the same salary, despite their nearly identical graduate degrees. Julie, as an 'international' staff person, was salaried in reference to what it was thought she could make 'at home' and, therefore, what it would take to keep her in Angola, a 'hardship post'. Maximino was offered a salary in reference to 'local standards' that, ideally, would neither shock nor inflate local economies, or compete with national institutions for national staff.[4] Within the development regime, Angola is not considered a hardship post for Angolans.

Maximino declined the offer of Helena's old position, but ended up working on the GGAP through one of the other INGOs in the consortium, which was able to offer him a much higher salary, though not quite as high as he would have liked. He was made supervisor of this INGO's field sites, replacing an international staff member. The municipal development advisor position (Helena's departed post) in the central office of the GGAP remained vacant during the entirety of my year-long study of the GGAP. Maximino was considered a demanding, high-maintenance—though very capable—colleague by many in the GGAP and, more broadly, in his hiring INGO, in part because of his initial salary negotiations.

The manner in which the negotiations played out, and the remarkable coincidence that Julie and Maximino had attended the same graduate programme and ended up working in the same development intervention in Luanda yet were not awarded equivalent positions, salaries or rights, provide evidence for my argument that, while cosmopolitan characteristics are commoditised in development work, the national origin of the professional in question remains a determining factor guiding the advancement and circulation of professionals throughout their careers. Julie was hired by the GGAP straight out of her Master's degree with no previous experience in development work and, in her first professional position, was awarded a salary nearly triple that of Helena's, who had years of experience. Julie's salary was also much higher than Maximino's, despite his equivalent degree and several years of highly relevant local experience. Helena and Maximino were considered as local hires, despite Maximino's being recently returned from studying in the UK. Julie, on the other hand, was an international hire and, more importantly, a developed-country national.

Much of the resentment and many of the practical differences and effects of the national–international staff categorisation in these three INGOs were material, as the above case illustrates. For instance, national staff members resented the access which international staff members had to work vehicles, particularly after office hours and at weekends. They resented the generous housing allowances which international staff members enjoyed, and the subsidised utilities, maintenance, furniture and other logistical support international staff received in matters of daily living.[5] Conversely, international staff members at times resented the opportunities that local staff members could pursue, including additional training and advanced degrees sponsored by the organisation; this was especially frustrating for those expatriates who were themselves citizens of other developing countries. Most (though not all) of these differences ran across the local/foreign divide and, for the organisations I studied, the majority of these policies were mandated by INGO international HQ offices, not in-country administrative staff.

Classifying international staff as a group of foreigners in an international organisation seemed fine to most of the Angolan professionals in my study, but they insisted that classifying Angolan staff as 'local' and then applying rules and limits that also applied to the local staff in Zambia, Bangladesh, Peru and elsewhere seemed entirely ridiculous to them. 'The Angolan context', they would tell me, 'is unique' (é único). But being 'local' in these international organisations was just 'local' as a generic category—not local-in-Angola, which could be different to being local-in-Zambia, for example. Glossing all developing countries as homogenously and equally 'developing' is one pillar of the development mobility regime: presuming locals to be immobile and, thus, in the example above, comparable only to other immobile locals in estimating the value of their contributions. That the staff make-up of the GGAP, the three supporting INGOs and the donor agency included many international staff members from other developing countries in addition to numerous Angolans who had trained or lived abroad did little to dissuade the organisations of this misleading binary. During my fieldwork, several Angolans confided that they longed for an opening in their specialty to come up in Portuguese-speaking Mozambique or

Guinea-Bissau, perhaps Brazil, where they might be competitive candidates because of their language abilities, and would be classified as international staff and treated accordingly.

Highlighting one's linguistic abilities, educational qualifications or practical experiences to win positions or promotions is a strategy of individual professionals, and organisations use similar tactics to portray their staff members, therefore themselves as institutions, in the best possible light in keeping with the imaginary of the development industry. Such strategies and tactics, though, also make use of concealment.

Maximino, 'Local' Development Professional

Following our disastrous first meeting at the National Assembly, my subsequent encounters with Maximino were much more productive and collegial. I learned that he had grown up partly in the central highlands of Angola and partly in the south, where his family had fled during the civil war. In the south, Maximino was educated at mission schools and first found employment with a local development NGO, working among the semi-nomadic tribes in the deeply rural south-east of the country. He speaks very competent English, elegant continental Portuguese and at least three indigenous languages. With the help of his first employer he was able to travel to England for a Master's degree. He now likes to discuss Robert Chambers on rural development (e.g. 1983) and, in the future, may pursue a doctoral degree in political science or government.

At our second encounter, we were preparing for a meeting between the foreign government donor that was funding the GGAP and a diamond company that was helping to fund the GGAP's operations in one of its provincial sites via contributions to the foreign government donor. The topic of the meeting was a three-year-old memorandum of understanding between the foreign government donor and the diamond company, in which each agreed to work together towards development in the province where the diamond firm had the bulk of its industrial interests. Evidently the diamond company had expressed concern about the donor's progress under the memorandum, and the donor, now under a new local director, had rapidly organised a meeting to address these concerns, additionally requesting that GGAP staff attend to present their work in the province.

Preparing for the meeting, I kept close to Maximino, to Osman—the GGAP's programme director—and Emile, a programmes officer for one of the consortium's INGOs and Maximino's new immediate supervisor. Osman had asked me to update his PowerPoint slides for the presentation and we spent a fair bit of time arranging where everyone would meet and figuring out who would need special permission to enter the foreign government embassy where the donor offices were located. It was agreed among the three that Maximino would deliver the main part of the presentation for the next day, and that it should be delivered in Portuguese, not English.

It was remarkable that Maximino, who was still new to his hiring INGO as well as to the GGAP and had not yet been to either of the provinces where he would be responsible for the programme, was being asked to present the programme's progress to date. It was unorthodox, to say the least, to have such a new staff member report on progress he had not witnessed, from a programme he had only just begun to read about and understand. Osman and Emile reasoned, though, that the presentation would be 'better received' by the donors if it were seen as 'locally owned' and 'Angolan'. They thought a presentation by an Angolan, in any language, would achieve that end far better than if either of them—Osman, from South Asia or Emile from Central Europe—were to lead the presentation. Osman was also insistent that the presentation be delivered in Portuguese, although they all knew most of the donor staff spoke English as a first language and that all attendees, even from the diamond company, would speak English fluently.

In the meeting the next day, Osman introduced Maximino as the new GGAP coordinator for one of the consortium partners, and stated that the programme was very pleased to have him. He then asked Maximino to say a few words about himself before beginning the presentation. Maximino, in his turn, thanked everyone for their attention and expressed his own pleasure at being a new participant in the GGAP, but suggested that the focus of the meeting should properly be on the programme, deflecting the request to speak about himself. He therewith began the formal presentation, never telling the donors about his prior experience in Angolan development or about his recently completed graduate degree. I would not imply that Maximino *intentionally* secreted his foreign educational credentials or perpetrated any type of fraud on his audience. Maximino is very modest in these sorts of situations, and truly thought attention should be on the programme presentation, rather than the presenter. Indeed, I think attendees at this meeting might have been impressed with his background. But the effect of his deflection was to conceal his international credentials and evidence of his international mobility. There was no way for the donors to know that Maximino spoke English or had a British graduate degree. In the development mobility regime, to be 'local' presumes stasis and may in fact require the absence of geographical mobility, though Maximino is in reality no less Angolan, no less knowledgeable and no less 'local' for his education and experience.

My next experience with Maximino was on a trip to a far northern province a few weeks later—both his first to the region and mine—where we spent just over a week in the remote diamond-mining area. His duty was to introduce himself as the new coordinator to the field staff and review with them the goals and methods of the programme. Emile came along to smooth the transition. Maximino spent the week lecturing, making work plans and setting up goals and accountability points for the four-person implementation team. His authority to do so came not just from his new position, however. In making introductory remarks on the first day of the visit, Emile explained that Maximino had just finished a Master's degree in England and that he had 'a knowledge and grasp of development and good governance processes that rivals those of the donors and architects of the programme'. What was arguably even better, Emile continued, was that Maximino knew the Angolan situation so well, being himself Angolan and having worked in development in the southern provinces for so long. On this authority Maximino then led the field staff: a combination of 'outside' education and knowledge and a type of 'inside' familiarity and legitimacy.

Maximino's identity remained flexible and dual, highly dependent on the context in which he was working. With collegial and institutional collusion, Maximino presented himself as local and incidentally not mobile, therefore credible, in the donor offices. Though he was not local to the province the GGAP was concerned with that day, and at that meeting had never visited there, he was sufficiently local for the donor's purposes because he was Angolan and spoke Portuguese. In the provincial field offices he was credible and authoritative because he was international—mobile, of course, and educated in Britain. Part of the strategy in introducing Maximino as 'international' to this field office may have been because he was replacing an international staff member. The man who previously held Maximino's position was Indonesian-American, with several years' work experience in Brazil. Making the case to the field teams that Maximino had the qualifications of an international staff member yet was also a 'local' Angolan was, in part, in reaction to problems and concerns remaining from the previous field coordinator.

The specific types of local and international experience which Maximino held and that his colleagues emphasised are also significant. Being something other than Angolan in that northern field office, for instance, from abroad but with the same education and experiences, I believe he would not have held the same authority, even though he knew little about the local language or culture, having never visited the region before. I believe he was also accorded greater respect because his degree was from Britain, not Brazil, Portugal or South Africa. This is not because Britain is a gloss for the generically global or the generically foreign but because, in Angola, Britain is considered to be among the 'most developed' nations. Finally, I believe Emile was anxious to replace his own French-Swiss internationality with Maximino's localness and British education because the northern provinces of Angola abut the Congo, where the international very often comes in a Francophone version and can be considered divisive on the Angolan side of the border (see Mandel 2008 for varieties of the foreign).

Maximino's case was one of many in which being local or being international changed depending on context and was something that could be manipulated depending on what one wanted to achieve. Even me, an American woman who might expect to be obviously international in Angola, came to be considered more or less local by dint of language ability, knowledge of Angola and the fact that my husband and son were also living in Angola. Being local, or 'like us' (como nós), is sometimes not an acknowledgement of belonging in terms of origin, but of belonging in terms of culture or, perhaps especially in a postwar political context, of commitment. But I wish to emphasise that belonging and not belonging each has its practical utilities. When an Angolan colleague in the central highlands was in a serious car accident, for instance, and others had a difficult time getting into her over-crowded municipal hospital ward to see her, I was brought along on their next visit. Staff and patients alike assumed I was a foreign physician, and we walked directly into the ward without being stopped. Being international as opposed to local can be a strategic decision, something one manipulates, or something one's colleagues or institution can manipulate for their own ends.

International Development as a Regime of Mobility

The ethnographic literature on cosmopolitanism is helpful in understanding the empirical situation of development professionals, because it pushes past essentialist discussions of local professionals as 'hybrid' or instrumentalist discussions of them as 'brokers' or 'translators' (Bierschenk *et al.* 2002; Mosse and Lewis 2006). James Clifford's (1992) influential essay, 'Traveling Cultures', is a seminal one for scholars seeking to examine the transnational patterns and experiences of the modern world; it interrogates who is, and who is not, a 'hybrid' of multiple cultures. Clifford discusses the 'uncanny' feeling that happens when one comes across something culturally familiar but unexpected:

> Perhaps I could start with a travel conjuncture that has, to my thinking at least, come to occupy a paradigmatic place. Call it the 'Squanto effect.' Squanto was, of course, the Indian who greeted the Pilgrims in 1620 in Plymouth, Massachusetts, who helped them through a hard winter and who spoke good English. To imagine the full effect, you have to remember what the 'New World' was like in 1620; you could smell the pines fifty miles out to sea. Think of coming into a new place like that and having the uncanny experience of running into a Patuxet just back from Europe (Clifford 1992: 97).

Clifford invokes the 'uncanny' example of a Patuxet recently returned from Europe: 'a disconcertingly hybrid "native" met at the ends of the earth: strangely familiar, and different precisely in that unprocessed familiarity' (Clifford 1992: 97). Clifford's thought experiment, wherein readers imagine themselves as pilgrims arriving in the New World and encountering Squanto, where they expect to find a stereotypical native, does evoke the uncanny; the interaction is 'strangely familiar' and 'disconcerting' in its hybridity of place, language and shared knowledge. In Clifford's telling, though, it is Squanto's individual hybridity that is disconcerting, not the overall encounter and not the social situation as a whole. As pilgrims landing at Plymouth, readers expect everything to be different, especially the people, but uncomfortably find some things not so different after all. Clifford aptly identifies 'unprocessed familiarity' as the source of discomfort, but neglects to consider exactly what is familiar and to whom.

It is not only that Squanto can explain New World concerns in English—how to get through a hard winter, etc.—that unsettles, but that he has travelled and can speak about European concerns as well. Like the contemporary development industry, these colonists presumed the 'local' and the locals to be static. This is not the underestimation of only the arriving foreigners, but an element of a global imaginary of the local and the foreign where all might erroneously consider the local to imply stasis and the foreign to imply mobility (see Glick Schiller and Salazar, this issue). Though Clifford does not push his readers to consider it from their perspective, the encounter between the arriving pilgrims and Squanto was, perhaps, just as unsettling for the local Wampanoag and Massachusett onlookers. Would it not be equally uncanny to witness a fellow native speaking incomprehensibly and getting on rather well with the strange new arrivals? What is unsettling here, considered from both sides of the encounter, is that Squanto's knowledge is 'out of place', to invoke Douglas' (1966) classic analysis of symbolic order and disorder. Here Clifford describes a situation in which a well-travelled[6] Patuxet is unsettling not because of the languages he speaks but because he knows things he is not supposed to know. He violates the order of the encounter by holding European knowledge in his Native American self. The local person is presumed to have always stayed in that local place, not to have gone and arrived back again.

Angolan and other professionals from developing countries present a similarly unsettling case for those engaged in development work, as well as for the anthropological literature. Perhaps the meeting attendees at the donor's offices would have been 'unsettled' had Maximino presented in English, with all the terminology and theory learnt in his graduate degree. To restate, within the institutional structures of international development, all Angolans working in Angola are considered local while those holding foreign passports are considered international staff. In daily life, however, the Angolan case sometimes admits finer distinctions than these: there are staff members from other African countries who are functionally 'more local' and staff from other Portuguese-speaking countries who are, in quotidian ways, 'less foreign' than other foreigners. The closest thing to an Angolan is a professional from another Portuguese-speaking African country, but the bureaucracy of INGOs looms above these practicalities of language and experience. The official classifications are rigid: Angolan passport-holders are local—to be treated as are other locals in other locales—and everyone else is international, to be treated as one international class. Development as a regime of mobility presumes the locals to have always been there and the internationals to have arrived from elsewhere, probably from their 'home' nation-state.

Observing development work on the ground reveals that not all Angolan professionals are local in the same way when working in Angola. Nor are all the foreign-born professionals working in Angola expats in the same way. Emile, Maximino's French-Swiss programmes director, for instance, has lived in Angola for more than 20 years, marrying an Angolan and raising his children there. Osman, the South Asian director of the GGAP, has extensive work experience elsewhere in Africa. In working to understand the modern Angolan experience—or the transnational society of development professionals and the larger development regime of mobility—these bureaucratic categories obscure more than they reveal and should not be adopted into the ethnographic literature uncritically. In addition to troubling categories of the foreign, the Angolan case reveals that the local is also complicated. The Angolan born and raised in the central highlands but then posted by his organisation to a northern province feels very much the outsider, despite his shared classification of 'national staff' with his provincial colleagues. Each of these cases might well demand an analytical, hybrid category, describing those who, like Squanto, possess knowledge out of place and gained through mobility.

Discussing individual or group knowledge, skills and experiences as though these things turn people into hybrid types, though, implies a permanence or essentialism, an ill-conceived naturalisation of difference which implies that certain knowledge belongs naturally to some while in others it is disconcerting. Consider Clifford's example again. Pilgrims speaking some Patuxet might be considered bilingual, not hybrid. If anthropology is to adequately describe the dislocations and relative characteristics of development workers, local or otherwise, calling some hybrid, transnational, bilingual or another term, simply will not do. In place of 'hybrid' for development studies, I turn to the literature on cosmopolitanism that identifies difference and considers how it is negotiated in the social world. I propose a concept of the *development cosmopolitan*, in which development professionals who work in the transnational social space of international NGOs, whether local or expatriate, developed- or developing-country national, are recognised as being a type of cosmopolitan.

The idea of the cosmopolitan is an appropriate substitute for concepts of the 'broker' or 'translator' that some scholars use to describe development professionals, as in Lewis and Mosse's collection (2006). Brokers, for these scholars, are the structurally in-between positions of consultants and gatekeepers: those 'social actors who specialise in the acquisition, control, and redistribution of development "revenue"' (Mosse and Lewis 2006: 12). Authors in the collection attempt to further 'a new ethnography of the social spaces that exist between aid funders and recipients' (Mosse and Lewis 2006: 12, citing Bierschenk *et al.* 2002). In focusing on this section of the development world, these analyses differ significantly from my view of the development apparatus through an implementation programme, the GGAP. In focusing on brokerage positions between whole communities and whole agencies, the Lewis and Mosse collection over-emphasises structural constraints, negotiations and manipulations, neglecting to consider the individual, lived experience of the folks inhabiting those positions (cf. Hindman and Fechter 2011). Furthermore, I believe that the productive friction (Tsing 2005) of international development for local communities lies more with implementation professionals than with the negotiators who are situated between aid agencies and NGO administrative staff.

Cosmopolitanism for development professionals is the most akin to Hannerz' (1996) definition; an enjoyment and capacity for foreign-ness and a competence and skill in working within foreign structures and systems. That this competence is perhaps selected for, cultivated within and rewarded by the structures of international development work, among other factors, is what leads me to identify the cosmopolitan-ness of my study informants as development cosmopolitanism.

On this point, Ferguson (1999) is helpful, as he considers the 'political economic compulsions' that have made rural–urban migration so necessary in his Zambian case studies. For local development professionals, like Ferguson's mine workers, there are often few options for employment and career development. Where Ferguson's mine-workers, though, find themselves becoming 'urbanised' and therefore reluctant to return to the rural homes they remember and imagine, local development workers may never leave home but work with people who, and in ways which, demand that they cultivate a certain cosmopolitan-ness, a certain facility for working with the foreign, to be successful.

The investigation of cosmopolitanism has become, in many ways, an investigation of difference and of how individuals and groups address their differences (Appiah 2006). In this formulation, cultural and social differences are often, but not necessarily, something achieved or produced by travel. Alternatively, the travel may be indicative of difference or a product of it rather than the thing that causes it. Additionally, the skills and knowledge of the cosmopolite may accrue more to those visited than to those visiting (Hawkins 2010; Notar 2008; Salazar 2010). Finally, the foreign may be—may originate or stay—literally next door (Brink-Danan 2011; Grant 2010). Recent work has uncovered a Eurocentric view in the literature, and part of the stream of adjectivised cosmopolitanisms (Holton 2009: Appendix 1) has been to make the point that we must distinguish among many cosmopolitans, not continue a fiction of one universal cosmopolitanism (Harvey 2009).

Conclusion

I have suggested in this paper that international development professionals should be considered as a type of 'cosmopolitan' professional, to change the language with which professionals working in the developmentalist configuration (Olivier de Sardan 2005) are compared and contrasted to one another and to recognise the uses to which certain elements of 'locality' and 'internationality' are put in the development mobility regime. My proposal argues against previous portrayals of local development workers as negative byproducts of development work—especially those who develop the skills and interests of more obviously 'international' staff. Mandel, for instance, considers local professionals to be part of 'the human fallout of international development aid' (2002: 279) and offers examples in which individuals have left Kazakhstan because their experiences in international aid work have 'rendered them unsuitable to work for their own governments' (2002: 279). In her critical study of programmes intended to increase civil society formation in Kazakhstan, Mandel provides brief 'snapshots' of six local USAID employees. She criticises the upward and outward mobility of these professionals as they strategically make use of the skills and contacts they gained working at USAID:

> [T]hese people do indeed possess social capital, but its deployment takes the form of writing grant proposals to study abroad, and knowing how to speak convincingly

in interviews with the vetting consular officials; this promotes only their own eventual deracinated cosmopolitanism. Western development aid personnel facilitate the dissolution of this precarious, indigenous professional class, by encouraging them on the road to self-improvement, and in many cases, exit from the region (Mandel 2002: 292).

While arguments to recognise vernacular and rooted cosmopolitans refute her criticism of a 'deracinated' cosmopolitanism, I also take issue with Mandel's myopic view in evaluating the effects of Kazakhstani professional mobility. I cannot agree that the 'international' here corrupts the 'local.' Would it be any worse that a Kazakhstani advances through the ranks of development work, leaving to run a programme in Latin America, say, than for a Canadian to do the same? This assertion reinforces global inequalities of opportunity and power and mistakes the development industry's emic concepts of national and international for analytic categories, an elision this themed issue of *JEMS* cautions against (see Glick Schiller and Salazar, this issue). I understand Mandel's (2002) point that perhaps Kazakhstan is in some way worse off for 'losing' these professionals, and Mandel concludes that foreign aid is working against itself in the region. I contend, however, that these professionals are not 'lost', but are circulating through the transnational development apparatus. Having more Kazakhstanis working in the wider professional world may, in fact, have great benefit for Kazakhstan in the modern, globalised era. Expecting all Kazakhstanis to stay put would seem detrimental to long-term change and development in the region. Mandel may have a point when she posits that foreign aid is working against itself in a broader sense, though, as these Kazakhstanis may be able to circulate only through certain, lower-status portions of the development machine. They may travel and become expatriates in, for example, Angola, but it is much less likely that they will travel to London, Brussels or New York, given their origins in Kazakhstan.

The literature on cosmopolitanism thus provides insight into the aesthetics and cultural characteristics of local development professionals as *development cosmopolitans*. Once local development professionals are recognised as cosmopolitans, as a class of persons with knowledge, experience and appreciation of the foreign, the analyst must define what sorts of knowledge and experience produce this particular cosmopolitanism. The genre of cosmopolitanism that this class inhabits is produced and bound by their participation in the international development regime, and is therefore a unique version. They are often but not necessarily an elite class, at least in comparison to the intended beneficiaries of the development work. Regarding a global elite, however, development professionals in Angola certainly do not consider themselves to be such, as they reserve that term for high-ranking state officials and those working for private international corporations. In this sense, international development professionals may be best analysed as being 'of the middle' of the transnational mobility scene (Clarke 2005).

This analysis of international development professionals and their commoditised cosmopolitan-ness acknowledges the limited opportunities open to those who come from developing countries, no matter their education or experience in development work. In studying the GGAP, I discovered that many of the so-called expatriate development professionals working on the programme or employed by a consortium INGO came originally from another developing country. As foreign to Angola as a Western professional might be, these developing-country nationals led, I believe, considerably more comfortable lives in Angola than they could afford to do at home by virtue of their status as international staff members. On a global scale, however, they remain living and working in a developing country, a situation many I spoke with hoped to work up and out of. Moreover, these development professionals, even Helena with her years of experience and Maximino with his British graduate degree, remain materially local and presumptively immobile, essentially the development industry's second-class citizens. The global aspirations and circulation patterns of development professionals in developing countries demonstrate that they are constrained by the same global inequalities which they would work to reduce, and by a type of development glass ceiling that limits their potential for social mobility. These patterns, presumptions and representations should be analysed as a regime of mobility, as described by Glick Schiller and Salazar (this issue), to reveal the dynamics of geographical and social mobility and stasis that reproduce global inequalities.

Notes

[1]   All names are pseudonyms.
[2]   The Good Governance in Angola Programme (a pseudonym) was implemented in five provinces of Angola, beginning in 2007, and was administered by a consortium of three INGOs, each headquartered in a different industrialised country. The programme's purpose was to increase the transparency of local municipal government practices and to empower local community groups to directly engage with their municipal governments.
[3]   Angola is roughly twice the size of France and, by 2008, had made little progress in repairing the damage of the civil war that ended in 2002. Travel outside Luanda was often difficult and time-consuming—one trip of Maximino's to an implementation site in the northern provinces had to be made overland when the regional airport closed for repairs, necessitating five full days of driving.
[4]   The Angolan case seems unique in this respect, perhaps because of the presence of several foreign oil corporations. The GGAP and many of the programmes and organisations I had contact with over the research period had a high personnel turnover, as staff continually left for better-paying positions in the oil companies, or for jobs with the state that were considered more stable than those in the international civil sector. Elsewhere, INGOs are often accused of 'poaching' qualified local people away from state and community groups. In Angola, the opposite would seem to be the case.
[5]   My estimation of Julie's salary in the recounting above does not take into account these added benefits, particularly the subsidised housing and transportation upon which I knew Julie to depend.
[6]   The term 'well-travelled' may give an inappropriate sense to Squanto's story. Squanto was trafficked against his will, being captured by English traders in 1605, returned, captured again in 1614 to be sold to Spaniards, rescued by Spanish friars, released to London and finally returned to New England in 1619, to find that his family and, indeed, his entire tribe, had fallen victim to smallpox during his second absence. I would not compare modern

development workers to Squanto as though they were victims of human trafficking, though the limited opportunities many local staff members have for employment could be seen as an element of compulsion in the cultivation of development cosmopolitanism, as Ferguson (1999) notes about Zambian mine-workers and urban migrants.

References

Appiah, K.A. (2006) *Cosmopolitanism: Ethics in a World of Strangers.* New York: W.W. Norton.

Bierschenk, T., Chauveau, J.-P. and Olivier de Sardan, J.-P. (2002) *Local Development Brokers in Africa: The Rise of a New Social Category.* Mainz: Johannes Gutenberg University, Working Paper No. 13.

Bornstein, E. (2003) *The Spirit of Development: Protestant NGOs, Morality, and Economics in Zimbabwe.* New York: Routledge.

Brink-Danan, M. (2011) 'Dangerous cosmopolitanism: erasing difference in Istanbul', *Anthropological Quarterly, 84*(2): 439–73.

Chambers, R. (1983) *Rural Development: Putting the Last First.* London: Longman.

Clarke, N. (2005) 'Detailing transnational lives of the middle: British working holiday-makers in Australia', *Journal of Ethnic and Migration Studies, 31*(2): 307–22.

Clifford, J. (1992) 'Traveling cultures', in Grossberg, L., Nelson, C. and Treichler, P.A. (eds) *Cultural Studies.* New York: Routledge, 96–116.

Coles, K. (2007) *Democratic Designs: International Intervention and Electoral Practices in Postwar Bosnia-Herzegovina.* Ann Arbor: University of Michigan Press.

Douglas, M. (1966) *Purity and Danger.* New York: Praeger.

Ferguson, J. (1999) *Expectations of Modernity: Myths and Meanings of Urban Life on the Zambian Copper Belt.* Berkeley: University of California Press.

Grant, B. (2010) 'Cosmopolitan Baku', *Ethnos, 75*(2): 123–47.

Hannerz, U. (1996) *Transnational Connections: Culture, People, Places.* London: Routledge.

Harvey, D. (2009) *Cosmopolitanism and the Geographies of Freedom.* New York: Columbia University Press.

Hawkins, S. (2010) 'Cosmopolitan hagglers or haggling locals? Salesmen, tourists, and cosmopolitan discourses in Tunis', *City and Society, 22*(1): 1–24.

Hilhorst, D. (2003) *The Real World of NGOs: Discourses, Diversity and Development.* London: Zed Books.

Hindman, H. and Fechter, A.M. (eds) (2011) *Inside the Everyday Lives of Development Workers: The Challenges and Futures of Aidland.* Sterling, VA: Kumarian Press.

Holton, R.J. (2009) *Cosmopolitanisms: New Thinking and New Directions.* New York: Palgrave Macmillan.

Kothari, U. (2005) 'Authority and expertise: the professionalisation of international development and the ordering of dissent', *Antipode, 37*(3): 425–46.

Kothari, U. (2006) 'Spatial practices and imaginaries: experiences of colonial officers and development professionals', *Singapore Journal of Tropical Geography, 27*(3): 235–53.

Lewis, D. and Mosse, D. (eds) (2006) *Development Brokers and Translators: The Ethnography of Aid and Agencies.* Bloomfield, CT: Kumarian Press.

Mandel, R. (2002) 'Seeding civil society', in Hann, C (ed.) *Postsocialism: Ideals, Ideologies and Practices in Eurasia.* London: Routledge, 279–96.

Mandel, R. (2008) *Cosmopolitan Anxieties: Turkish Challenges to Citizenship and Belonging in Germany.* Durham, NC: Duke University Press.

Mosse, D. and Lewis, D. (2006) 'Theoretical approaches to brokerage and translation in development', in Lewis, D. and Mosse, D. (eds) *Development Brokers and Translators: The Ethnography of Aid and Agencies.* Bloomfield, CT: Kumarian Press, 1–26.

Notar, B. (2008) 'Producing cosmopolitanism at the borderlands: lonely planeteers and "local" cosmopolitans in southwest China', *Anthropological Quarterly, 81*(3): 615–50.

Olivier de Sardan, J.-P. (2005) *Anthropology and Development: Understanding Contemporary Social Change.* London: Zed Books.

Salazar, N.B. (2010) 'Tourism and cosmopolitanism: a view from below', *International Journal of Tourism Anthropology, 1*(1): 55–69.

Tamas, P.A. (2007) 'Spoken moments of a pernicious discourse? Querying Foucauldian critics' representations of development professionals', *Third World Quarterly, 28*(5): 901–16.

Tsing, A. (2005) *Friction: An Ethnography of Global Connection.* Princeton: Princeton University Press.

Yarrow, T. (2008) 'Negotiating difference: discourses of indigenous knowledge and development in Ghana', *PoLAR: Political and Legal Anthropology Review, 31*(2): 224–42.

Jembe Hero: West African Drummers, Global Mobility and Cosmopolitanism as Status

Pascal Gaudette

In Guinea, West Africa, the status attributed to the musicians who play the wooden, goat-skinned jembe drum has historically been very low. But, over the last 60 years, the jembe *has progressively 'gone global', and today some master drummers earn a living by teaching* jembe *workshops to amateur aficionados everywhere. In Asia one week, Europe the next and North America the following, these masters build global social networks, opening and plying the trade routes for the commodification of their roots. In this paper, I describe how the modern fetish for African drumming has created an alternative economy of status for* jembe *musicians. I examine how, against significantly increasing barriers, young musicians in Guinea are leveraging this economy to follow their elders into global mobility, attempting to achieve a cosmopolitanism through which they, too, can inscribe themselves into West African imaginaries of heroism. And I show how their life paths in turn can allow us to reconsider the notion of cosmopolitan citizenship, in a very unequal world.*

Introduction

Historian Frederick Cooper has claimed that 'In Africa, the encounters of the past are very much part of the present. Africa still faces the problems of building networks and institutions capable [...] of struggling against and engaging with the structures of power in the world today' (1994: 1545). Cooper's point about past and present encounters is well taken. But though they certainly still face problems and obstacles, some Africans have been doing just what Cooper suggests: engaging with global structures of power, by launching themselves into global mobility and actively building, maintaining and leveraging long-distance social networks. This paper examines the example of one such group: those West African musicians who play the *jembe* drum—the *jembefolas*.

I draw on anthropological fieldwork within a transnational network of *jembefolas* in order to describe a pattern of out-migration and global movement which I have dubbed 'the *jembefola's* path'.[1] Although this pattern is dependent upon the historically recent development, outside of Africa, of an alternative economy of status for *jembe* musicians, it inscribes itself in West African notions of heroism through migration that largely predate the current trend towards the study of mobility in the social sciences. By adopting a relational approach (Glick Schiller and Salazar, this issue) and seeing how global flows of power influence the microdynamics of social relations on the ground, I am led to argue that practices of mobility, and the failures of such practices, can be used as diagnostics of power in a globalised but very unequal world. I conclude by proposing a model of cosmopolitanism as status rather than, as is often the case, as citizenship.

Fadouba: A Rooted Cosmopolitan *Jembefola*

The *jembe* is a powerful, wooden, goat-skinned hand drum that has its origins in a region of West Africa known today as the Mande. This cultural area reflects the former reach of the Mali empire, from the thirteenth to the fifteenth centuries. It encompasses regions in Guinea, Mali, the Ivory Coast, Burkina Faso, Senegal and Gambia, and its heartland straddles the contemporary Guinea–Mali border.[2] The *jembe* is still played in the Mande. It prompts masks to come out and dance, it encourages field labourers, it underlines the intensity of initiation ceremonies and it provides the music for dancing celebrations of various kinds (Charry 2000). So when, in 2005, I set out to do some fieldwork with one of the greatest Guinean masters of the *jembe*, I naturally headed straight to . . . Germany.

Fadouba[3]—the drum master himself—and his wife were my hosts there. A few days before I arrived, Fadouba had also flown in, returning from a teaching tour that included cities in France, Portugal, Italy and Israel. He and his wife picked me up at the airport and, in the car, Fadouba immediately started telling me stories and observations from his tour, and we reminisced a little about our previous meetings in Canada and Guinea. Once we reached his European home, he showed me some video footage of his most recent concert tour to Japan.

But what struck me the most over the next few days, as we walked and bicycled the quiet streets of the small, southern German town that Fadouba calls home for half of the year, was the man's anonymity. The scene there was a complete contrast both to what happens when Fadouba teaches a drum workshop—where he is recognised and treated as a grandmaster—and especially to what happened when, three years earlier, I accompanied Fadouba to his hometown of Sirakoro, in Upper Guinea.

I still vividly remember our arrival in Sirakoro in the middle of the night, after a gruelling 12-hour ride that had started in the capital (Conakry) and had involved two minibuses. Our group included Fadouba, members of his family, some of his

Guinean musical apprentices, his European manager/wife, his North American manager and the 15 or so participants of the drum workshop of which this trip was the culmination. That night when we arrived, as large wooden canoes took us across the Niger river, as we walked under the giant, moonlit baobab tree that marked the village entrance, and as we reached Fadouba's compound, the village was eerily quiet. It would not long remain so. Over the next few days, whenever Fadouba walked, clouds of dust were raised by the cohorts—both of locals and of visitors— accompanying him. Wherever he sat, a crowd would assemble. Of course, drum and dance demonstrations and celebrations were held for the workshop participants. But people also gave Fadouba letters of supplication asking for money for a sick relative or for themselves. Ground was broken for the construction of a new wing of the village school, a project for which the North American manager had been raising funds. Praise singers called *griots* sang, and a bull was sacrificed during a large and lengthy ceremony on the village square.

It only lasted a few days and, before long, we returned—even more exhausted—to the compound in Conakry that Fadouba calls home for those months of the year that he spends in Guinea—usually from December to March. And yet that short trip vividly underscored the status that Fadouba has acquired for the people in his native village. For them, he has become a veritable '*jembe* hero'.

West African and Mande Heroism

Imaginaries of heroism in the Mande revolve around the inescapable figure of Soundjata, the mythical-historical founder of the thirteenth-century Mali Empire and canonical Mande hero. The epic of Soundjata is recognised as one of the masterpieces of African 'oral literature' (Austen 1999; Conrad and Condé 2004; Jansen 2001). As the story goes, Soundjata was born the crippled son of a king in thirteenth-century Mande. Upon his birth, his ascendancy as a great king is predicted by seers. Yet despite the wishes of his father that Soundjata inherit the throne, it is Soundjata's half-brother who is crowned instead, and Soundjata is eventually sent into exile, along with his mother. Only after overcoming his handicap and fighting many heroic battles will he be able to build an army, return to the Mande and defeat the evil king who, during Soundjata's exile, subjugates the Mande and declares himself, by force of arms, its new king. Through his victory, Soundjata gains the crown and transforms the Mande into an empire of unsurpassed riches and glory.

There are many versions of the Soundjata epic and they do vary in some respects. But for our purposes there are two central points about it that need to be stressed. The first is that this mythical-historical story forms an ideological bedrock in Mande societies. As Charry puts it:

> The epic recounting of the founding of the Mali empire is one of the primary
> sources of the musical repertory of Mandenka musicians [...]. The role of the

115

Sunjata epic in forming modern Maninka identity and the national identities of Mali and Guinea cannot be overestimated (2000: 41).

The second crucial point is that Soundjata's story, which now serves as a model for would-be Mande heroes, is one of exile followed by triumphant return. As Bird and Kendall state in a classic article on Mande heroism:

> The figures preserved in history are those who broke with the traditions of their villages, [...] travelled to foreign lands searching for special powers and material rewards, but just as importantly, they are also the ones who returned to the villages [...]. This image of the rebel hero who breaks with, but ultimately returns to his people is not without relevance to the modern Mande child. [...] Its effect has been to spin the headstrong youth out in to the world of adventure (1980: 22).

Indeed, similar models of adventure and heroism through some form of exile (hopefully) followed by a subsequent triumphant return are common throughout West Africa (Bredeloup 2008). These models very much pre-date the current trend in the social sciences towards the study of mobility. Filmed in the early 1950s, Jean Rouch's acclaimed work of 'ethnofiction', *Jaguar* (1967), tackles such a story by following three young adventurers from their home in Niger (at the periphery of the Mande), as they travel to prosperous cities in Ghana looking for economic opportunity, and as they return home from their adventures. In the film, the young, eventually successful heroes describe themselves as *jaguars*—agile, mobile and powerful. Rouch's metaphor was more recently taken up by Stoller in his own ethnography of Nigerien Hausa traders (2002). But, in keeping with the times, Stoller's subjects travel a bit further than Rouch's characters: they ply their trade and live their adventures in New York City.

It is easy to see how Fadouba's life path of artistic exile conforms to such models of heroism, and to the story of Soundjata in particular. Born under French colonial rule quite a few years before Guinea's 1958 independence, Fadouba now represents a consummate example of what Appiah (2005) has dubbed a 'rooted cosmopolitan'. Though he travels the world teaching his instrument, and despite his home in Europe, he remains deeply committed to both his native country and his village. And when he returns—yearly now, and usually bringing with him a group of Western drum students and cultural tourists—he brings the kinds of riches and generates the kind of welcome that qualify him as a West African *jembe* hero, one who has left and returned triumphantly. However, when he was born some 60 years ago, this would have seemed an extremely unlikely fate for a drummer.

The Development of an Alternative Economy of Status for *Jembe* Musicians

The link between drumming, dancing and Africa—between *rhythm* and Africa—is one of the principal stereotypes associated with the continent. It may go as far back as the eleventh century, and extends into the present (Agawu 1992, 1995). In the late-nineteenth and early-twentieth centuries, the French colonial government had already made exhibitions of dancing and drumming part of the spectacle of colonial exhibitions (Bancel *et al.* 2004; Lindfors 1999).

The perception of Africa as a radical Other to the West's alienating modernity (Ebron 2002; Torgovnick 1990) constitutes a central factor in the development of the *jembe* drum's global popularity. The fetishisation of African rhythm and of the embodied practice of African hand-drumming as a way to escape or relieve Western alienation forms a core part of the instrument's appeal for its Western practitioners. It confers upon the instrument and its players an aura of prestige that, ironically, was until recently completely absent in the drummers' birthplaces.

Indeed, scholars agree that the level of status traditionally accorded to *jembefolas* in their own societies is quite low. For example, in a well-known book on Malinke praise singers, Camara states: 'Drummers, in general, get very little consideration. To call someone *jèbèfóla* is equivalent to calling them a nobody, *mòfú*' (1992: 120, my translation). Charry, in his detailed exploration of Mande music, talks about the 'stigma' associated with *jembe* playing (2000: 199). Knight, too, in his ethnomusi-cological discussion of Mande performance contexts, contrasts the respective visibility of the praise singer ('*jali*') and the drummer: 'The privileged status of the jali, his association with royalty and other people of influence [...] all combine to make him a highly visible figure in Manding society. This is not so with the drummer' (1984: 66). Thus, *jembe* playing is a traditionally low-status activity, and *jembe* drummers unlikely candidates for heroism. In order to gain a potential for upward social mobility, drummers had to find a social context in which their skill would be much more highly valued. Following Bramadat (2001), I refer to such a context as an 'alternative economy of status'.

If one wanted to pick a historical marker for the development of an alternative economy of status for *jembe* players, one could do worse than point to the founding, not in Africa, but rather in the Paris of the late 1940s, of a theatre troupe named 'Le Théâtre Africain de Keita Fodéba'.[4] Keita's theatrical productions can be directly linked to his earlier passage at the William Ponty colonial school in Dakar, where the first experiments in 'mixing' European-style theatre with African arts and myths were performed (Aggarwal 1999; Mouralis 1986). Keita's troupe eventually changed its format, shifting towards dance performance while retaining only some theatrical elements. By 1954, the group had been renamed 'Les Ballets Africains de Keita Fodéba'. In 1956, after a year-long recruitment trip to West Africa, the newly professionalised troupe unveiled a brand new show and already that year, it toured 36 cities in France, England, Ireland, Belgium, Italy, Holland, Switzerland and Germany (Ballets Africains 1956; Keita 1957; Rouget 1956).

After Guinea's independence from France in 1958, the troupe's founder, Fodéba Keita, would be asked by President Sékou Touré to join the new government, and shortly thereafter the troupe would become the premier national ensemble of the country, touring the world and becoming a key foreign representative for a government that would place art and culture at the forefront of its pan-Africanist cultural policies (Touré 1969).[5] Through Les Ballets Africains and the other national ballets which it inspired from the 1960s—in Mali and Senegal, for instance (Zanetti 1996: 174–5)—the *jembe* drum, thanks to the central role it was given within these ensembles, acquired a much-increased visibility on the world's stages, at a time when African culture was being revalorised.

Other developments of the 1960s and 1970s—such as the introduction of African dance classes at the American Center in Paris (Delanöe 1994), the progressive arrival of national-level Guinean artists in places like Dakar (Senegal), Abidjan (Ivory Coast) and Banjul (Gambia) and the influence in the USA of such artists as former Ballets Africains soloist 'Papa' Ladji Camara and Nigerian Babatunde Olatunji—all contributed to the exposure and popularity of African hand drumming, and merit further scholarly attention. Yet it was only after the mid-1980s that the *jembe*'s rise in global popularity would truly start to accelerate. Two major events more or less coincided at that time and provide a historical inflection point for the *jembe*'s globalisation. The first of these was a change of regime following the death, in March 1984, of Guinea's dictatorial president, Sékou Touré. The new regime of Lansana Conté realigned the country with Western economic policies and institutions, and both radically diminished state support for the arts and opened up the country's borders to adventurous tourists (Bender 1992: 22). The second major event was the late-1980s surge in popularity of 'world music', which led to a multiplication of music festivals and a significant increase in both exposure and demand for African artists (Taylor 1997).

Thus, to return to our main character, it was in 1986 that a small group of Germans found Fadouba in Conakry at the rehearsal of one of Guinea's most prestigious national troupes, where he had been the lead soloist for many years. Soon the Germans were staying at Fadouba's house, and Fadouba was, for the first time, teaching *jembe* music to non-Africans. They invited him to visit them in Germany for a performance and teaching tour and, within a few years, Fadouba was regularly touring Europe. During the dry season, the visit of Europeans to Fadouba's house in Conakry became a regular occurrence, as Fadouba and his main European collaborators started organising intensive three- or four-week teaching workshops in Guinea.

Fadouba and many of his peers eventually established European homes in such places as Germany, Belgium and France. These drum masters first converted their roots—their culture, their 'traditional' music—into routes of travel, patterns of physical mobility and circulation[6]. They leveraged and further developed these routes into an alternative economy of status for *jembe* drummers, by means of which they could find recognition abroad. With this recognition, that is with the riches it brought them, they could then convert physical mobility into social mobility by coming back home to be recognised as heroes.[7] And the riches—the capital—they brought back consisted not just of money *per se*, but also of 'wealth in people' (Guyer 1993), in the form of Western students travelling *to* 'Africa' with their master as he returns. So important has this phenomenon become that at least one of the scene's commentators dubbed the 1990s 'the *jembe* years' (Kokeleare 1997). The drummers of Fadouba's 'generation' inaugurated a pattern of out-migration and global circulation that endures to this day, and that has now brought this powerful wooden drum to most corners of the earth (Polak 2000; Zanetti 1996). One of my informants eloquently summed things up:

> Thanks to the *jembe*, I can say that now we have become...something. Here in Africa, a *jembefola*, he's nothing! The man who hits the skin—his hands are wrecked! But now, thanks to the *jembe*, we can go wherever we want. With a little piece of wood! This is why I have a lot of respect for my drum (Fodé, interview, January 2006, my translation).

I have dubbed this pattern of out-migration 'the *jembefola*'s path'.

The *Jembefola*'s Path: Gaining Mobility

The globalisation of the *jembe* has thus created an alternative economy of status for *jembe* drummers, and this development inserts itself very well within West African models of heroism through exile and subsequent triumphant return. But how, exactly, does one travel along the *jembefola*'s path? How does one go from being a young village drummer in Upper Guinea, to teaching a drumming workshop to a group of Germans or Australians? And what makes the migration of *jembe* drummers different from other migratory movements of Africans?

Although it would be possible to get an idea of the 'geography' of the path by considering the complete life-history of someone like Fadouba, I believe it is also possible, even preferable, to build a more synchronic picture of the *jembefola*'s path by considering four different characters that I met during my fieldwork. Each person exemplifies a different point along a path of increasing mobility and status. They all aspire to eventually attain the 'end point (exemplified by Fadouba). When put together, these four characters provide us with a kind of 'human geography' of the *jembefola*'s path, as follows:

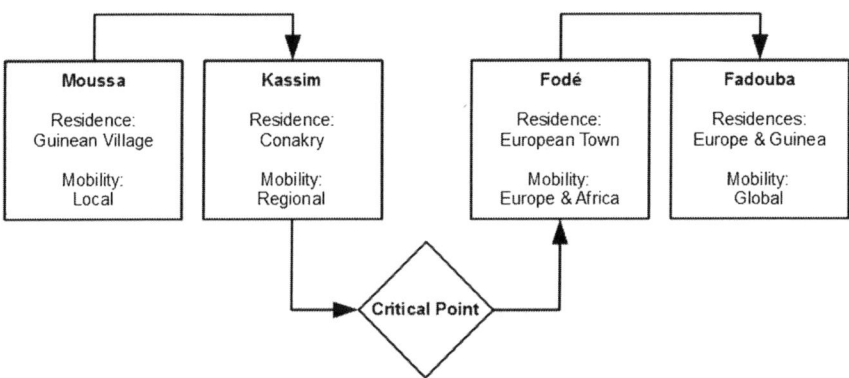

Figure 1. The *jembefola*'s path (translated from Gaudette 2007: 129).

As mentioned above, Fadouba is at the end-point of the path: he has become a consummate cosmopolitan, a world-recognised master of the *jembe*, a Mande hero. He is the model that his apprentices and his apprentices' apprentices are attempting to emulate. In order to tell you about the other characters in this diagram and before discussing what I have identified as the critical point in the path, I need to take you back to my fieldwork, this time not to Germany but to Conakry, the capital of the Republic of Guinea.

All successful *jembefola* now residing in Europe or North America of whom I am aware organise, usually once a year, a trip to West Africa for their students. The tourist season occurs at the height of the dry season, or roughly from the beginning of December to the end of February. Students of the *jembe* are on a quest for the authenticity of musical expression, and so a workshop not only with a source musician, but also in Africa, is a privileged moment in the learning process. For 'first-timers', the trip to Africa serves as a kind of rite of passage that marks a change of status within their own community upon their return. Western students of the *jembe* do not need to spend much time reflecting on the extraordinary mobility—shall we say, the 'cosmopolitan capital'—that their first world passport affords them. The visa application filled out as part of a trip to, say, Guinea is but a very small administrative detail. Barely a blip on the radar. There is a great asymmetry of power at work here.

While I was in Conakry I not only visited and observed Fadouba's own classes, but I also participated in a three-week workshop organised by someone else: one of Fadouba's senior apprentices, Fodé. Much younger than Fadouba, Fodé is himself a world-class artist, though he does not like to be referred to as a 'master'. Fodé also now resides in Europe for most of the year and, like Fadouba, has a European wife. But his status there is still precarious. For one thing, he has only been there a short while, and has yet to achieve either citizenship or permanent resident status in his host country (Belgium). His mobility is thus still fairly restricted. For another, he has not had the experience that Fadouba had, and that has been leveraged by many others, of touring the world with one of Guinea's national drum and dance troupes. He cannot rely on such credentials to prove his mastery, and is still in the process of building his own reputation as an artist. He teaches and performs in Belgium, but his only other international experience so far has been in Spain, where he was called upon by Fadouba to take over a series of workshops. Fodé is still a fairly marginal person in the context of European society, but when he comes back to Conakry, with students in tow, he's already a 'Big Man'.[8]

Now, it quickly became obvious that, format- and content-wise, Fadouba's workshops are all quite similar, whether they are held in Germany or Guinea. So it was not entirely surprising to find Fodé following a similar model. But it is what happens *around* the workshops that is different between Europe and Conakry. And it is this activity that holds a particular interest for us, namely an intense jockeying for positions of brokerage—all forms of brokerage—economic, social and, especially, cultural. Which brings us to our third character: Kassim.

Since I had arrived almost two weeks before the start of Fodé's workshop, I arranged to take private drum classes in the meantime. Fodé directed me towards Kassim. Not only was Fodé too busy to teach private classes, but I also believe this was a way for him to re-invest some of the *human* capital (Guyer 1993) that he was bringing back to Conakry with him—a way to spread the opportunities, so to speak.

Kassim is just a little bit younger than Fodé, but has never left West Africa. He was hired by Fodé to help out with the workshop by serving as accompanist. This means he was part of a small group of musicians who would, as required, play those musical parts in the ensemble that were not what Fodé was teaching his students at any particular moment. Of the five musicians who did this regularly, Kassim was the strongest. Fodé even asked him to teach us one musical piece himself, which made him one of three guest teachers in the workshop. All these factors put him in a very strategic position from which to face the critical juncture in the *jembefola*'s path: the moment when one must attempt to increase one's mobility beyond the confines of the African continent.

Kassim became a frequent companion. I found him to be an excellent teacher. He accompanied me to the market to buy supplies, he walked with me to the Internet café. I started to learn a little about him and even helped him to write a couple of pleading, romantic emails to two different women—one Japanese and one American—whom he had met during workshops the previous year. One evening during the workshop, when Fodé organised a concert with the 'house band', Kassim really went all out to 'show' himself, taking a quite disproportionate quantity of solos, to the visible disapproval of some of the other members of the group. On a subsequent evening, he asked me (I paraphrase): 'So, how's the situation for visas in Canada? How does it work? Is it hard?' My answer was evasive...

But I was not the only card that Kassim could play, and Pedro, a Spaniard, soon muddied the waters for me. He wanted to buy drums—something I was not doing, and a significant economic opportunity for Kassim. After the end of the workshop, my private classes with Kassim resumed, but they became semi-private classes— Pedro was joining us. Then one evening, Kassim exited Pedro's room and, quite literally, jumped for joy. Pedro had said the magic words: he had agreed to help Kassim (try to) obtain a visa to Spain. From that point on, Kassim had very little time for me, though Pedro kept me informed of the vagaries of their relation.

I got the impression that his involvement with Pedro was the most serious opportunity Kassim had ever had. However, once they started looking into the necessary procedures, it quickly became apparent that the road ahead was still fairly steep. Kassim grew up in Abidjan (Ivory Coast) after his father, a trucker and Fadouba's brother, moved there because of the (at the time) greater economic opportunities. It was only after his father passed away that Kassim came back to Conakry and joined Fadouba's household. As it turned out, he had no passport, nor even a valid form of identification, or anything like a birth certificate, let alone a bank account. Yet, on top of the mandatory letter of invitation from Pedro, these were all bureaucratic prerequisites to even submit a visa *application* to the Spanish embassy.

Huddles of strangers started appearing around Pedro and Kassim, earnestly discussing how to normalise his ID situation or what the appropriate procedure was for opening a bank account. Complications ensued and the costs for Pedro started to significantly add up. After many surprising twists and turns, things soured, and Pedro severed all ties to Kassim. Although he did not get a visa to Spain, Kassim did end up with the money for several drums which were never delivered to Pedro.

Kassim may not have played his cards quite optimally. Or maybe he actually did, and he really got the most he could hope for out of a difficult situation. Perhaps he and I would not even agree on what the rules of the game are. The *jembefola*'s path is strewn with intercultural challenges of the first order. But Kassim still managed to be in the right place at the right time: as a key cultural broker during a drumming workshop in Conakry. Of all the workshops held in Guinea, the vast majority are held in, or within a short distance of, the capital. This fact is not lost on those even less further along on the *jembefola*'s path, and many can only dream of eventually getting an opportunity like Kassim's.

One such person is Moussa, a young drummer in Sirakoro, Fadouba's native village—completely at the other end of Guinea with respect to Conakry. I first met him as a young teenager, during the return visit by Fadouba which I described at the beginning of this article. At Fadouba's request, the youngest generation of musicians demonstrated for us a masked dance, an event for which Moussa was the lead drummer.

The second time I met Moussa, in 2006, he was a much taller and much more muscular young man, but still a village drummer in Sirakoro. I was travelling with Fodé and, though we stayed in Sirakoro for only a few days, I was able to record an interview in February with Moussa. Through an interpreter, he was quite clear in his desires, and very lucid about the path ahead:

> *Interpreter:* He wants to go to Conakry and learn even more about the *jembe*, and also to become a little familiar with the behaviour of Whites. Where he is now, like this, night and day he thinks about going to Conakry, but how to go? He has no means, he has no support.[. . .]
> *PG:* And if he succeeds in making it to Conakry, would he then want to go to Europe?
> *Interpreter:* He says, if God gives him the chance, and if he finds a way, truly, he wants to go abroad. . . . To play *jembe* over there.
> *PG:* And how will he benefit from playing over there?
> *Interpreter:* When you play the *jembe* here, it's our parents, they don't earn anything. And playing *jembe*, it hurts a little. It tires a man too. And here, your parents, your elders, when you are done playing, they will say 'Thank you, thank you', but they have nothing. This is why all the drummers here fight to go abroad. Because once you are there, if you work a little, even if it's small, you will get some money that you can send and give to your parents (my translation).

Thus Moussa is looking to join Kassim in Conakry, Kassim is trying to make the critical jump overseas that Fodé has already achieved, and Fodé is attempting to obtain citizenship (or permanent residency) in his host country, and expand his network of contacts in order to achieve the same kind of global mobility and recognition that Fadouba enjoys.

Power at the Critical Point

We can now return to Kassim's position at the critical point in the path. Not only is he in a place which I argue is revelatory of global flows of power, but his story is one of the failure of movement. And, sometimes, failures can be more revealing than successes, because failures clearly highlight obstacles. As Glick Schiller and Salazar state in their introductory paper to this special issue of *JEMS*:

> In US and contemporary global migration narratives, the unspoken, unacknow-ledged underpinnings of migrant success are the processes of capitalist accumula-tion, which are always emplaced. [...] There are a few winners and many losers. This is not to validate stasis but to argue for a regimes of mobility studies that constantly theorises the relationships of unequal power within which relative stasis and different forms of mobility are constructed and negotiated.

If we consider the range of options that are available to Kassim, we see that travelling to Senegal, Gambia or (back to) the Ivory Coast are all possibilities for him, presenting modest logistical and financial hurdles, and little in the way of political-legal issues. One must find and pay for ground transportation and transit through reasonably porous border controls and find a place to stay at the destination. And those Guineans who do not find their luck in Conakry sometimes make such a move. But the only real way forward is to reach the alternative economy of status outside of Africa. Such a continental jump presents a challenge of quite a different order, and one which is now near-impossible to realise by drawing only on local resources. An alliance needs to be made. Someone must help the hero. Had he obtained his visa and been flown to Spain by Pedro, Kassim would have achieved through legal means an outcome which, for the vast majority of West Africans, can only be reached through the highly dangerous, covert means of human smuggling.

In 2006, an unprecedented wave of over 30,000 African migrants reached the Canary Islands—Spanish territory—in overcrowded wooden boats, travelling from the coast of West Africa (mostly from Senegal and Mauritania). An estimated 6,000 people lost their lives that year attempting to make the 1,500 km journey, and another 5,000 were intercepted by the Spanish Coast Guard (BBC News 2006). This wave came as flying bullets and immediate deportation started becoming more-commonplace occurrences for migrants attempting to cross the fences that mark the borders to Spanish enclaves in Morocco (BBC News 2005). The human wave of migrants to the Canaries prompted European immigration authorities to step up patrols and to enter into various patrol and repatriation agreements with West African coastal states (ARB 2006). And it seems to have worked. The flow of migrants started decreasing, so much so that it has now slowed to a trickle (laopinion.es 2010).

The adjunct director of the European Union's Frontex border agency even recently declared 'The route to the Canary Islands is practically dead' (quoted in LAHT 2010). Although this would not seem physically possible (Willems 2007), in collaboration European and West African states have, for all practical purposes, built a wall in the sea.

What makes the *jembefola*'s path special is that it provides a route through this apparatus of exclusion and towards what I will call below 'cosmopolitan status'. The challenges of the *jembefola*'s path make clear where the barriers to physical mobility are in the world system. Much as Abu-Lughod suggests for practices of resistance (1990), we can use practices of mobility, and the challenges to such practices, as 'diagnostics of power'. We can do this because global power dynamics have a direct influence on the relations between the various actors of the *jembe* scene and on the microdynamics of power in social relations.

In theory, the relationship between Western *jembe* drumming students and their West African teachers inverses the typical colonial and developmental direction of power and knowledge flow. Westerners are the students, and a West African artist is the expert, the 'master'. And mostly, if one looks at my relation to Fadouba or Fodé, this is reflected in the dynamics of movement we have with respect to one another. I go to them. I follow them around. But, until Pedro muddied the waters, it was *Kassim* who followed *me*. *He* walked with *me* to the Internet café. *He* came to see *me* in the morning to ask what my plans were for the day.

Kassim has reached a point in his path where, in order to move forward, he needs help. It could come from me, from Pedro or even from Fadouba. Yet the power dynamics of global mobility are such that he is faced with a situation which he is unlikely to be able to solve strictly through his own resourcefulness. Though he, too, was my teacher, this predicament significantly alters the dynamics of power between us. Interestingly, there is a parallel to this in the story of Soundjata who, at the critical point, faces an enemy which he is unable to defeat by himself. Only through the intervention of an outsider—Fakoli, the nephew of the enemy king, who crosses sides in order to join Soundjata—is the hero finally able to prevail. And what does Soundjata offer in return for this help? Just as the drummer offers his music, Soundjata offers a song, called the *Janjon* (Bird and Kendall 1980: 20). In both cases a trade for cultural capital is made, but today's trade involves cosmopolitan capital instead of military might—today's is a different kind of warfare.

Conclusion: Cosmopolitanism as Status in an Unequal World

What does Kassim's story tell us about cosmopolitanism? Being a cosmopolitan is often likened to being a 'citizen of the world'. Discussions of cosmopolitanism frequently centre on issues related to the 'world' part of this expression: issues of nomadism, intercultural contact, hybridity, the ability to adapt to various cultural surroundings and openness towards the Other (Hannerz 1990; Skrbis *et al.* 2004: 116–17). Indeed, it is interesting to note that 'world' is also the term that has been used to associate these things to music. Thus, the label 'world music' designates music that is often hybrid, results from intercultural contact and demonstrates (the musicians' and buyers') openness towards the Other. But let us consider for a moment the other word—not 'music', but 'citizen'.

An integral part of citizenship is freedom of movement.[9] If we want to consider our small planet as a single place, as a 'global village', then I believe we must conclude that, a bit like in ancient Athens, not all the inhabitants of this 'village' are granted citizenship. In trying to move from their home towards Europe, African would-be migrants face a very real apparatus of violence, repression and exclusion. They are neither wanted nor welcomed outside their 'enclave', their 'homeland'. They are not citizens of the world system. Ferguson (2006) comes to precisely such a conclusion while reflecting on the sad fate of two Guinean boys who, in 1998, were found dead in the landing gear of a plane arriving in Brussels from Conakry. Referring to the posthumous letter the boys left behind, he ends '[...] the gentle last words of these two young men make a moral claim to something like global citizenship [...], they appeal poignantly, desperately, for a "graciousness and solidarity" that are, in the West as presently constituted, chillingly absent' (2006: 175).

In his influential work on mobility, sociologist John Urry uses the concept of citizenship in a more elaborate manner (2000, 2007). He talks about 'a wide variety of citizenships developing in the contemporary world' (2000: 167). In particular, he distinguishes 'cosmopolitan citizenship' from 'mobility citizenship' by restricting the notion of cosmopolitanism to the development of an '*orientation* to other citizens, societies and cultures across the globe' (2000, my emphasis). While I agree with such a distinction, it is the use of 'citizenship' to which I want to suggest an alternative.

Applying the notion 'citizenship' to global mobility and cosmopolitanism points towards models of (universal) rights, and is both illuminating and ethically useful. But to the extent that existing state citizenship is explicitly controlled through socially recognised normative authorities (nation-states), and that there is no such authority for the world as a whole, I suggest that an even more appropriate model than 'citizenship' might be that of 'status'. Treating cosmopolitanism as status deliberately draws on a class schema along with a generalised notion of capital (Bourdieu 1984; Marx 1990; see also Calhoun 2002). Thus, '[...] the ability and legal right to travel become one of the criteria by which class is defined and class privilege upheld' (Glick Schiller and Salazar, this issue).

So, rather than a cosmopolitan citizenship, one might achieve, instead, a cosmopolitan *status*. And if one cannot acquire the actual physical mobility this entails (the cosmopolitan *capital*), one could only then demonstrate a cosmopolitan *orientation*. As Ferguson states:

> [...] in a world of non-serialized political economic *statuses*, the key questions are no longer temporal ones of societal becoming (development, modernization), but spatialized ones of guarding the edges of a *status group*—hence, the new prominence of walls, borders and processes of social exclusion in an era that likes to imagine itself as characterized by an ever expanding connection and communication (2006: 192, my emphasis).

Leaving open some possibility of upward social mobility (even though requiring heroic action), this 'status' model is tuned to register global power dynamics and their fluctuations. It illuminates global regimes of mobilities (Glick Schiller and Salazar, this issue).

By trading on the cultural capital accrued through their roots and their training, and by the establishment of crucial strategic alliances, many *jembefolas* are attempting to punch through a considerable apparatus of exclusion and negotiate the route leading to a veritable status of cosmopolitan or, as anthropologist Jean Rouch might have called it, the route towards becoming cosmopolitan jaguars. Along the *jembefola's* path, successes and failures are illustrative not only of the commodifying effects of globalisation on culture, but also of the great desirability and empowered nature of the cosmopolitan status. This is the critical ingredient that makes it so special to become a *jembe* hero.

Notes

[1]   My fieldwork was carried out in 2005–06 (3 months in Germany, Italy and Guinea) and 2010–11 (14 months, mostly in France and Guinea). I also draw on my personal experience of the global *jembe* drumming scene since the year 2000 (see Gaudette 2007).

[2]   For an encyclopedic consideration of Mande music, see Charry (2000).

[3]   The names of people and of some places in this article are pseudonyms.

[4]   Note that, as is the case here, West Africans often give the patronym—'Keita'— first when indicating a name.

[5]   For more on the early days of Les Ballets Africains, see Cohen (2012).

[6]   On roots and routes, see Clifford (1997) and, *a contrario*, Friedman (1998, 2002).

[7]   Pelican, and Glick Schiller and Salazar (all in this issue) also discuss the links between physical and social mobility.

[8]   I am borrowing here a (classical) concept from Melanesian anthropology (Lindstrom 1981), but one which has already found much purchase within the African context (e.g. Price 1974; White 2008).

[9]   See Article 13 of the Universal Declaration of Human Rights (UN 2011 [1948]: http://www.un.org/en/documents/udhr/).

References

Abu-Lughod, L. (1990) 'The romance of resistance: tracing transformations of power through Bedouin women', *American Ethnologist*, 17(1): 41–55.

Agawu, K. (1992) 'Representing African music', *Critical Inquiry*, 18(2): 245–66.

Agawu, K. (1995) 'The invention of "African rhythm"', *Journal of the American Musicological Society*, 48(3): 380–95.

Appiah, K.A. (2005) 'Rooted cosmopolitanism', in Appiah, K.A., *The Ethics of Identity*. Princeton: Princeton University Press, 213–72.

ARB (2006) 'AFRICA–EUROPE: illegal immigration', *Africa Research Bulletin*, 43(8): 16766A–8B.

Aggarwal, K. (1999) 'L'africanisme dans l'enseignement colonial: le cas de l'École William Ponty', in Aggarwal, K., *Amadou Hampâté Bâ et l'Africanisme: De la Recherche Anthropologique à l'Exercice de la Fonction Auctoriale*. Paris: L'Harmattan, 109–23.

Austen, R.A. (ed.) (1999) *In Search of Sunjata. The Mande Oral Epic as History, Literature, and Performance*. Bloomington: Indiana University Press.

Ballets Africains (1956) *Les Ballets Africains de Keita Fodeba: Bilan 1956*. Dakar: Archives Nationales du Sénégal, lot O 680(31).

Bancel, N., Blanchard, P., Boetsch, G., Deroo, E. and Lemaire, S. (2004) *Zoos Humains: Au Temps des Exhibitions Humaines*. Paris: La Découverte.

BBC News (2005) 'Six killed near Spain's enclave', *BBC News Europe*, 6 October, http://news.bbc.co.uk/2/hi/4316702.stm.

BBC News (2006) 'Canaries migrant death toll soars', *BBC News Europe*, 28 December, http://news.bbc.co.uk/2/hi/europe/6213495.stm.

Bender, W. (1992) *La Musique Africaine Contemporaine*. Paris: L'Harmattan.

Bird, C.S. and Kendall, M.B. (1980) 'The Mande hero: text and context', in Karp, I. and Bird, C.S. (eds) *Explorations in African Systems of Thought*. Bloomington: Indiana University Press, 13–26.

Bourdieu, P. (1984) *Distinction. A Social Critique of the Judgment of Taste*. London: Routledge and Kegan Paul.

Bramadat, P.A. (2001) 'Shows, selves and solidarity: ethnic identity and cultural spectacle in Canada', *Canadian Ethnic Studies*, 33(3): 78–98.

Bredeloup, S. (2008) 'L'aventurier, une figure de la migration africaine', *Cahiers Internationaux de Sociologie*, 125(2): 281–306.

Calhoun, C. (2002) 'The class consciousness of frequent travellers: toward a critique of actually existing cosmopolitanism', *South Atlantic Quarterly*, 101(4): 869–97.

Camara, S. (1992) *Gens de la Parole: Essai sur la Condition et le Rôle des Griots dans la Société Malinké*. Paris and Conakry: Karthala and SAEC.

Charry, E. (2000) *Mande Music: Traditional and Modern Music of the Maninka and Mandinka of Western Africa*. Chicago: University of Chicago Press.

Clifford, J. (1997) *Routes: Travel and Translation in the Late Twentieth Century*. Cambridge, MA: Harvard University Press.

Cohen, J. (2012) 'Stages in transition: Les Ballets Africains and independence, 1959–60', *Journal of Black Studies*, 43(1): 11–48.

Conrad, D.C. and Condé, D.T. (2004) *Sunjata: A West African Epic of the Mande Peoples*. Indianapolis: Hackett.

Cooper, F. (1994) 'Conflict and connection: rethinking colonial African history', *American Historical Review*, 99(5): 1516–45.

Delanöe, N. (1994) *Le Raspail Vert: l'American Center à Paris, 1934–94*. Paris: Seghers.

Ebron, P. (2002) *Performing Africa*. Princeton and Oxford: Princeton University Press.

Ferguson, J. (2006) *Global Shadows. Africa and the Neoliberal World Order*. Durham and London: Duke University Press.

Friedman, J. (1998) 'Routing roots and rooting routes: a cosmopolitan paradox', *Current Anthropology*, 39(5): 733–4.

Friedman, J. (1997) 'From roots to routes: tropes for trippers', *Anthropological Theory*, 2(1): 21–36.

Gaudette, P. (2007) Le Djembé, Enjeux: Eléments d'une Mondialisation à Grandeur Humaine. Montreal: University of Montreal, unpublished MSc. dissertation.

Guyer, J.I. (1993) 'Wealth in people and self-realization in Equatorial Africa', *Man*, 28(2): 243–65.

Hannerz, U. (1990) 'Cosmopolitans and locals in world culture', *Theory, Culture and Society*, 7(2): 237–51.

Jansen, J. (2001) 'The Sunjata epic: the ultimate version', *Research in African Literatures*, 32(1): 14–46.

Keita, F. (1957) 'La danse africaine et la scène', *Présence Africaine*, 14–15: 202–9.

Knight, R. (1984) 'Music in Africa: the Manding contexts', in Béhague, G. (ed.) *Performance Practice: Ethnomusicological Perspectives*. Westport: Greenwood Press, 53–90.

Kokelaere, F. (1997) '1990: Les années «djembé»', http://www.heureduthe.com/Textes-ansDjembe.html.

LAHT (2010) 'Most illegal migrants arrive in Spain by plane', *Latin American Herald Tribune*, 21 July, http://www.laht.com/article.asp?ArticleId=360868&CategoryId=12395.

Laopinion.es. (2010) 'Los inmigrantes dejan de venir', *La Opinión de Tenerife*, 22 July, http://www.laopinion.es/canarias/2010/07/22/inmigrantes-dejan-venir/295756.html.

Lindfors, B. (1999) *Africans On Stage: Studies in Ethnological Show Business*. Bloomington: Indiana University Press.

Lindstrom, L. (1981) '"Big Man": a short terminological history', *American Anthropologist*, 83(4): 900–5.

Marx, K. (1990) *Capital*. London: Penguin.

Mouralis, B. (1986) 'William Ponty drama', in Gérard, A.S. (ed.) *European-Language Writing in Sub-Saharan Africa*. Budapest: Akadémiai Kiadó, 130–40.

Niane, D.T. (1960) *Soundjata ou l'Épopée Mandingue*. Paris: Présence Africaine.

Polak, R. (2000) 'A musical instrument travels around the world: jembe playing in Bamako, West Africa, and beyond', *The World of Music*, 42(3): 7–46.

Price, R. (1974) 'Politics and culture in contemporary Ghana: the Big-Man Small-Boy syndrome', *Journal of African Studies*, 1(2): 173–204.

Rouch, J. (1967) *Jaguar*. Paris: Les Films de la Pléiade.

Rouget, G. (1956) 'La musique', *Présence Africaine*, April/May: 138–41.

Skrbis, Z., Kendall, G. and Woodward, I. (2004) 'Locating cosmopolitanism: between humanist ideal and grounded social category', *Theory, Culture and Society*, 21(6): 115–36.

Stoller, P. (2002) *Money Has No Smell: The Africanization of New York City*. Chicago and London: University of Chicago Press.

Taylor, T.D. (1997) *Global Pop: World Music, World Markets*. New York: Routledge.

Torgovnick, M. (1990) *Gone Primitive: Savage Intellects, Modern Lives*. Chicago: University of Chicago Press.

Touré, A.S. (1969) *La Révolution Culturelle*. Conakry: Imprimerie Nationale 'Patrice Lumumba'.

Urry, J. (2000) *Sociology Beyond Societies: Mobilities for the Twenty-First Century*. London and New York: Routledge.

Urry, J. (2007) *Mobilities*. Cambridge: Polity Press.

White, B. (2008) *Rumba Rules: The Politics of Dance Music in Mobutu's Zaire*. Durham and London: Duke University Press.

Willems, R. (2007) 'They cannot build a wall in the sea': West Africans fighting for the right to migrate'. New York: Paper presented at the African Studies Association Annual Meeting, 18–21 October.

Zanetti, V. (1996) 'De la place du village aux scènes internationales: l'évolution du jembe et de son répertoire', *Cahiers de Musiques Traditionnelles*, 9(1): 167–87.

Moving Subjects, Stagnant Paradigms: Can the 'Mobilities Paradigm' Transcend Methodological Nationalism?

Barak Kalir

This article contends that an emerging 'mobilities paradigm' within the social sciences reproduces an analytical gaze that is predominantly fixated on the movement of people across national borders. This privileging of state borders and categories in many of the mobilities studies should alert us to the extent to which it brings novelty to our examination of human mobility in the world. By analysing the flow of migrant workers from rural China to Israel, this article demonstrates how new insights regarding the importance and meaning of crossing national borders can be generated by looking at mobilities through the eyes of those involved in them, allowing state categories and national borders to prefigure in the analysis to an extent and form that are relevant for migrants. The article depicts the mobility-ridden life of Tseng, who comes from a small village in Fujian province and who, after migrating internally in China several times, decides to go to Israel. Highlighting the importance of unequal capital accumulation in shaping human mobility, the article questions some taken-for-granted assumptions about the motivation and situation of those who exercise international mobility; it particularly upsets a prevalent association in migration studies between physical and socio-economic mobility.

Introduction

This article argues that the analytical gaze in much of the emerging mobilities paradigm within the social sciences has been persistently fixated on a segment in people's life trajectories in which they become mobile across national borders. This bias towards international mobilities applies to all sorts of 'people on the move': migrants, refugees, businesspeople and tourists (Urry 2007: 10–11). While it is true that the subjects of our studies become mobile, and we often travel with them (Burawoy *et al.* 2000; Marcus 1995; Tsing 2004), our gaze largely remains stagnant. At the root of this stagnation lies a pervasive methodological nationalism that shapes our research locations, populations and questions (Wimmer and Glick Schiller 2002).

A recurring reference to national borders and an emphasis on states as points of departure and arrival for both migrants and our analysis of them keeps the mobilities paradigm captured within the perceived omnipresence of the state with its interests and categories. If the mobilities paradigm is to breathe new life into migration studies it is by offering new points of departure and innovative methodologies for studying the experiences of 'moving subjects'. One way to generate new perspectives, as this article shows, is by looking at regimes of mobility from the eyes of those involved in them, allowing state categories and national borders to prefigure in the analysis to an extent and form that are relevant for migrants.

A regimes-of-mobility approach that is grounded in the views and experiences of less- and more-mobile subjects encourages us to interrogate the ways in which a powerfully global, neo-liberal economic and political regime moulds the spatial strategies of individuals in different social positions and geographical locations, as they choose (or not) to move in and across any number of scales (local, regional, national and international). From this perspective, mobility is more broadly analysed in view of an unequal distribution of power resources, and the accumulation and destruction of capital within emplaced economic networks and social configurations (Harvey 2007). States, it then becomes clearer, struggle not simply with the regulation of mobility within and across their national borders but, and perhaps more importantly, with maintaining the hegemonic idea that crossing international borders constitutes the most significant type of human mobility in our world.

This article results from my reflections on a research project that is *par excellence* a product of the mobilities paradigm. For three years I studied the migration of Chinese temporary workers to Israel. My project was part of a larger research programme entitled 'Illegal But Licit: Transnational Flows and Permissive Polities in Asia' which examined flows of people and goods across national borders, and interrogated the changing role of states in controlling them.[1]

Israel is an exemplary case of a state that, while extremely preoccupied with protecting its territorial borders and maintaining the ethno-national composition of its population, is nevertheless pushed by the forces of a global economy to open its labour market to migrant workers. Studying the flow of Chinese workers to Israel, the state has clearly been a major unit of analysis in my writings focusing on the formal regulation of this flow, and highlighting developments that reshaped the power of the Israeli state *vis-à-vis* NGOs and an emerging global discourse of rights.

Yet, in retrospect, I believe that the greater insights emerging from my research were generated by documenting the life histories of some of my Chinese interlocutors, taking stock of their mobility before and after migration to Israel. Examining international mobility through the eyes of some Chinese workers sheds a different light on the importance and meaning of crossing national borders, and upsets some taken-for-granted assumptions about the motivation and situation of contemporary labour migrants. For example, a deeply ingrained link is assumed in much of the popular and the academic literature between physical and socio-economic mobility. This is epitomised by idioms, such as 'left behind' or 'staying put', that describe—always somewhat condescendingly—those who did not go abroad. Yet, for some Chinese workers in Israel, mobility across national borders was more of a 'consolation prize' for not managing to move fast enough in their own country and, rather than taking care of those who are 'left behind', migrant workers were often cared for by their relatives who, while 'staying put' in China, have experienced more intense social mobility.[2]

This article expands on this and other insights by ethnographically depicting the mobility-ridden life of Tseng, who comes from a small village in Fujian province and, after migrating internally in China several times, decided to go to Israel as a temporary migrant worker. First, however, I position my intervention within a broader debate around an emerging mobilities paradigm in the social sciences.

New Paradigm, Old Questions

The mobilities paradigm is largely the conjectural child of a feeble marriage between theories of globalisation and those of deterritorialisation. It has often been criticised for celebrating an ever-increasing global fluidity of ideas, capital, goods and people (Appadurai 1996; Urry 2001) rather than painstakingly showing the concrete consequences that such fluidity carries for different people in different positions and localities (e.g. Bude and Dürrschmidt 2010; Favell 2001; Friedman 2007; Wimmer and Glick Schiller 2002).

Human mobility itself arguably presents the biggest hurdle in the way of the mobilities paradigm to claim ever-less-restrained global fluidity. Whereas the movement of ideas, goods and capital has been facilitated by bilateral, regional and international treaties, and by institutional restructuration and technological advancements, the mobility of people, conversely, has been restricted and put under the increasing scrutiny of beleaguered states, despite impressive technological advancement in transportation (Cornelius *et al.* 2004; Shamir 2005). Therefore, most of the literature on migration in recent decades has focused on *international* migration, in a marked shift from previous decades and for no substantial empirical ground. As King and Skeldon (2010), who convincingly make this point, note, 'Castles and Miller's *Age of Migration*, first published in 1993, is an age of international migration' (2010: 1620). We focus on people who cross national borders, because we perceive their movement to be economically significant and potentially upsetting for conventional links between territoriality, sovereignty, or national belonging.

Trying to tame an over-emphasis on international migration, many critics point out that less than 3 per cent of the world population actually reside outside their country of birth (Friedman 2007). Yet this waving of facts in the face of a largely rhetorically asserted fluidity on a global scale is missing the point as, in line with the mobilities paradigm, it accepts an understanding that mobility across national borders is the most significant. A similar mistake is committed by scholars who try to cool down those who herald the deterritorialisation of the world, by emphasising that we should rather speak of 'bi-territoriality' or 'multi-territoriality' (Hannerz 2002). Here, again, the basic assumption that a global process of deterritorialisation in terms of a splitting of one's being-ness between different national territorialities, disregards the perspective of the individuals involved in which deterritorialisation or cosmopolitisation can take place within a certain locality or region (Notar 2008). As Pries (2005) eloquently argues, we continuously design research projects that take note of people who move across national borders in order to show that these borders are less relevant.

A tendency to neglect power fields is also characteristic of a mobilities paradigm that mimics a penchant in globalisation theory for using aquatic metaphors—such as flows, waves and streams—which provide little insight for the lived realities of those who practice mobility in different positions, gradations and temporalities (Favell 2001). The aquatic metaphor of flows seems too often to wash away an important distinction between the many losers and few winners among those who exercise mobility. Maps of the world with arrows marking the direction and volume of migratory movements across the globe are commonly used to illustrate copious flows (Castles and Miller 1998: 7), yet these maps lack any indication of an underlying grid of power that determines the situation of crossers and the conditions for crossing, except from the taken-for-granted assumption that people from poor countries make their way to rich ones. Thus, in celebrating global mobility, we sometimes confuse the cruel working of capital's subordination of labour with an allegedly emancipating human mobility (de Genova 2010). It is therefore necessary for a regimes-of-mobility approach to problematise a somewhat naïve equation of greater mobility with increased freedom (Glick Schiller and Salazar, this issue).

When one accounts for power grids in the constitution and ramifications of international mobilities, it quickly becomes clear that migratory flows are increasing, but mostly within channels that are structured by big business and handmaid states that serve the interests of global capital instead of protecting the rights of mobile workers (Mezzadra 2011). This often results in the systematic exploitation of cheap labour at the hands of agile global capital and the world's privileged middle and upper classes. The landscape of extreme capital accumulation and severe inequality of redistribution by states is, by now, a global phenomenon (Harvey 2007). These kinds of topography of capital accumulation significantly shape migratory paths and, as the case of China strongly evidences, they often do so more powerfully within, rather than across, national borders (Solinger 1999).

Metaphorically speaking, the dominant gaze within the mobilities paradigm simulates a speed camera that is placed at a certain segment of the highway which is notoriously problematic (from the state viewpoint), and is taking note of those who are passing through it at a speed that exceeds the limit (specified by the state). The purpose of the speed camera is to enhance control and normalise the behaviour of certain individuals (allegedly for their and for society's general sake).

Almost two decades after the first warning about the potential hazards of methodological nationalism (Glick Schiller *et al.* 1992), we are still in need of new paradigms and terminologies with which to analyse mobilities without recidivating to the state as our major unit of analysis. Acknowledging the important advances that have been made in developing alternative views and methodologies for relativising the centrality of the state (e.g. Appadurai 1996; Beck 2000; Gluck and Tsing 2009), we should wonder about the extent to which they have influenced our research designs in a way that is conducive to breaking loose from the grip of methodological nationalism.

As this article demonstrates, one significant way to generate a new perspective on mobilities is by realising that, instead of locating our gaze near the speed camera, we should step into the car and sit next to the driver, accompanying her/him not only when passing through or avoiding speed cameras, but documenting the full course of the journey, which begins long before and ends much after the speed cameras' location. The state should not be ignored in our analysis, not least because it often looms large in the eyes of mobile subjects; however, it is a very different image of the state that we then encounter (Kalir and Sur 2012). It is, for example, an image of a predatory state that favours agile capital in its quest to subordinate labour in a global market; it is a state that is mostly avoided by mobile workers, who have little faith in institutions and officials when it comes to the protection of their rights; it is a state that, counter-intuitively, makes little effort to enforce its own laws for regulating migratory flows, thereby leaving much of this regulation to an informal migration industry (Kalir 2011).

Building a Jewish State: Chinese Labour Migrants in Israel

As a Jewish state, Israel's declared purpose has been to serve as a 'home' for Jews worldwide. Accordingly, Israel encourages the immigration of Jews, while ideologically rejecting that of non-Jews. Nevertheless, in the early 1990s, as the first *Intifada* led to a dramatic reduction in the number of Palestinian workers from the Occupied Territories entering Israel, it was the first time in the country's history that powerful lobbies of Israeli employers seeking alternative cheap labour increased pressure on the government to engage in the importation of non-Jewish migrant workers.[3]

From 1993, Israel began recruiting temporary migrant workers from countries in Asia (e.g. Thailand, the Philippines, Nepal, India and China) and Eastern Europe (e.g. Romania, Bulgaria, Moldova). Migrant workers were mainly employed in construction, agriculture and care-giving for the elderly. By the year 2000, there were

113,000 migrant workers in Israel, comprising 11.5 per cent of the total Israeli workforce in the private sector (Bank of Israel 2000). Throughout the 2000s, the number and proportion of migrant workers have remained steady.

Israel relegated the recruitment of migrant workers to privately owned manpower agencies. Israeli law forbids manpower agencies from charging workers for the right to work in Israel. The profit of agencies should come from the fees that they charge to the Israeli employers who contract their services. Yet, in practice, Israeli agencies, often working together with local recruitment agencies abroad, made huge profits from charging illegally informal fees to recruited workers (Hotline for Migrant Workers and Kav La'oved 2007). In the early 2000s, Israeli agencies were making an estimated average profit of US$3,000 for each migrant worker they provided Israeli employers with (State Comptroller 2003: 649).

In 1992, Israel and China officially established diplomatic relations. Soon afterwards, Chinese workers started to reach Israel. More than 30,000 Chinese workers came to Israel on a work visa in the period between 1995 and 2004 to fill jobs in the construction sector (Ministry of Labor 2005). This recruitment of Chinese workers should be seen in the broader context of exponentially growing economic ties between the two countries. The Sino-Israeli bilateral trade increased from US$50 million in 1992 to US$3 billion in 2005; more than 800 Israeli companies are currently doing business in China.[4]

Of all migrant workers in Israel, Chinese workers pay the highest informal fee to recruitment companies (Hotline for Migrant Workers and Kav La'oved 2007); this fee stood in China at around US$5,000 in the mid-1990s, US$10,000 in the year 2000, and as much as US$30,000 in 2010 (Kalir 2011). To pay this informal fee, almost all Chinese workers depend significantly on loans from usurers who charge an interest rate of 1–3 per cent per month.

Chinese workers in Israel are principally men in the age group 30–44 years who were initially recruited mainly from villages across the southern province of Fujian. In later years recruitment has spread to other provinces like Jiangsu, Anhui and Hubei. Chinese workers mostly come from a poor economic and educational background; commonly leaving school at an early age to work for their household's income. For many, their pre-migration salary was around US$100 per month for work in construction or agriculture (Kalir 2009; Li 2012).

It usually takes Chinese migrants around one and a half years to return the loan they took out to pay the informal fee. Since their work visas are limited to a maximum of five years, they operate under enormous pressure to make their migration economically successful.

A Work Place Called Israel: Tseng's Story

Tseng and I first met in Israel when I arrived by car on a Friday afternoon to pick up his best friend, Lai, from the so-called 'Chinatown' in south Tel Aviv. As a matter of fact, there *is* no Chinatown in Israel. Historically, as in the present, Israel has forestalled the settlement of non-Jewish immigrants, including Chinese ones, and thereby prevented the development of a Chinese community. Nevertheless, the formation of a Chinese zone in south Tel Aviv is evident. Israeli owners of supermarkets and butchers' shops put up signs detailing their products in Chinese, and the streets are full of flashy advertisements and posters in Chinese, along with improvised ads in Chinese handwriting offering films, music, medicine and contraceptives. Bars broadcast CCTV4 on their TV sets to attract Chinese migrants who come there to drink, and some apartments on side streets have been converted into informal Chinese gambling dens and brothels. At weekends and on holidays this embryonic Chinatown is visited by hundreds and even thousands of Chinese workers.

I parked my car near the bustling market and rang Lai on his mobile phone to indicate my location. After a few seconds Lai and Tseng approached me, their hands full of bags. Tseng feebly shook my hand and we greeted each other. In the car, during the ride to the compound[5] where the two friends lived, Tseng hardly said a word. I first attributed the silence to his suspicion towards me, although I was pretty sure that Lai had told him that my intentions were 'academic'. I also thought that Tseng might speak Hebrew poorly, and could thus not follow and join in the conversation Lai and I were having. It took a long night of eating and drinking before the ice between Tseng and I broke.

Tseng talked in a calm and composed manner. It quickly became clear that the man I thought to be timid and reserved was in fact open, self-confident, assertive and distinctly warm and curious. His command of Hebrew was outstanding. Tseng showed much interest in my research project, and respected my position at a university. 'I want my son to go to university when he finishes school. I hope that he achieves high grades and that I have enough money to pay [for university studies]'.

Tseng was born in 1969 in a small village in Fujian province. He was 12 years old when his father, who was the only breadwinner in the family, suddenly died. After the death of his father the economic situation of the family, which was meagre to begin with, deteriorated further. His mother was not in paid employment, and Tseng could vividly recall the many days in which he, his younger sister and his older brother, had little to eat. At the age of 13, Tseng was forced to leave school because his mother could no longer afford to pay the annual tuition fee, which stood at what would today equal US$5. Tseng joined Wu, his older brother, in working on a nearby arable farm in exchange for food, which barely sustained the family. Two years later Wu left the village to work on another farm in a bigger village some hours away. After a few months on the new farm Wu, who was by now earning a modest salary for his work, arranged for his brother to join him there. This was the first time that Tseng, then only a teenager, had migrated away from home. For a few years in the new village, the two brothers were clocking up 16–18-hour work days, seven days a week. Only a couple of times a year were they able to visit their home village and family.

With a reputation for being a hard worker with well-developed social skills, Wu established a good rapport with employers and 'important people' in the new village, and was eventually offered a job at a bakehouse in the city of Ganzhou. The pattern repeated itself as, after some months in Ganzhou, Wu called his younger brother to join him there and arranged for Tseng to work in the same bakehouse. Tseng migrated to Ganzhou. He worked very hard and was able to save money for the first time in his life. After four years in Ganzhou, Tseng returned to his home village to marry and start his own family. In the meantime, Wu advanced further with his entrepreneurial ambitions, and was now able to open his own modest bakehouse in a town near Ganzhou. Tseng migrated again to join his brother's business. After two more years, Wu opened a second bakehouse, putting Tseng in charge. For the next three years Tseng was working around the clock and managing six other employees. Tseng earned well, according to his own understanding, but the business did not grow as expected.

In 2001 Tseng was told by Lai, a friend from his home village, about the possibility of working in Israel for a monthly salary of US$800. Tseng consulted with Wu, who approved of the idea and lent Tseng the money to pay an informal fee of US$14,000 to agents from the provincial labour export company. Tseng and Lai had to pass an exam, demanded by the Israeli company, to guarantee them as qualified construction workers. Since the two friends never before worked in construction, they were given a short demonstration by someone from the Chinese labour export company about what they needed to do in the exam. They passed the exam successfully and were sent to Israel. It is interesting to note that, for Tseng to 'jump scale' from a city in China to a job in Israel, he first needed to return to his home village from which workers were recruited.

I asked Tseng several times about his decision to go to Israel. I remember that what struck me most in our first conversations was the nonchalant way in which he talked about it. Israel was just another work place for him. 'I knew nothing about Israel and it didn't really bother me. I only needed to know how much I could earn and for how long I would work there. I then made some calculations and saw that it was a good opportunity'. I asked Tseng if he was not afraid to go to a place where a war could break out at any time. 'From my village in China, if you go to the seaside you can see Taiwan. There are military bases all around in the place I live. If a war starts with Taiwan we are likely to get bombed and die. But nobody is afraid. Same here. You never know when you die, but why be afraid?'. He then told me how, two years ago, when Israel was distributing gas masks to all civilians in preparation for a possible war with Iran, Chinese workers could also get a mask; 'We only had to pay US$50 for it', he remarked.

Migrant workers in Israel cannot be joined by their families. Fearing that it would promote their settlement, Israel prohibited the partners, and particularly the children, of migrant workers from joining them. The separation from their families is undoubtedly emotionally draining for Chinese and all other migrants. The Spring Festival, for example, has become known among some Chinese in Israel as 'The Red Eyes Day', referring to the many tears that the Chinese shed during this festivity while talking on the telephone with their families in China.

When I met Tseng he had been living in Israel for almost four years. 'When you leave, you make a knot [illustrating with his hands the action of knotting close to his heart] and you try to keep it out of your head. Not to think about it. It helps to work hard, many hours, because then you don't think [about it]'. Once, after speaking on the phone with his wife, who told him that their son was doing poorly in school and was not listening to her, Tseng was upset. 'It is a problem. When I'm not there he doesn't listen. He only listens to me. I try to tell him [on the phone] that it is important to do well in school, but I'm not there'. For a few seconds Tseng searched my face for a sign of understanding, and then said one more sentence before he stood up and reached for his cigarettes pack: 'In China I was also away for years from my village'. I said, 'But you could go back to visit once in a while, no?'. Tseng replied, 'Yes but that only makes it harder. Here in Israel you can also go back to visit every year. Some people do it but I prefer to stay the full 5 years and then maybe leave a bit earlier before my contract ends. If you go in the middle it is all open again [illustrating with his hands the untangling of a knot], much more difficult to start again afterwards'. According to Israeli regulations, migrant workers are allowed to visit their home once a year during the maximum five-year term. Some Chinese workers use this right, very few use it twice and the majority prefers not to make use of it at all.

Migrant workers in the construction sector must work a minimum of nine hours per day, which earns them a monthly salary of around US$900. However, most Chinese migrants choose to work 12 hours a day, thereby increasing their wages to around US$1,200. Many also 'moonlight' in the evenings and/or at weekends in the private houses of Israelis (painting, laying tiles, etc.). When I asked Hua, one of my closest informants who regularly 'moonlighted', how he physically managed his workload with only five hours of sleep each night, he answered in an offhand way: 'I'll have all the time I want for sleeping when I'm back in China'. Tseng and Lai were not feeling overworked and they often joked about the work ethics of Israelis. Tseng was amused as he drew a comparison with the kind of work he was used to from an early age: 'In China you work 16–18 hours a day and you only break once to eat. Israelis come to work late in the morning and the first thing they do is drink coffee for half an hour. Then they work two hours, then they drink coffee again, work another two hours, eat lunch. And all the time they talk about how hard they work'.

In order to save most of their salary, Chinese workers adopt a very frugal lifestyle; many carefully monitored their expenditure on food each week, and some even counted the number of cigarettes they smoked each day. After paying off their debts, most Chinese migrants use their savings to build a new house in their home village. Tseng initially planned to build a big house for his family but, as the price of raw materials and the salary of construction workers went up in China during the time Tseng spent in Israel, Wu—who supervised the construction of the house—advised Tseng to go for a modest house and keep some of his savings for investing in a business upon his return.

'Controlled' Labour Flows: Seeing the State as a Migrant Labourer

Allegedly to ensure that migrant workers would not settle down, Israel authorised their work only in a designated job and for an exclusive Israeli employer, whose name appeared on a migrant's work visa. If dismissed by their employer, for whatever reason, migrant workers had their work visa instantly invalidated, and they were forced to return home. The bureaucratic cageing of migrant workers rendered them 'captive labour' (Calavita 1992)—in an extremely vulnerable position when Israeli employers began to violate signed contracts, and threatened with dismissal and deportation if they complained to the police. Fearing deportation, many migrant workers endured severe working conditions and harsh exploitation. Those who did complain to the Israeli police quickly learned that such an attempt was more likely to result in their own deportation rather than in the enforcement of laws on employers.[6] The Israeli police appeared to be uninterested in enforcing the law when it came to the protection of migrant workers' rights. It was, for example, well known to the police that a Chinese mafia operated in Israel among workers, collecting 'protection fees' and debts from illegal gambling. Despite many violent incidents in which these *mafiosi* severely injured workers, the police clearly chose to look the other way. As one senior police officer told me, 'As long as their actions and violence are contained within their own community, we usually don't intervene'.

Tseng, as all my other Chinese interlocutors, was subjected to grave exploitation; he was underpaid regularly and unpaid for several months. He needed to change company three times before he managed to establish a decent working relationship with an Israeli employer. Yet, to my surprise, when we talked about the rampant exploitation of Chinese workers, Tseng often insisted on putting the issue in a broader context:

> It's not true that here in Israel employers are all bad. Employers are like that everywhere. Some are good, some are bad. It is the same in China, I tell you. The state and big bosses are like one [entwining his fingers in synergy]. If you are a big boss you can do things and the state doesn't interfere.

According to Israeli regulations, migrant workers must sign a detailed contract before they reach Israel, and receive a copy of it in their own language. Yet, Chinese recruitment companies take advantage of the fact that many Chinese workers are illiterate and/or desperate to emigrate, by not offering written contracts to migrants who are too afraid to insist on it or are ignorant about their right to one. From a survey conducted by Israeli NGOs among 43 Chinese workers it appeared that 12 per cent of them never signed a written contract and among those who did sign a contract, 45 per cent never received a copy of it (Hotline for Migrant Workers and Kav La'ved 2007: 22). Supervision for the signing of contracts could easily have been enforced, for example, by the Israeli embassy in Beijing before it issued work visas. However, as the Israeli consul in Beijing told me: 'I never know what kind of contracts they sign and what is written in them. For me, such contracts do not exist' (interview, December 2007). In fact, most Chinese workers in Israel do not pin their hopes on any written contract, except on an informal one with the recruitment company which they sign in China. This contract is a sort of 'insurance policy' that specifies the responsibility of the recruitment company to repay part of the informal fee if workers are deported from Israel during the first year of work.

China could undoubtedly exercise some political and economic leverage on Israel in trying to influence the exploitative treatment of Chinese workers. It is nevertheless clear that China chooses not to interfere with the Israeli practices. In my interview with the Chinese consul in Tel Aviv, he offered the official Chinese view:

> In China we call it a win-win-win situation. All sides win out, China is able to export workers, Israel is happy to receive cheap workers who are willing to do the jobs Israelis don't want to do, and the migrants can earn and save a lot of money for their families.

When I asked the consul whether he was aware of the widespread exploitation of Chinese workers by Israeli employers, he opined that 'Everything goes well if they [Chinese workers] don't do illegal things'. I asked the consul about the informal fees which workers pay recruitment companies in China. He first dismissed my claim as sheer rumour but, when I insisted that I had first-hand knowledge of this matter, the consul said:

> Listen, in China we have now a free market economy. You probably know that lately we even joined the WTO. It is the market which decides if people will go abroad, not the government. So they pay these fees to agencies, but they still earn a lot of money, otherwise they wouldn't have come here, right? People know how much they have to pay and they can decide if it is good for them to emigrate.

Most Chinese workers in Israel unsurprisingly never contact their embassy when in trouble. Echoing a prevailing understanding among Chinese workers, one of my interlocutors once vented: 'They [Chinese officials] work together with Israeli officials. They don't care about us, they only want us not to become a problem for them'.

Given their vulnerable position, which exposed them to rampant exploitation with little protection of their rights, most Chinese workers did not desire settlement in Israel.[7] In addition, they often mentioned the inability to bring their families to Israel as a reason for returning. Yet for some it was their limited employment opportunities that pushed them to pin their hopes on a return to China. For Tseng it was clear that Israel was an important stepping-stone in his economic progression, but that his future was in China:

> In Israel I can earn good money but I can never do anything else but work in construction. With the money I earn here I can maybe start my own business or manage a team of workers in China. I will never work there [in China] like I work here.

At that time, he already knew that his brother Wu was planning for Tseng to enter his new business—developing his entrepreneurial ambitions successfully in China, Wu was now the owner of three restaurants in Shanghai.

Two months before his five-year term as a legal migrant worker ended, Tseng returned to China. Amit, his Israeli employer during the previous three years, tried to convince Tseng to postpone his return and remain as an undocumented migrant (not an uncommon practice). Tseng's professionalism, familiarity with the Israeli construction sector and remarkable command of Hebrew made him a pivotal employee in the sub-contracting company owned by Amit, who offered Tseng a better salary and an easier job as a supervisor. He also promised to protect Tseng from the immigration police. Tseng politely declined the offer and returned to China as he had planned.

The New China, the New Tseng

Two months after his return to China I visited Tseng in his home village in Fujian. Before my visit I checked with Tseng that he would have time to spend with me. 'I'm not busy at all. I'm now on vacation', he laughed on the phone and extended a warm invitation for me to stay with him. Picking me up from the central bus station in PuTian, Tseng was all smiles and looked relaxed and energetic. 'I'm now on holiday until the [Chinese] New Year, then I will have to start working again, but first I need to rest from the five years I worked in Israel'. I stayed at Tseng's new house for a week. He showed me around, and we visited many of his relatives and friends.

After one of our plentiful meals at a restaurant, I asked Tseng about his future plans and whether he would have liked to return to Israel if he had the opportunity (in practice it is impossible for migrant workers to reach Israel for a second term). Tseng sounded almost polite as he replied:

> Israel was good to me, I like this country very much, but I'm finished with working in construction like in Israel. I need now to think well, to use my brain. I have some money that I should invest in a business. I don't know yet. There are some possibilities. I will probably go to Shanghai with Wu after the New Year, and see if I can work in his business. [He paused for a while and then laughingly added] I want to go back to Israel but as a tourist. I want to go back and visit all the places that I didn't see, and stay in hotels.

Tseng and I stayed in touch in the months thereafter. We communicated by phone and, after he bought a computer, via online video and phone calls.

As in the years before his migration to Israel, Tseng again followed in his elder brother Wu's footsteps. Tseng and his wife Yang moved to Shanghai, where they lived in Wu's house and worked in one of his three restaurants for six months, to learn the trade. Meanwhile, Wu looked for a place for Tseng to open his own restaurant. When he found a place and agreed a price, Wu helped Tseng with the initial investment. The first months of work as a restaurant owner were very tough; Tseng and Yang worked

16-hour days, doing everything from cutting vegetables to cleaning the floor. The couple saved on accommodation costs by sleeping in the restaurant on mattresses. The business quickly became a success, and soon Tseng had four employees working for him in the restaurant. After a few months the business became profitable. Wu never charged his brother any interest on the loan he had extended to him, and Tseng could repay Wu at his own pace.

A year after he had opened his restaurant in Shanghai, I paid Tseng another visit. It was a reformed Tseng I met. He was now wearing a jacket over a smart black shirt and had elegant shoes on. During the six days we spent together, Tseng never allowed me, sometimes despite fierce insistence on my part, to pay for a single taxi ride, foot massage, dinner or drinks at the trendy karaoke bar we frequented every night. Whenever we went out, Tseng rang his friends, who were all in the restaurant business, to join us. They also called some female 'friends', whom they paid for 'keeping us company'.

Wu, who heard from Tseng about my visit and wanted to meet me, came to pick us up one night with his luxurious Chevrolet jeep. We went out for dinner with a few more of Wu's friends to an upmarket restaurant, and later enjoyed VIP treatment in a fancy night club. In the days after our night out with Wu, Tseng apologised for being unable to match the kind of hospitality his brother showed. 'I'm still a small boss', Tseng giggled, slightly embarrassed, 'I need to work hard to reach the level of my brother'. While he often explained to me that knowing the right people was essential to doing business in China, Tseng was now attending a professional business management course 'to understand better how I can develop further my business'.

Before I left Shanghai I asked Tseng again about his future plans. This time he seemed to be resolute:

> I first have to make sure that my restaurant keeps on turning increasing profits, but I'm already looking, together with Wu, for a place for my second restaurant. You always have to think ahead. China is developing very fast. If you stand still, it is like you are going backwards. Other people will move ahead faster than you. So you have to think and dare to move ahead. If you don't dare in doing business, you will never succeed. [He lit a cigarette with his sybaritic lighter] What I need to do very soon is buy a car. I need to have a car so that I can be mobile, go quickly to meetings and check new possible places for a new restaurant.

Tseng asked me if I was still visiting Israel occasionally. I said I was. He then smiled and said: 'I will go to Israel in two–three years, when I'm more settled. We'll plan it so that you are there as well. We'll stay in good hotels, take a car, and go to all places. What do you say?'

The Mobilities Paradigm: Is There a Way Out?

The life-story of Tseng is one of hypermobility. Tseng has moved significantly in almost every direction in life. Geographically, he moved from the small village where he was born to other villages and cities in the same province, to other provinces in China, and then to Israel. Economically, he started off as the youngest son of a deprived peasant family and has now become a successful restaurant owner in one of the world's biggest metropolises. Culturally, he was a poorly educated teenager and is now someone who has travelled the world, speaks a foreign language, attends business management courses, and adopts the ultramodern and hedonistic lifestyle of Shanghai as his own. Socially, he has climbed from the status of a poor rural habitant to the position of a successful businessman.

Seeking to study flows and mobilities in Asia, it seems that my research project was well designed, as it led me to Tseng and many other Chinese migrants. Yet it is precisely this hypermobility, characteristic of Tseng's generation, that leads me to think that my project's success has been severely contained by a mobilities paradigm that strongly directs our attention to those who cross national borders. After all, Tseng entered my research because he moved to Israel. Wu, his brother, did not. Yet on all the parameters by which I measure Tseng's mobility, Wu fairs more impressively. In fact, it was Wu who always moved first, and Tseng who simply followed in his footsteps once the ground was ready. The move to Israel was in this respect an exception to the rule, and one which Wu, already being successfully mobile in China, did not need to undertake.

If studying mobilities in Asia was my aim, would I not have been better off focusing on mobile workers in Fujian? And instead of following workers from rural China in Israel, would it not be more revealing to compare the mobilities of Chinese villagers with those of villagers in Israel or elsewhere in Asia? I am not suggesting that studying temporary Chinese workers in Israel is unimportant or uninteresting, simply that migration and mobilities studies have been saturated in recent decades with this type of research project, whose core questions are overdetermined by the state and its interests. For example, it is perhaps not surprising that Israel, like most receiving states, invested much energy and effort in preventing Chinese and other migrant workers from settling down in the country. It is, however, surprising and certainly not self-evident that social scientists have paid much attention to this same concern, as if it were the single most important issue that defined this human mobility. Attention to the potential settlement of Chinese workers is all the more surprising since their systematic exploitation, by Israeli employers and under the auspices of the state, led most workers to make their ordeal in Israel economically successful and return home.

By methodologically favouring the vantage viewpoint of mobile subjects and non-state actors, we open our analysis to different questions and insights (Glick Schiller and Salazar, this issue). In the case of Tseng, by taking into account his mobility-ridden life-course, before and after his migration to Israel, we can better understand the significance of this particular move. Tseng was clearly able to relativise his decision ('Israel is just another work place') and his experiences there ('Employers are like that everywhere', 'In China I was also away for years from my village'). For Tseng, a process of deterritorialisation shaped his understanding of place in the world as an exploited worker before he went to Israel. For Tseng, migration to Israel was not the most significant move in his life. Israel was a stepping-stone and not a desired destination. Settling down there, or establishing transnational links, was never part of Tseng's ambition.

For poor villagers in China, like Tseng used to be, moving abroad to Israel clearly meant 'moving up'; yet for highly mobile workers and small business entrepreneurs in booming China, the group to which Tseng belonged at the time he left for Israel, moving abroad as a construction worker actually meant 'moving down' with respect to one's mobility. Instead of writing-off internal migration in a quest to demonstrate global fluidity, we should recognise that, in a world of unequal capital accumulation . . .

> internal and international mobility may be alternative responses to the same set of conditions; the selection of internal versus international mobilities can be viewed as competing strategies in a matrix of opportunities open to potential migrants (King and Skeldon 2010: 1640).

In China, internal migration can thus be both a preferable option, as in Wu's case, or a highly difficult and taxing one for millions of other villagers to pursue (Chan and Buckingham 2008; Fan 2008).

In this article I have demonstrated that it is time for a mobilities paradigm to generate research projects which study human mobility holistically, privilege the perspective of moving subjects, explore the impact of movement on the lived realities of involved actors and 'bring in the state' as people experience it. While examples of such reorientation are evident (cf. Glick Schiller and Çağlar 2009; Lindquist 2009), detrimental to this potentiality are the clogs of methodological nationalism, which prevent a study of human mobility that is removed from the centrality of the state in determining from the very beginning that which counts as significant mobilities. One of the risks in celebrating and embracing a mobilities paradigm that reinforces undesirable tendencies in migration and globalisation studies is that, while we might think that we engage in a critical analysis of the state and its changing control over populations and territory, we often, in fact, contribute to the reproduction of the state as a prime unit of analysis.

Notes

[1] The research programme included sub-projects that studied flows between Afghanistan and Pakistan, Bangladesh and India, China and Israel and Southern India and the Golf States.

[2] Bude and Dürrschmidt (2010: 493) highlight the analytical pitfalls of thinking about 'home' as a 'freezing locality', and about the 'immobilised' who stay behind in relation to the figure of the 'homecomer'.

[3] For more on the process that led the Israeli government to take this decision, see Kalir (2010) and Schnell (1999).

[4] See http://www.Chinaembassy.org.il/eng/.

[5]   Most Chinese workers in Israel live in makeshift residential units—made up of converted cargo containers and located in fields outside big cities.

[6]   For more information on the lack of enforcement on Israeli employers by the police, see Hotline for Migrant Workers and Kav La'oved (2003) and Kalir (2010, 2011).

[7]   In practice it is extremely difficult for non-Jewish migrant workers to settle in Israel. Nevertheless, since 2006, Israel has awarded some undocumented migrants, who have raised families in Israel, permanent residency status leading to full citizenship (see Kalir 2010).

References

Appadurai, A. (1996) *Modernity At Large: Cultural Dimensions of Globalization.* Minneapolis: University of Minnesota Press.

Bank of Israel (2000) *Press Release,* December (Hebrew).

Beck, U. (2000) 'The cosmopolitan perspective: sociology of the second age of modernity', *British Journal of Sociology,* 51(1): 79–105.

Bude, H. and Dürrschmidt, J. (2010) 'What's wrong with globalization?: contra "flow speak"—towards an existential turn in the theory of globalization', *European Journal of Social Theory,* 13(4): 481–500.

Burawoy, M., Blum, J.A., George, S., Gille, Z., Gowan, T., Haney, L., Klawiter, M., Lopez, S.H., ÓRiain, S. and Thayer, M. (2000) *Global Ethnography: Forces, Connections, and Imaginations in a Postmodern World.* Berkeley: University of California Press.

Calavita, K. (1992) *Inside the State: The Bracero Program, Immigration and the INS.* New York: Routledge.

Castles, S. and Miller, M.J. (1998) *The Age of Migration: International Population Movements in the Modern World.* London: Guilford Press.

Chan, K.W. and Buckingham, W. (2008) 'Is China abolishing the *Hukou* system?', *The China Quarterly,* 195: 582–606.

Cornelius, W.A., Tsuda, T., Martin, P.L. and Hollifield, J.F. (2004) *Controlling Immigration: A Global Perspective.* Stanford, CA: Stanford University Press.

de Genova, N. (2010) 'Theoretical overview', in de Genova, N. and Peutz, N. (eds) *The Deportation Regime: Sovereignty, Space, and the Freedom of Movement.* Durham, NC: Duke University Press, 33–65.

Fan, C.C. (2008) *China on the Move: Migration, the State and the Household.* New York: Routledge.

Favell, A. (2001) 'Migration, mobility and globaloney: metaphors and rhetoric in the sociology of globalisation', *Global Networks,* 1(4): 389–98.

Friedman, J. (2007) 'Global systems, globalization, and anthropological theory', in Rossi, I. (ed.) *Frontiers of Globalization Research: Theoretical and Methodological Approaches.* New York: Springer, 109–32.

Glick Schiller, N. and Çağlar, A. (2009) 'Towards a comparative theory of locality in migration studies: migrant incorporation and city scale', *Journal of Ethnic and Migration Studies,* 35(2): 177–202.

Glick Schiller, N., Basch, L. and Szanton Blanc, C. (1992) *Towards a Transnational Perspective on Migration: Race, Class, Ethnicity, and Nationalism Reconsidered.* New York: New York Academy of Sciences.

Gluck, C. and Tsing, A. (2009) *Words in Motion: Toward a Global Lexicon.* Durham, NC: Duke University Press.

Hannerz, U. (2002) 'Where we are and who we want to be', in Hedetoft, U. and Hjort, M. (eds) *The Postnational Self: Belonging and Identity.* Minneapolis: University of Minnesota Press, 217–32.

Harvey, D. (2007) 'Neoliberalism as creative destruction', *Annals of the American Academy of Political and Social Science,* 610: 22–44.

Hotline for Migrant Workers and Kav La'oved (2003) *Immigration Administration or Expulsion Unit?* www.hotline.org.il/english/pdf/Hotline_and_Kav_Laoved_paper_on_Immigration_Police_May_2003_Eng.pdf.

Hotline for Migrant Workers and Kav La'oved (2007) *Freedom Inc.: Binding Migrant Workers to Manpower Corporations in Israel.* http://www.hotline.org.il/english/pdf/Corporations_Report_072507_Eng.pdf.

Kalir, B. (2009) 'Finding Jesus in the Holy Land and taking Him to China: Chinese temporary migrant workers in Israel converting to Evangelical Christianity', *Sociology of Religion, 70*(2): 130–56.

Kalir, B. (2010) *Latino Migrants in the Jewish State: Undocumented Lives in Israel.* Bloomington: Indiana University Press.

Kalir, B. (2011) 'Uncovering the legal cachet of labor migration to Israel', in Kyle, D. and Koslowski, R. (eds) *Global Human Smuggling: Comparative Perspectives.* Baltimore: Johns Hopkins University Press, 273–304.

Kalir, B. and Sur, M. (2012) *Transnational Flows and Permissive Polities: Ethnographies of Human Mobilities in Asia.* Amsterdam: Amsterdam University Press.

King, R. and Skeldon, R. (2010) '"Mind the gap!" Integrating approaches to internal and international migration', *Journal of Ethnic and Migration Studies, 36*(10): 1619–46.

Li, M. (2012) '"Playing edge ball": transnational migration brokerage in China', in Kalir, B. and Sur, M. (eds) *Transnational Flows and Permissive Polities: Ethnographies of Human Mobilities in Asia.* Amsterdam: Amsterdam University Press, 207–27.

Lindquist, J. (2009) *The Anxieties of Mobility Migration and Tourism in the Indonesian Borderlands.* Honolulu: University of Hawai'i Press.

Marcus, G.E. (1995) 'Ethnography in/of the world system: the emergence of multi-sited ethnography', *Annual Review of Anthropology, 24*: 95–117.

Mezzadra, S. (2011) 'The gaze of autonomy. capitalism, migration and social struggles', in Squire, V. (ed.) *The Contested Politics of Mobility: Borderzones and Irregularity.* London: Routledge, 121–42.

Ministry of Labor (Israel) (2005) *Newsletter 46* (Hebrew).

Notar, B.E. (2008) 'Producing cosmopolitanism at the borderlands: lonely planeteers and "local" cosmopolitans in southwest China', *Anthropological Quarterly, 81*(3): 615–50.

Pries, L. (2005) 'Configurations of geographic and societal space: a sociological proposal between "methodological nationalism" and the "space of flows"', *Global Networks, 5*(2): 167–90.

Schnell, I. (1999) *Guidelines for Policy Making Towards Foreign Workers in Israel.* Jerusalem: The Israeli Centre for Political and Social Research (Hebrew).

Shamir, R. (2005) 'Without borders? Notes on globalization as a mobility regime', *Sociological Theory, 23*(2): 197–217.

Solinger, D.J. (1999) *Contesting Citizenship in Urban China: Peasant Migrants, the State, and the Logic of the Market.* Berkeley: University of California Press.

State Comptroller (Israel) (2003) *Annual Report No. 53.* Jerusalem: State Comptroller (Hebrew).

Tsing, A (2004) *Friction: An Ethnography of Global Encounters.* Princeton: Princeton University Press.

Urry, J. (2001) *Sociology Beyond Societies: Mobilities for the Twenty-First Century.* London: Routledge.

Urry, J. (2007) *Mobilities.* Cambridge: Polity Press.

Wimmer, A. and Glick Schiller, N. (2002) 'Methodological nationalism and beyond: nation-state building, migration and the social sciences', *Global Networks, 2*(4): 301–34.

Index

INDEX

INDEX